P9-DFW-266

THE HUMAN RIGHTS OF STREET
AND WORKING CHILDREN

Dedication

The cover design reproduces the handprints of a small boy who may still live with his mother on the streets of a large African city. His mother had AIDS, but her child is strong and healthy.

This book is dedicated to the following people:

Babli
Luis Alberto Granada
Clara
Nahaman
Wagner dos Santos
Krishna Prasad
Masouruwa
Kim
Manolito
The children of Cambodia
A child on the street: Amsterdam 1944
Guillermo
Elizabeth and Agnes
A group of vibrant young artists at
Estrela Nova,
Ibeji and Barraca da Amistade

Paul Erum-Akai
Leia Erum-Akai
Stephen Erum-Akai
B. Vittal
Budi
James Wambugu
A child who worked: Germany 1947
Vasilica Hariton
Laura
The children of South Africa
Rosê
Sr. Chako
Father George Kollashani
The Global Marchers
The Bogota YMCA Prevention Team
Jeff Anderson

In memory of
Gabriel Benitez de Thomas (1962–1996)

'Where, after all, do universal human rights begin? In small places,
close to home . . .'

Eleanor Roosevelt

The Human Rights of Street and Working Children

A practical manual

for advocates

IAIN BYRNE

Consortium for Street Children UK

Foreword by PRESIDENT NELSON MANDELA

INTERMEDIATE TECHNOLOGY PUBLICATIONS 1998

Intermediate Technology Publications Ltd
103–105 Southampton Row, London WC1B 4HH, UK

© Consortium for Street Children UK 1998

A CIP record for this book is available from the British Library

ISBN 185339 449 1

Table on pages 249–56 reproduced with kind permission of the
International Labour Organisation

Cover design: Wendy Jones

Funded by: The Social Development Department, Department for
International Development
The Human Rights Policy Department, Foreign and Commonwealth
Office
Peter and Annette Duckworth
David and Patricia Maidment
H.P. and Surina Narula

Typeset by Dorwyn Ltd, Rowlands Castle, Hants
Printed in UK by SRP, Exeter

Contents

Foreword

Nelson Mandela
CHILDREN'S FUND

"Protecting the human rights of street and working children :
A Practical Manual"

The legal handbook on the protection of the human rights of street and working children is a commendable publication. It is hoped that it will enable organisations worldwide to obtain legal information in relation to human rights abuses against children.

South Africa is proud to be a party to the International Convention on the Rights of the Child. Despite the problems arising from poverty, domestic violence and other issues, we are strongly committed to the enhancement of the quality of life for all children in our society.

NELSON R MANDELA
Founder & Chairperson

Fundraising Number: 011013370008
E-mail: nmcf@mail.icon.co.za   Web address: http://www.web.co.za/mandela/children
P.O. Box 797, Highlands North, 2037   33 Scott Street, Waverley, 2090 Telefax: (+27 11) 786-9197   Tel: (+27 11) 786-9140

Introduction

Why you should use this manual

BEFORE 1945 THERE was very little formal recognition that human beings had rights and that it was the duty of states to uphold and protect them – a notable exception being the 1924 Geneva Declaration of the Rights of the Child. This situation was to change forever with the creation of the United Nations and the international resolve to ensure that the horrors of the Second World War were not repeated.

In the past 50 years there has been a plethora of international and regional human rights treaties, together with permanent monitoring systems established by the UN. The result is that, in theory, everybody in the world – no matter where they live – should have their basic human rights protected. The reality – particularly for marginalized and vulnerable groups such as street and working children – is often very different. Fine-sounding words about rights and freedoms are of little use when a street child faces death or torture, or a child domestic servant is abused and exploited by her employer.

Even if action can be taken against a violating state it can often take years and there may be little or no remedy for the victim at the end of the process. As you will see from this manual, none of the systems designed to monitor and take action on human rights abuses is perfect – some use outdated and limited sets of standards, others have little or no enforcement power, some are subject to political pressure. In these circumstances why bother using such mechanisms at all?

Using such systems as part of your overall campaigning and advocacy system can, however, have a number of advantages:

○ information and statements from government and NGO reports can be used to support campaigns
○ international monitoring committees' conclusions and criticisms provide a powerful case for those pressing for legislative reform or an end to particular violations
○ the questioning of a state or the upholding of a victim's complaint can provide valuable publicity within the country itself
○ participation in human rights gives the opportunity to link up with other national and international NGOs and to exchange information.

But perhaps the best reason to make use of international and regional human rights mechanisms is that doing so will help to make them more effective. If a state becomes a party to an international treaty (see Section C:3) it makes a legally binding commitment to implement that treaty in accordance with the provisions contained therein. Therefore, for whatever reason a government originally signed up to a human rights treaty, it should be held to account if it fails to meet any commitments under it.

This practical manual can help to bring governments to account for failing to protect the rights of street and working children. It is not an academic text book, but a step-by-step guide to many of the most important human rights that should be enjoyed by street and working children and the various mechanisms that can be used to enforce these rights.

We hope readers will seek to update information as new developments in human rights law occur. New treaties and mechanisms are being introduced year by year and it is important to be aware of fresh opportunities for bringing states to account for violations as they arise.

Above all, this manual shows the variety of human rights systems that exist over and above the Convention on the Rights of Child, which are designed to protect street and working children when domestic means of redress prove inadequate.

Acknowledgements

The production of this book has involved the work and synergy of many people. We would like to express particular thanks to the Department for International Development, the Human Rights Policy Department of the Foreign and Commonwealth Office, Peter and Annette Duckworth, David and Patricia Maidment, and H.P. and Surina Narula for their financial support. Within the Foreign and Commonwealth Office we would like to thank Ron Nash and Neil Angel of the Human Rights Policy Department for their help and encouragement; thanks also to Pat Holden, formerly Social Development Advisor of DFID, whose commitment to children's issues has made much of the Consortium's work possible. Thanks to Robyn Callagher of Kleinwort Benson, who provided generous help in kind.

We would especially like to thank Geraldine van Bueren and Professor Kevin Boyle for their very valuable comments and support for this project. The production of this book would have been difficult without them, as it would have been without Rute Pinto and Christina Janke.

We would like to thank President Nelson Mandela, whose care for children extends well beyond the borders of his native country, for providing the foreword to this publication.

Thanks to the staff of the Nelson Mandela Children's Fund, especially Meiline Englebrecht and Jeremy Richardson, for their help throughout.

A number of people gave generously of their time and effort. These include Jonathan Blagbrough, Ana Capaldi, Martha Cadell, Emma Cain, Neide Cassaninga, Trudy Davies, Sarah de Benitez, Dr Agnes Camacho, Dr Judith Ennew, Bruce Harris, Wendy Jones, Caroline Levaux, Anabel Loyd, Catherine Maidment, David Maidment, Misael Marceliano, Dr Elizabeth Protacio Marcelino, Brian Milne, Francisco Pilotti, Becky Purbrick, Dr Irene Rizzini, Richard Wakelam, Alan Whaites and David Westwood.

Finally, thanks to Gill Allmond, Neal Burton, Jane Lanigan and David Stevens of Intermediate Technology for bringing the book to the light of day.

Iain Byrne – *Author*
Anita Schrader – *Project Co-ordinator*
Consortium for Street Children UK

How to use this manual

This manual is divided into three main sections:

SECTION A: Substantive Rights
SECTION B: Human Rights Systems
SECTION C: Information Appendices.

Each of these is further subdivided into numbered subsections: e.g. Section A:3 covers empowerment rights; Section B:3 the African human rights system. Some are further subdivided (e.g. B:4.1 Petitioning the Commission), to help readers find their way around the information more easily.

Some text has been **highlighted in bold** to indicate particular significance and to enable easy identification of key words and documents.

Every so often there will be a reference to another subsection in the text: for example [>**C:7**]. This means that further information – it may be a contact name and address or a particular treaty article – can be found in that subsection. The arrow indicates whether the reader need to turn forwards > or backwards < in this book.

Information in ***bold italics*** summarizes particular important points.
For example:

The victims must be identified when submitting collective and general petitions under the Inter-American Convention.

If the manual is being used for the first time it would be a good idea to read the 'Some basic points' section first (on pp. 4–5) , and then Section A on Substantive Rights which details some of the relevant human rights issues surrounding street and working children. A glossary of some of the more technical terms used can be found in Section C:1.

The manual is not designed to be either an exhaustive guide to child rights or to international human rights law. The two books upon which much of it is based provide a more complete picture: *The International Law on the Rights of the Child*, Geraldine Van Bueren (Martinus Nijhoff/Save the Children 1994) and the *Guide to International Human Rights Practice* edited by Hurst Hannum (University of Pennsylvania Press 1992). However, this manual should provide a practical base upon which to build human rights experience. Once the sources of information – such as the UN Human Rights Centre in Geneva – are known we hope it will be possible to update the manual. New treaties come into force, new mechanisms are introduced and states will continue to accept new obligations.

Finally, if anybody has any comments or suggestions for how the manual could be updated or improved we would be delighted to hear from them.

Some basic points

○ International law, of which human rights law is a part, is mainly made up of treaty law and custom.

○ Both states and individuals are subjects of international human rights law. Only states (or non-state entities that have the powers of states) can violate a person's human rights, but it is also up to the state to protect those rights.

○ As well as having their own special treaties – for example, the Convention on the Rights of the Child – children enjoy the same protection as adults under all the general human rights treaties.

○ Most of the law discussed in this manual is treaty law – standards laid down in international agreements drawn up by the United Nations (UN) and other international and regional bodies.

○ As well as international and regional treaty systems the UN has set up its own non-treaty system – all states are subject to this system, whether they have become parties to certain treaties or not.

○ In most circumstances (apart from when the Security Council becomes involved because human rights abuses threaten international peace and security) the ultimate UN body for the protection of human rights is the General Assembly to which both the treaty and non-treaty bodies must report. However, it has delegated many of its powers to a body called the Economic and Social Council (ECOSOC) which in turn has established other bodies such as the Human Rights Commission to assist it with its work.

○ An example of an international treaty is the Convention on the Rights of the Child.

○ An example of a regional treaty is the African Charter on Human and People's Rights.

○ An example of custom is freedom from slavery which as a principle has existed for so long and is so widely accepted by states that it cannot be disputed.

○ For states to be subject to a treaty after initially acceding to it they must ratify it: i.e. it is accepted by parliaments and governments – they are then bound by its terms (unless they choose to derogate or make reservations [>C:1]).

○ Once a state has ratified a treaty it will have various obligations to fulfil. The minimum for most international treaties is to provide regular reports to the treaty monitoring bodies showing how it is implementing and protecting each right. NGOs can obtain copies of these reports before they are considered, submit their own reports and usually attend Committee sessions.

○ Some treaties allow individuals to bring complaints against states if their rights have been violated. If a victim is going to bring a complaint against a state he or she must always show that he or she has used the domestic courts and administrative procedures in their own country before using the international one, or demonstrate a good reason why he or she cannot (for example, because they are ineffective). International and regional mechanisms are meant to be used as a last resort.

References

Hannum, H. (ed.) (1992) *Guide to International Human Rights Practice* (University of Pennsylvania Press)

Van Bueren, G. (1994) *The International Law on the Rights of the Child* (Martinus Nijhoff/Save the Children)

Fundamental principles

'A child means every human being below the age of 18 unless under the law applicable to the child, the majority is attained earlier.'

[Article 1 Convention on the Rights of the Child]

'The States Parties shall respect and ensure the rights set forth in the Convention to each child within their respective jurisdiction without discrimination of any kind, irrespective of the child's or his or her parent's or legal guardian's race, colour, sex, language, religion, political or other opinion, national, ethnic or social origin, property, disability, birth or other status.'

'In all actions concerning children, whether undertaken by public or private social welfare institutions, courts of law, administrative authorities or legislative bodies, the best interests of the child shall be a primary consideration.'

[Article 3(1) Convention on the Rights of the Child]

'1. States Parties undertake to respect the right of the child to preserve his or her identity, including nationality, name and family relations as recognized by law without unlawful interference.

2. Where a child is illegally deprived of some or all of the elements of his or her identity, States Parties shall provide appropriate assistance and protection, with a view to speedily re-establishing his or her identity.'

[Article 8 Convention on the Rights of the Child]

'1. States Parties shall assure to the child who is capable of forming his or her own views the right to express those views freely in all matters affecting the child, the views of the child being given due weight in accordance with the age and maturity of the child.

2. For this purpose, the child shall in particular be provided the opportunity to be heard in any judicial and administrative proceedings affecting the child, either directly, or through a representative or an appropriate body, in a manner consistent with the procedural rules of national law.'

[Article 12 Convention on the Rights of the Child]

SECTION A
Substantive Rights

A1: Survival

THIS SECTION LISTS those rights that are fundamental to the basic survival of street and working children and without which their lives are often placed in jeopardy.

1.1 Right to Life

Naturally, this is the most basic right of all which is the precondition for the enjoyment of all others. Indeed, in many provisions it is described as an inherent right which cannot be derogated from in any circumstances **[>C:1]**.

1.1.1 Treaty Provisions Because of its fundamental nature this right is widely protected in many of the major international human rights treaties and in all of the regional documents:

○ ART 6 **Convention on the Rights of the Child (CRC) [>B:1.1]**
○ ART 6 **International Covenant on Civil and Political Rights (ICCPR) [>B:1.2]**
○ ART 4 **African Charter on People's and Human Rights (AfCHR) [>B:3]**
○ ART 4 **American Convention on Human Rights (AmCHR) [>B:4]**
○ ART 2 **European Convention on Human Rights (ECHR) [>B:5]**.

It may also be found in ART 3 of the **Universal Declaration of Human Rights (UNDHR)** and as such has the status of customary international law **[>C:1]**.

1.1.2 Protecting the Right Many factors can threaten a street and working child's right to life. Some can take the form of **violating acts** by the state and its agents:

○ extrajudicial executions
○ 'disappearances'.

Because such actions are considered to violate a child's civil rights it has been possible to bring states to account under both the international and regional systems which are described in Section B. Indeed, they even have their own specialist mechanisms within the UN system **[>B:2.6]**.
   However, other equally serious threats to the right to life can take the form of **omissions** which fail to protect certain basic economic and social rights, resulting in:

○ poverty
○ malnutrition
○ lack of decent health care
○ lack of adequate shelter.

The remainder of this section focuses on these economic and social rights, which have traditionally been neglected both by states and the international community but for which there is now growing pressure to ensure greater protection within the human rights system.
   Any, or a combination, of these factors result in the deaths of thousands of street and working children world-wide every day. Hence, to bring a state to

account for its failings as well as its definite abuses, it is important to be aware of the responsibilities that a state has in each area and any special duties it has in respect of children.

✓ 1.2 Right to an Adequate Standard of Living

As with the right to life, this incorporates a number of concepts reflected in the variety of definitions adopted by different international treaties and declarations:

- ○ ART 25(1) **UNDHR**: food, clothing, housing, medical care, necessary social services and social security
- ○ ART 11(1) **International Covenant on Economic, Social and Cultural Rights (ICESCR)**: food, clothing and housing
- ○ ART 27(1) **CRC**: links a child's standard of living to his physical, mental, spiritual, moral and social development.

Both the Preamble of the CRC and Art 27(3) discuss the need to provide assistance to those children 'living in exceptionally difficult conditions'.

In addition to this general standard, each of its component rights also receives its own protection to a greater or lesser degree under international law.

✓ 1.3 Right to Adequate Nutrition and Clean Water

Although the **ICESCR** is the main substantive document for the protection of economic and social rights, it is noticeable that ART 11, which focuses on the right to food, does not explicitly mention the importance of nutritious food nor the need for access to clean drinking water. This is despite the fact that ART 11(2) highlights the importance of disseminating information on the principles of nutrition.

For the most comprehensive protection for children in this area we must look instead to:

- ○ ART 27(2)(c) **CRC** – states that one crucial way of combating disease and malnutrition is to provide adequate nutritious foods and clean drinking-water which is not subject to environmental pollution
- ○ ○ART 14(2)(c) **African Charter on the Rights and Welfare of the Child** – again guarantees a child's right to adequate nutrition and safe drinking-water.

When the African Charter comes into force it will provide the opportunity for children and their representatives to enforce such rights through individual complaints to a Committee of Experts **[>B:3]**, something that the existing economic and social rights system does not permit **[>B:1.3]**.

✗*Economic and social rights are justiciable*

For **pregnant street girls** malnutrition is a particular danger as they are already weakened by their condition. This interdependence of adequate food and well-being is reflected in ART 24 of **CRC** which sees appropriate nutrition as a vital component of primary health care programmes and calls for the dissemination of information about it to be included within health education.

✓ 1.4 Right to Decent Health Care

The marginalization of street and working children limits their access to even the most basic health services, which are sometimes the only facilities many developing states have to offer. Their inability to attend school often means they miss out on the regular health checks and immunization programmes that are carried out there.

However, ART 24(1) of the **CRC** clearly indicates that **no child shall be deprived of access to the highest attainable standard of health available**. This taken together with the general non-discrimination indicated in ART 2(1) means that even those children on the fringes of society – indeed *especially* those children because of their greater susceptibility to disease and ill health – should be able to receive the same standard of treatment as every other child.

The **CRC** again goes further than the **ICESCR** in defining exactly what the right to decent health care means, reflecting the passage of time between the two treaties. ART 24 talks of the importance of **preventative work** and **primary health care**, taking into account the level of health service technology appropriate to the developing world. In contrast, ART 12 of the ICESCR adopts a much more limited approach.

Note also ART 24(2)(d) of the **CRC**, which focuses on the need to provide ante-natal and post-natal services for mothers implicitly including pregnant girls.

A similar approach to the **CRC** may again be found in the **African Charter on the Rights and Welfare of the Child** (ART 14) which, raises the **possibility of bringing states** (and perhaps ultimately the international community for its failure to provide adequate resources) **to account** for their failure to make a range of health care services available for all their children.

1.5 Right to Adequate Shelter

By definition, many (but not all) street and working children are denied adequate shelter through their exclusion from a family home or the lack of any suitable temporary or permanent accommodation provided through state agencies or NGOs. Living and sleeping on the streets can quickly have a detrimental effect on a child's health – particularly in those countries where extremes of temperature are commonplace.

Despite its fundamental importance, this issue does not receive separate protection under the **ICESCR** but is merely listed in ART 11(1) as one of those rights necessary to ensure a person enjoys an adequate standard of living. Hence, the right is not defined further and no basic standards laid down.

The obligations upon states are elaborated in slightly more detail in ART 27(3) of the **CRC**, where it states that in relation to enabling a child to enjoy an adequate standard of living it '**... shall in the case of need, provide material assistance and support programmes, particularly with regard to nutrition, clothing and housing'.** Implicit in this clause is the recognition that unless states adopt an integrated approach to providing enjoyment of certain fundamental economic and social rights then the neglect of any one could threaten the right to life.

A2: Fair Treatment

THIS SECTION LOOKS at those rights that are designed to ensure that street and working children are not badly treated or exploited – they could also be labelled the **protection** or **equal respect rights**.

Street and working children can often find themselves in a number of situations where their rights are not being respected by either commercial institutions, agents of the state or private individuals.

The introduction of the **CRC**, which builds upon the existing UN **International Labour Organisation (ILO)** and regional human rights law, now means that there is a sufficient set of standards to make it clear that **marginalized children have the right not to be sexually or commercially exploited or inhumanely treated under any circumstances**. The implementation of these rights – as with all human rights – is another matter, but through skilful reconceptualization (see below) even this can begin to be addressed by NGOs and advocates.

Six areas involve particular threats to the fair and equal treatment of street and working children:

○ right not to be tortured or suffer inhumane and degrading treatment
○ right to fair treatment while in detention
○ right to fair treatment under the law
○ right not to be commercially exploited
○ right not to be sexually exploited
○ right not to be socially exploited.

2.1 Torture

Like the right to life, the right not to be tortured or suffer cruel, inhumane or degrading treatment is a fundamental freedom which cannot be derogated from in any circumstances. However, it is only too apparent that for many countries torture remains a routine – sometimes systematic – practice which is often the first recourse for police and security forces who deal with street children.

The right is protected by all the main general treaties we are concerned with:

○ ART 37 **CRC**
○ ART 7 **ICCPR**
○ ART 5 **AfCHR**
○ ART 5(2) **AmCHR**
○ ART 3 **ECHR**.

It also benefits from having its own treaty – the **Convention Against Torture [>C:2]** together with **a monitoring committee** with some unique powers of investigation **[>B:1.4]** and an individual expert (special rapporteur) appointed by the UN **[>B:2.6]**. The result is that victims of torture have a number of options to bring violators to account, depending of course upon which treaties the particular state has ratified **[>C:3]**.

Given the wide range of protection that exists it is not surprising that the different aspects of ill treatment have been analysed quite closely by different human rights bodies:

Torture Inhuman treatment with a purpose such as obtaining information or confessions ... generally an aggravated form of inhuman treatment.

Inhuman Treatment At least [that which] ...deliberately causes suffering, mental or physical, which in the particular situation is unjustifiable.

Degrading Treatment Grossly humiliates [an individual] before others or drives him to act against his will or conscience.

[European Commission in *Denmark et al. v. Greece*]

The majority of treaties define the right in a similar way. However, note that the ECHR omits the word 'cruel' which, given that some treatment or punishment may amount to cruelty while not being considered torture or inhumane, may be a drawback when considering bringing a case under that system **[>B:5]**.

However, in most cases the choice will probably depend more upon the relative effectiveness of each protection system (speed, openness, result) than the substantive wording. More than one system can be used, provided the relevant rules are followed about which can be used first or at the same time.

2.2 Treatment while in Detention

Many street children are regularly held without charge, often in terrible conditions, as a means of 'cleaning' them off the streets. Even if they are found guilty of crimes such as stealing or drug abuse and imprisoned – an act which is still not outlawed by international law – the standards of their detention often fall well below that laid down by international guidelines such as the Body of Principles for the Protection of All Persons under Any form of Detention or Imprisonment, the United Nations Standard Minimum Rules of the Administration of Juvenile Justice [The Beijing Rules] or (most importantly) **the Standard Minimum Rules for the Protection of Juveniles Deprived of their Liberty 1990** (contact the UN Centre for Human Rights or Defence for Children International – who also provide a free commentary – **[>C:5]** for copies, or they may be found in *International Documents on Children* (edited by Geraldine Van Bueren 1993) but note that, unlike the **CRC**, these are not binding law).

Until the Standard Minimum Rules in 1990 and the **CRC**, international law had not catered for detained children as well as it had for adults. However, there is now a body of standards designed to ensure that if children are detained this must be done in accordance with the rule of law and humanely.

ART 37(b) of the **CRC** establishes that **detention should be used only as a means of last resort** – as does Rule 1 of the 1990 Standard Minimum Rules. This is a higher standard than in treaties which apply equally to adults and children, such as the ICCPR which prohibits pre-trial detention only 'as a general rule' (ART 9(3)) – therefore the CRC standard should always be quoted provided the state is a party to it.

As Van Bueren points out [1994 p. 210] there is a **particular danger for street children** that courts will use pre-trial detention as the only option to secure their whereabouts until trial, given that they will be unable to supply an address and will not be able to meet any bail payment. However, routine use of detention without the state seeking to provide any alternative through other agencies, such as social services, will surely be a breach of the 'last resort' clause of ART 37(b).

ART 37(c) provides the framework within which states must operate when choosing to detain children:

*Every child deprived of liberty shall be **treated with humanity and respect** for the inherent dignity of the human person, and in a manner which takes into account the needs of persons of their age. In particular, every child deprived of liberty shall be **separated from adults** unless it is considered in the child's best interest not to do so and shall have the right to maintain contact with his or her family through correspondence and visits, save in exceptional circumstances.*

Although this does not lay down a **minimum age** at which children may be detained, a further duty on states in ART 40(3) obliges them to 'seek to promote' the establishment of a minimum age 'below which children shall be presumed not to have the capacity to infringe the penal law' – in other words, also below which they should not be detained.

As pointed out above, although the needs of detained children are clearly different from adults the relevant general treaty provisions also apply to them and may be found in the following articles:

○ ART 10 **ICCPR**
○ ART 5(2) **AmCHR**.

2.3 Treatment under the Law

It is one of the foundations of a civilized state that the rule of law should prevail and that justice should be administered fairly and consistently. Again, juvenile justice has traditionally been neglected in regard to standard setting compared to its adult counterpart.

Articles 10(2)(b) and 14 of the ICCPR **[>C:2.2]** do offer some safeguards for children who are subject to the criminal justice system, but it was not until the introduction of the **Beijing Rules in 1985 [<2.2]** and then **Article 40 of the CRC [>C:2.1]** that there was recognition that children require special protection due to their particular vulnerability. This is even more the case as regards street and working children who in most countries are viewed with suspicion and hostility by the authorities and who because of their lack of education are in an even weaker position than their family-based peers.

This marginalized position is considered to some extent by ART 40(2)(b)(III) which seeks to ensure that courts take into account the situation of the child when determining the case, and the more general provision of ART 40(1) which, echoing ART 39 **[>2.7]**, discusses the need to treat the child in accordance with his or her 'sense of dignity and worth' and to promote their reintegration into society. Above all, Article 40 is designed to ensure that the child should be subject to natural justice throughout the entire legal process and that this should include:

○ access to suitable legal representation
○ enjoying the benefit of the presumption of innocence
○ not to be forced into giving testimony or making a confession
○ if found guilty, to be subject to the most appropriate disposition taking into account his or her circumstances (with institutional care as only one option among many).

However, Article 40 does not provide an exhaustive list of safeguards – the Beijing Rules although not binding do provide more detailed standards (e.g. the right to silence as 'a basic safeguard') while the general protection offered under ART 14 of the ICCPR to both juveniles and adults ensures that the child can understand the charge against him or her (ART 14(3)(b)).

Other general protection clauses can be found in:

○ ART 15 **CEDAW [>C:2.6]** – fair treatment for women before the law
○ ART 7 **AfCHR**
○ ART 8 **AmCHR**
○ ART 5 **ECHR**.

2.4 Commercial/Economic Exploitation

Many marginalized children need to carry out some form of work to survive, and not all of this is necessarily exploitative. Anti-Slavery International sees the issue of child labour as a continuum with many grey areas in the middle. At one end of the spectrum there is:

○ **child work** (which is not necessarily exploitative, but can play a positive role in a child's development if consistent with the child's evolving mental and physical capabilities)
○ **child labour** towards the middle (which is exploitative and where the work being undertaken is hazardous, or the conditions of work (long hours, etc.) interfere with a child's education, or physical or mental well-being, or socialization)
○ **child slavery** at the furthest end of the spectrum (where the child is taken or otherwise handed over by his or her guardians to work, or made to pay off loans given as advances through the use of their labour (debt bondage), or where the child is in extremely hazardous employment, such as child prostitution).

The situation of street and working children in many countries is such that they have no recourse but to engage in some form of work. It is therefore **not a question of trying to implement blanket bans** on any form of work, but instead ensuring that children are not being exploited or put at risk.

This is reflected in the large amount of international law in this area, much of it developed by the ILO, which even for permitted levels of work, has introduced regulations regarding minimum age and the types of activity to be engaged in.

UNICEF, in its 1986 report on working and street children, highlighted a number of factors involved in child work that can have a detrimental effect:

○ beginning full-time work at too early an age
○ working too long hours
○ inadequate remuneration
○ excessive physical and social strain
○ working and living on the streets
○ excessive responsibility at too early an age
○ the hampering of the psychological and social development of the child
○ the inhibiting of the child's self-esteem.

[UNICEF Executive Board Paper – Exploitation of Working and Street Children 1986.]

Hence, it is important when considering taking action in this area to analyse the situation that children find themselves in, and identify those elements that amount to an abuse of child rights under international law.

The general framework for these standards may be found in some of the UN treaties, but for more detailed definitions it will be necessary to refer to the various ILO Conventions ratified by each state [>C:5 for ILO contact address].

The ICESCR prohibits exploitative work in ART 10(3) as part of an article concerned with the protection of the family:

> *Special measures of protection and assistance should be taken on behalf of all children and young persons without any discrimination for reasons of parentage or other conditions. Children and young persons should be protected from economic and social exploitation. Their employment in work harmful to their morals or health or dangerous to life or likely to hamper their normal development should be punishable by law. States should also set age limits below which the paid employment of child labour should be prohibited and punishable by law.*

In terms of defining what type of work and conditions are exploitative, this does not take us very far. However, it should be noted that it expressly refers to **social exploitation**, which is of particular relevance for street children (see below).

ART 32 of the **CRC** adopts similar language, specifically adding the threat to a child's education by undertaking such work and the need for states to take action in a number of areas – legislative, administrative, social and educational measures – reflecting the fact that the problem of child labour cannot be tackled in isolation by one means, but needs the co-operation of a number of agencies.

However, beyond stating that minimum admission ages and maximum hour limits must be set by each state the Convention does not provide any further guidance as to what these should be. It was no doubt felt that a sufficient regulatory system already existed, as devised and developed by the ILO.

There are currently 27 ILO Conventions and 14 Recommendations that discuss child employment. The **International Labour Office in Geneva [>C:5]** is able to provide a complete list and gives advice on what standards are most applicable to the particular situation in question. Here we briefly examine some of the most important areas.

2.4.1 Minimum Age

ILO Convention No. 138 on the Minimum Age for Admission to Employment (1973) encourages states both to develop policies for abolishing child labour and to progressively raise the minimum ages when children can legally begin work (ART 1). The full text can be found in *International Documents on Children* (Van Bueren, 1993).

However, in ART 2 the Convention then goes beyond these general requirements to provide some benchmarks for states to adhere to:

○ the age should not be less than **the age when compulsory schooling ends** and in any event should not be less than **15**
○ per ART 2(4), those states whose economies are not sufficiently developed are allowed to set the age at 14.

BUT this can only be transitional.

AND under **ILO Recommendation No 146** it is stipulated that where the minimum age is less than 15, states should be seeking to raise it as a matter of urgency and that the ultimate aim for all states is to raise it to 16 in all economic areas.

Note the formal linking of the right to finish education with the permitted entry stage to begin work.

Permitted Exceptions

○ States are permitted by ART 4(1) to exclude certain categories of child workers where this might create problems – e.g. family businesses and domestic service.

BUT the state has to justify any exclusion and cannot exclude any type of work where the child's well-being could be put at risk (see ART 4(2) and (3)).

○ States whose economies are not sufficiently developed can nominate certain types of economic activity should not be included under ART 5.

BUT this does not apply to certain industries – e.g. **manufacturing and mining**. The table in **C:4** shows the minimum ages set by some states for hazardous industries.

○ ART 7 permits children aged 13–15 to be employed in 'light work' provided it does not affect their schooling.

The exceptions to Convention No. 138 change periodically. The ILO has information on all of these in addition to which states have ratified it.

2.4.2 Working Conditions

Because of its **hazardous nature**, certain types of work should be carried out only by adults (i.e. those who are 18 or over). Convention 138 allows states to define what types of work this might be, based upon their own international treaty commitments and current scientific data. However, other ILO Conventions focus on three particular areas which indicate that the child might be at risk by engaging in them:

○ night-time work
○ work requiring regular medical check-ups
○ occupations that are inherently dangerous.

In terms of regional protection it is worth noting that the **American Protocol of San Salvador** prohibits night-work completely, while the **European Social Charter** does permit certain **exceptions**.

ILO Recommendation 146 (PARA 12(1)) places a duty on states to ensure that working conditions for all those under 18 are maintained to a satisfactory standard and that these are checked regularly and closely.

In order to prove a case where it is believed that children are working in an industry where conditions are prejudicial to their health, but which has been exempted under Convention 138, it is necessary to obtain relevant medical scientific evidence.

2.4.3 Remuneration

One child rights lawyer and academic highlights the potential importance of trying to press for **equal pay for equal work** for child workers, since cheap wages is one of the most significant reasons why people employ children [van Bueren 1994 p.271].

Support for the principle may be found in Paragraph 13 of the **European Social Chapter**.

2.4.4 The Issue of Domestic Service

Because of their situation in private homes working for their 'adopted families', child domestic servants remain one of the most hidden groups of human rights victims. Unfortunately, this position is reinforced by the ILO machinery, which does not cater for activity which is not formally considered 'work'.

17

Often exempted by states under ART 4 of Convention 138 [see 2.4.1 above], domestic service places marginalized children, particularly girls, in positions of extreme vulnerability. The only technical ILO standard that children can rely on is the age limits set in ART 7 of Convention 138 for 'light work' [see 2.4.1], into which category domestic service has traditionally (and bizarrely) fallen.

However, as Van Bueren points out [p.266] the general prohibitions on all forms of economic exploitation introduced by ART 32 of the **CRC** should enable the ILO, under pressure from NGOs, trade unions and sympathetic states, to review the existing framework which allows domestic service to be excluded from much of the protection machinery.

Anti-Slavery suggests quoting ART 19 of the CRC in preference to ART 32 because of its stronger language in placing duties upon states to outlaw all forms of abuse and exploitation against children **[>2.5]**. In any event, it is clear that much domestic service violates both Articles. Indeed, for many children domestic service is **akin to slavery** which was outlawed long before other human rights abuses were tackled by the international community.

The following section describes the international standards introduced to address this issue.

2.4.5 Forced Labour/Slavery

Not only is any form of forced labour or slavery prohibited by all the major international and regional treaties:

○ ART 4 **UNDHR**
○ ARTs 4 and 8 **ICCPR**
○ ART 5 **AfCHR**
○ ART 6 **AmCHR**
○ ART 4 **ECHR**

but it is also the subject of two specific international treaties which have been widely ratified:

○ **The Slavery Convention 1926**
○ **The Supplementary Convention on the Abolition of Slavery, the Slave Trade, and Institutions and Practices Similar to Slavery 1956**.

Although these two treaties do not have their own monitoring bodies, if a state has ratified them it is still under a legal duty to adhere to them, and they should be cited if it is suspected that violations are occurring. Moreover, there is a **UN Working Group on Contemporary Forms of Slavery** which meets in Geneva every year to receive reports on standards, rehabilitation and violations from both governments and NGOs. In its yearly report the Working Group makes recommendations concerning implementation of the standards. Although the Group is little known, NGOs can make both oral reports at its sessions or send in written material to its Secretary, at the Palais des Nations in Geneva.

One of the most typical situations that many children find themselves in is **bonded labour** [see ART 1(a) of Supplementary Convention 1956] whereby they have been forced to work to pay off their families' debt or loan. This practice can continue for several generations.

Given the endemic nature of this practice in many developing countries, where governments have done little *de facto* to outlaw it, it could potentially be the subject of a **1503 procedure [>B:2.5]** as an example of a gross and systematic violation.

18

2.5 Sexual Exploitation

Given the commercial nature of child prostitution, pornography and trafficking, and the fact that vulnerable children are forced into industry through poverty, it is clear that this form of abuse also amounts to economic exploitation and is therefore a violation of ART 32 of the CRC [<2.4].

However, specific protection may be found in ART 34:

States Parties undertake to protect the child from all forms of sexual exploitation and sexual abuse. For these purposes, States Parties shall in particular take all appropriate national, bilateral and multilateral measures to prevent:

a) *The inducement or coercion of a child to engage in any unlawful sexual activity;*

b) *The exploitative use of children in prostitution or other unlawful sexual practices;*

c) *The exploitative use of children in pornographic performances and materials.*

2.5.1 The Need to Reconceptualize Child Sexual Exploitation

Traditionally the right not to be sexually exploited has been classified as an economic and social right, given the reference to 'work harmful to morals or health' in ART 10(3) of the **ICESCR**.

However, this has two drawbacks for those wishing to take action on abuses:

○ states have a duty under both the CRC and the ICESCR only to 'progressively realise' economic and social rights instead of taking immediate action to correct abuses

○ violations cannot be the subject of individual complaints as under the ICCPR or regional treaties which address only civil and political rights.

One potential answer to both problems is to reconceptualize child sexual exploitation as **degrading treatment** and therefore a violation of ART 7 of the ICCPR or ART 3 of the ECHR or ART 5 of the AmCHR [see Van Bueren 1994 p.279].

Another suggestion is to view keeping a child brothel as a practice which is **in effect slavery** and therefore contrary to customary international human rights law. This means that no matter what treaty obligations the state is under (and there are many which outlaw slavery) it should not allow this practice to continue [Sunga 1992].

Both ideas show the imaginative approach that needs to be taken in order to overcome the barriers that currently exist to protecting economic and social rights.

2.6 Social Exploitation

Many street children are not subject to direct economic or sexual exploitation. However, their neglect by the community still means they are exploited through their lack of equal access to public services and the opportunity to participate fully in society.

This social exclusion is recognized explicitly by ART 10(3) of the **ICESCR**, and implicitly by ART 36 of the **CRC**, which states:

States Parties shall protect the child against all other forms of exploitation prejudicial to any aspect of the child's welfare.

Their lifestyles often mean that **they have greater need of state services** than those children who are part of a permanent family unit, attend school and receive medical care upon demand.

The inclusivity of the **CRC** to **embrace all children** **without discrimination** places a duty upon states to devise both protective and social programmes for those children living on the margins of society. Governments' failures to do so should be brought to account through the reporting mechanisms of the CRC and the ICESCR [>**B:1**] and, in due course, through the individual complaints system of the African Charter on the Rights and Welfare of the Child [>**B:3**], for example.

2.7 Rehabilitation and Reintegration

An important provision of the CRC, which is worth noting in relation to violations under any of the six areas covered above, is ARTICLE 39 which places a duty on states to assist in the rehabilitation and reintegration within society of child victims of abuse and/or exploitation:

> *States Parties shall take all appropriate measures to promote physical and psychological recovery and social reintegration of a child victim of any form of neglect, exploitation, or abuse; torture or any other form of cruel, inhuman or degrading treatment or punishment; or armed conflicts. Such recovery and reintegration shall take place in an environment which fosters the health, self-respect and dignity of the child.*

The **potential importance of this provision for street and working children** should not be underestimated since it includes both omissions by states as well as direct violations. Indeed, its inclusive message can be applied to the whole range of violations suffered by street and working children, emphasizing as it does that no child should be excluded from society through abuse or neglect.

As Van Bueren states:

They captured national and media attention precisely because it was the children who met and marched about the problems they faced.

[Van Bueren 1994 p144]

Freedom of association may be found in the following treaties:

○ ART 8 ICESCR
○ ARTs 21 and 22 ICCPR
○ ART 15 CRC
○ ART 10 AfCHR
○ ART 16 AmCHR
○ ART 11 ECHR.

Note that the freedom is found in both the ICESCR (where it is formulated as a specific right to join trade unions) and the ICCPR, hence enabling it to transcend the traditionally artificial boundaries of economic and social rights and civil and political rights and again undermining the argument that the former cannot be the subject of individual complaints.

ART 15 of the **CRC** does not redefine the right as expressed in other treaties:

1. States Parties recognise the rights of the child to freedom of association and to freedom of peaceful assembly.

2. No restrictions may be placed on the exercise of these rights other than those imposed in conformity with the law and which are necessary in a democratic society in the interests of national security or public order (ordre public), *the protection of public health or morals or the protection of the rights and freedoms of others.*

BUT its **symbolic importance** should not be underestimated as it gives express recognition to such a right for children that was only ever implied (and denied by some governments) previously.

Hence, states can no longer deny children working on or above the minimum age for employment the right to form trade unions to protect their interests. Of course, in practice many states will continue to prevent such activity, as they do for adults, through intimidation, arrests and even murder. However, such violations for a state party to the CRC can now be the subject of NGO reports to the Committee on the Rights of the Child.

Empowerment rights matter – they enable street and working children to take control of their own lives.

3.3 Freedom of Thought, Conscience and Religion

This right is particularly important in countries where the relationship between the state and one established religion is particularly close and there is a consequent lack of pluralism.

Although at first glance such a right may seem of less importance for street and working children, since even the most powerful of states cannot prevent people holding particular thoughts, it is the prevention of the manifestation of those beliefs and the very fact that somebody is identified as holding certain beliefs that can result in widespread abuses against certain minorities.

If children are being discriminated against because of their beliefs the following texts may be cited:

- ○ ART 18 ICCPR
- ○ ART 14 CRC
- ○ ART 8 AfCHR
- ○ ART 12 AmCHR
- ○ ART 9 ECHR.

3.4 Education

Those who work with street and working children know that one of the things many of them miss most is the chance to receive an education. Even the most basic tuition will provide them with useful skills in literacy and numeracy, while opportunities to receive a higher level of education could transform their lives completely. Many street kids projects seek to provide some form of informal education, but this does not reduce the duty on states to educate all their children up to a certain standard.

ART 13 of the ICESCR establishes the **right of education for all, with primary education compulsory and freely available**. However, given the Covenant's caveat for the implementation of all economic and social rights – that they should be 'progressively realized' according to the available resources of each state – the complete introduction of this right is somewhat limited by the subsequent ART 14, which allows a state two years to devise plans for progressive implementation over a number of years. The demands to put in place secondary and higher education are even less stringent (see Art 13(2)(b) and (c)) **[>C:2.3]**.

The duties contained in ART 28 of the CRC **[>C:2.1]** do not lessen states' responsibilities, but merely reinforce those of the ICESCR, leading one child rights writer to conclude:

Treaty law is clear. All children who live in states which are party either to the International Covenant on Economic, Social and Cultural Rights or to the Convention on the Rights of the Child are entitled to receive free primary education.

[Van Bueren 1994 p.235]

although she doubts whether existing international law provides a right to free education at higher levels (note that ART 12 of the American Declaration – not a binding treaty – states that 'at least primary education' should be free). Nevertheless, given that most children in the developing world will not progress further than the primary stage (if they receive any education at all), this principle of free and accessible basic education is an important one.

ART 28 contains one further requirement for state education which is of significance for marginalized children – that it should be implemented on the basis of **equal opportunity** which, given the profile of many schools, clearly does not occur. However, the need to combat discrimination has been further taken up by the Committee on Economic, Social and Cultural Rights **[>B:1.3]** which now requests states to provide information in their regular reports on discrimination against groups of children most likely to be the subject of discrimination.

The Committee welcomes information on the degree to which children have access to education.

Further anti-discrimination measures can be found in:

- ○ UNESCO Convention against Discrimination in Education [contact UNESCO's offices in Paris **[>C:5]** for a copy]
- ○ ART 10 CEDAW **[>C:2.6]** – tackling discrimination against girls
- ○ ART 11(3)(e) African Charter on Rights and Welfare of the Child **[>C:2.10]**.

SECTION B
Human Rights Systems

B1: International Human Rights Treaty Systems

How many international human rights treaties are there?

If all the International Labour Organisation conventions are included there are over 200. However, within the United Nations system there is a need to be aware of only the following six, here listed in chronological order, since these are the only ones to have any form of monitoring mechanism and, in some cases, the powers to receive individual complaints:

○ International Covenant on Civil and Political Rights (ICCPR)
○ International Covenant on Economic, Social and Cultural Rights (ICESCR)
○ International Convention on the Elimination of All Forms of Racial Discrimination (CERD)
○ Convention against Torture and Other Cruel, Inhuman or Degrading Treatment or Punishment (CAT)
○ International Convention on the Elimination of All Forms of Discrimination against Women (CEDAW)
○ Convention on the Rights of the Child (CRC).

But surely there is only really a need to know about the Convention on the Rights of the Child?

The CRC is undoubtedly a major breakthrough in the protection of children's rights, especially because of the large number of countries that have ratified it [>C:3] and the new and more comprehensive set of rights that it has introduced. However, it is important to realise that:

○ the **rights that are included in other treaties apply equally to children** as well as adults. Children should not be 'ghettoized' into the CRC, but where appropriate, be the subject of actions under all relevant mechanisms – both treaty and non-treaty
○ as we shall see, unlike the CRC, **some of the other treaties have individual complaints procedures** which can be used by children or their representatives if their rights have been violated
○ some of the other treaties have **stronger monitoring procedures** because they have been enforced longer.

Appendix C:3 details the various human rights treaties ratified by each state.

That seems to make sense, but do all these different treaties not lead to duplication?

It is true that many people who work in human rights – lawyers, activists, academics, UN officials – think there are often too many mechanisms dealing with the same subject matter. For example, torture could be reported under the ICCPR, CAT and CRC and an individual complaint can be brought under the first two. However, the danger is that if we try to dispense with some of the mechanisms, governments may, through their UN representatives, try to get rid of the stronger procedures and retain the weaker ones.

Based upon their particular resources – both human and financial – and what they are trying to achieve, each NGO must decide which is the best strategy to adopt, considering the relative advantages and disadvantages of not only the different UN treaty bodies listed here, but also the non-treaty and regional mechanisms described in the next two sections. Unless there are specific rules to the contrary, there is nothing to stop an NGO using one procedure until it is completed and then pursuing another, or in some circumstances using more than one at the same time. This section shows that some procedures are stronger in some areas compared with others, and, based upon their own experiences and that of colleagues, each person will need to devise their own effective strategy to get the most from them.

It is only by greater and more consistent use by both individuals and NGOs of all the different mechanisms that they will become more effective.

1.1 Convention on the Rights of the Child (CRC)

When did it come into force?
September 1990 – only ten months after being adopted by the UN General Assembly.
Isn't it good news that so many states have ratified it?
Yes, it is, but this is only half the story. It is easy to agree to be bound by a document – the difficult part is implementing it effectively, particularly in the case of the CRC which involves such a wide range of rights for children – 34 substantive articles compared with the ICCPR's 21 **[>C:2]**.

It has been suggested that the reason so many states have ratified the CRC is because of the opportunity to receive UN resources through the provision of 'technical advice and assistance' **[>1.1.3]**. Whatever the reasons for a state's acceptance – self-serving or humanitarian – once it has ratified an international treaty such as the CRC it is under a **binding duty** to implement it.
How does the UN ensure that states are implementing their promises?
As with all the main international treaties, a committee has been established to monitor state progress. The **Committee on the Rights of the Child** consists of ten experts who serve in an independent, personal capacity.

Despite some arguable deficiencies – it has no Islamic members or children – the Committee does have eight people with comprehensive experience in child rights and a balanced number of men and women.
How often does the Committee meet?
Three times a year (in January, April and September for between two and three weeks) at the United Nations Palais des Nations building in Geneva **[>C:5]**. It reports every two years to the UN General Assembly.
What are its main functions?
These are:

○ to receive state **reports** on how they are implementing the CRC (ART 44)
○ to devise and recommend **innovative methods of implementation** (ART 42)
○ to provide **technical advice and assistance** (ART 45)
○ to make specific **recommendations** and to commission **studies** to be carried out by the Secretary General (ARTS 44+45).

1.1.1 Reporting
How long after ratification must a state submit a report?
Within **two years** and **then every five years**. However, as is the case with all the reporting systems, many states are already behind the Committee's schedule, having failed to file their first report **[>C:3]**.

What should the report cover?

It should cover how each of the substantive articles of the CRC is being implemented and the difficulties encountered. Ideally it should form a framework within which politicians, NGOs and concerned individuals can discuss progress within the country and what are the future priorities and the measures needed to tackle them – administrative, judicial and legislative at national, regional and local level.

It should include **statistical information** such as:

o estimated numbers of homeless children
o the numbers of children taken into protective custody
o breakdowns by gender/ethnic/rural/urban divisions.

As well as demonstrating how national laws are being brought into line with the CRC, it should also show how the state is **publicizing and disseminating information about the Convention**.

The state must show that **rights are being enforced on behalf of all children without discrimination**, a point that is particularly important for street and working children and other marginalized young people.

But shouldn't some rights take priority over others?

By including both civil and political rights and economic, social and cultural rights, the drafters of the CRC endeavoured to ensure that an integrated approach would be adopted towards children's rights. In order to enable a child fully to enjoy one right he or she must often enjoy the benefit of another – e.g. the right to education cannot be enjoyed by a sick or hungry child.

Rights are interdependent and the boundaries between them are increasingly blurred. The Committee is therefore concerned with **progress on all rights under the Convention**, (even though, as has been the tradition with other UN treaty bodies [>1.2], it will be recognized that those requiring more resources will be implemented over a longer period of time).

Are states the only source of information?

The Committee is empowered under ARTICLE 45, to receive information from UNICEF and other specialized agencies and competent bodies – e.g. the World Bank – in order to have access to comparable data.

Where do NGOs come in?

The Committee has **recognized the significant role that NGOs can play in the monitoring process**. NGOs played a large part in drafting the Convention and met with the Committee at its first session to discuss effective implementation of its procedures. Under ARTICLE 45 it has been agreed that the Committee's ability to receive information from 'competent bodies' includes NGOs. Therefore there is the opportunity **to submit reports at the same time** as State Parties for consideration by the Committee.

This process is greatly assisted by the **NGO Group for the Convention on the Rights of the Child**, which is also based in Geneva [>C:5] and acts as a conduit for NGO information into the Committee. Contact the Secretariat for more information about how they can assist NGOs both to submit reports and with funding to attend pre-sessional working groups of the Committee.

What is the most effective way of submitting a report?

[NB: All of the following advice applies to the other treaty bodies covered in this section]

NGOs should not try to submit a report in isolation. Once they know that a state's report is due for consideration by the next meeting of the Committee they should:

○ endeavour to obtain a copy of the state report – states are under a duty to make the document public and widely available
○ contact other local and, if possible, international NGOs with similar concerns
○ coordinate activities and submit a joint report responding particularly to those areas of the state report which are inaccurate or which highlight omissions. This will avoid duplication, enable pooling of resources and have much more impact
○ ensure they have a presence at the Committee's session – either directly or through a partner NGO.

What information should be provided?
When preparing the report NGOs should ensure that wherever possible:

○ information is presented under the **relevant Treaty article(s)** which they consider to have been violated
○ reference is made to and **quotes are taken from the government's report** where they are making counter claims
○ **Committee members should not be requested to ask questions** on their behalf unless they have a personal contact
○ **individual cases should not be referred to** unless they can show that they are part of a systematic pattern of violations
○ **specific recommendations** are made for government action
○ mention is made that **information has been submitted to other treaty bodies** (for example, the Human Rights Committee or Committee Against Torture) if this has happened and the fact that the government has failed to take any suitable action.

The NGO should **make sure there are sufficient number of copies** for each Committee member and one additional copy for the Human Rights Centre (for example, 11 in the case of the CRC, 19 in the case of the Human Rights Commitee [>1.2]). The copies of the reports, should be sent for the attention of the Committee, care of the Centre in Geneva [>C:5] **at least one month in advance** of the next session.

What happens next?
The Committee examines state reports in **open public session**, during which state representatives will make opening statements, answer questions from Commitee members (or submit them later in writing), listen to the latter's observations on the record of implementation to date and then make a concluding address.

Inadequate responses or unanswered questions will be requested by the Committee to be addressed in the next report – providing useful indicators for NGOs – or possibly to the UN Secretariat in the interim if the issue is more urgent.

The **concluding remarks** of the Committee should be analysed carefully as these will provide a good summary of members' particular concerns that require state follow-up action.

Individual Committee reports subsequently form part of the main report submitted every two years to the UN General Assembly.

Can NGOs intervene during the consideration of the report?
Only if the matter does not concern examination of a state report (!)

BUT, unlike some other Committees, the CRC does permit NGOs to make **formal written interventions**.

What sanctions does the Committee have if a state ignores its conclusions?

Apart from international shame – which should not be underestimated – none.

Then what does the whole process actually achieve?

The reporting process is seen as part of **a 'constructive on-going dialogue'** between the state and the international community within which the two sides and other interested parties – specialist agencies and NGOs – can engage without the threat of judicial punishment.

It enables the state to monitor its own progress in implementation, reflect upon its deficiencies in an impartial arena, request international help to overcome them and (hopefully) take specific action to improve the situation: for example, setting economic and social targets.

It enables the international community both to monitor individual states' progress and to discover whether there are common problems and themes, learn of innovative solutions that could be applied elsewhere and to receive comparative information.

However, given the large number of reports the Committee has to deal with and the fact that after the initial report the state has to submit only every five years, it is certainly questionable how much can be achieved, both in terms of detailed examination and regular discussion. These are common problems for all the treaty bodies, but given that the Committee on the Rights of the Child has more substantive rights and country reports to examine than any other it is particularly serious. Only more resources and a review of its internal procedures can hope to improve the situation.

1.1.2 Innovative Implementation

ART 42 provides the framework within which the CRC recognizes the importance of states adopting original and effective means of implementing a children's human rights treaty:

> *States Parties undertake to make the principles and provisions of the Convention widely known, by appropriate and active means, to adults and children alike.*

States must be able to show that they are actively involving children in developing and promoting their child rights policies.

But how will this affect street and working children?

As we saw in **A:3**, part of the CRC's mandate is to empower children – *all* children – and while it may be naïve to think that such marginalized children will immediately begin playing such a role, the state should be devising strategies with bodies such as NGOs both to inform them about their rights and, more importantly, how they should be able to enjoy them.

1.1.3 Technical Advice and Assistance

Why should states receive such help from the UN?

Since its founding, the UN has seen that one of its roles is to help states implement their treaty commitments effectively since this is in everyone's interest. **It does not lessen the obligations that the state has.**

Any state request for assistance is passed through the Committee to the UN. Help coordinated by the Human Rights Centre in Geneva, can take the form of:

- ○ training on how to better prepare state reports
- ○ distribution of human rights materials
- ○ regional seminars on focused themes such as child exploitation.

NGOs are playing an increasingly important role in providing such assistance – the Human Rights Centre can be contacted for more details.

1.1.4 Recommendations and Studies

ARTS 44 and 45 allow the Committee to make specific recommendations to states on implementing the CRC and to request the UN General Assembly to commission the Secretary General to undertake specific studies.

Note that the **study does not need to relate to a right protected under the CRC** (see ART 45(c)) nor to the CRC state parties.

1.2 International Covenant on Civil and Political Rights (ICCPR)

Why are there two separate covenants?

At the time the Covenants were drafted in the mid-1960s the debate between the supremacy of civil and political rights compared with economic, social and cultural rights reflected the Cold War divide, with the West tending towards the former and the Eastern bloc towards the latter. Unlike today, where there is wider consensus about the need to adopt a holistic approach towards human rights, it was felt impossible to include all rights in one document.

However, taken together – and most countries have now ratified both **[>C:3]** – they are seen to represent an International Bill of Rights. This reflects the fact that both Covenants are products of the original Universal Declaration of Human Rights, which, although not a binding treaty, is now widely accepted as being a part of customary international law (and therefore applicable in all circumstances **[>C:1]**).

What is the name and function of the ICCPR monitoring body?

The implementation of the ICCPR is supervised by the **Human Rights Committee**. It has 18 members of high moral character who serve in an independent personal capacity. It meets for two three-week sessions in **Geneva (July and October/November)** and **New York (March/April)**. The International Service for Human Rights provides up-to-date information on dates of meetings and countries under consideration.

The Committee:

- ○ examines state reports every five years
- ○ receives and considers inter-state complaints
- ○ receives and considers individual complaints from countries that have signed the Optional Protocol
- ○ makes general comments on the implementation of the ICCPR.

1.2.1 Reporting

How should state reports be set out?

The Committee's general guidelines stipulate that **initial reports** should include an **introductory section** describing the general legal framework within which human rights are protected which is in line with the UN consolidated guidelines [see UN Centre for Human Rights and UN Institute for Training and Research (UNITAR) *Manual on Human Rights Reporting* UN Sales No. E.91 XIV.1 (1991) p.35] and a **second section** setting out for each article of the ICCPR:

o the legislative, administrative or other measures in force with regard to each right
o any restrictions imposed, however temporary
o any other factors or difficulties affecting the enjoyment of the right
o any other relevant information on progress made.

With regard to **periodic reports**, states should concentrate on the developments occurring since the previous report and address earlier Committee concerns.

The Committee uses essentially the same process as the Committee on the Rights of the Child to examine a state report **[<1.1.1]**
BUT note that the Committee **does not permit NGOs to make any written or oral interventions** during its session.

Does the Committee's examination become less rigorous as time passes?

On the contrary, it will scrutinize subsequent reports much more closely than initial submissions as it will expect the state to have taken action on its remarks. The initial report provides an opportunity to introduce the state to the Committee's procedures and to begin the process of dialogue.

If that's the case is there any point in commenting on initial state reports?

Yes. This will be the first opportunity that the most important UN treaty body has had to analyse a state's human rights record. NGOs can use the opportunity to focus publicity on the issues that they want addressing (bearing in mind it will be another five years before the Committee will comment again).

Any recognition by international human rights bodies that a state is failing to protect the rights of street and working children adequately can only be of benefit when campaigning at a local and national level for the equal respect and treatment such children deserve from the rest of society.

1.2.2 Inter-state Complaints
Will states be reluctant to bring complaints against each other?

Yes, unless they can count on strong diplomatic support from others. For this reason it is not surprising that to date the procedure has never been used under the ICCPR, although it has been used a few times under the European Convention.

1.2.3 Individual Complaints
Can anybody bring an individual complaint against any country that has ratified the Covenant?

It is possible to petition the Committee alleging a violation of the Covenant by a state only if the latter has, in addition to ratifying the ICCPR, also ratified **the first Optional Protocol (OP)**.

To date, 84 of the 131 state parties to the ICCPR have ratified the OP **[>C:3]**.
So are there any other restrictions?

According to Article 1 of the OP the Committee may receive complaints only from '**individuals subject to the State Party's jurisdiction who claim to be victims** of a violation by that State Party of any of the rights set forth in the Covenant'.

However, the **victim's representative** may submit a complaint on his or her behalf, or if the victim is unable to lodge the complaint himself (for example, if he or she has disappeared) his or her **close relative** may do so.

Note that the **burden rests with the representative** to show that there is a sufficiently close connection between him or herself and the victim to permit acting on the victim's behalf, otherwise the application could be declared inadmissible. Moreover, it will be necessary to:

- ○ ensure that whoever is the author of the petition **signs and dates it**
- ○ have **exhausted all domestic remedies** or be able to explain how they are ineffective
- ○ not to use the procedure to make a general challenge against an unjust law by bringing an *actio popularis* – **it is necessary to show that there has been a specific violation**
- ○ ensure that the complaint is not an abuse of the right of petition – **by not using offensive language or making a political attack on the state**.

Does the victim need to be a citizen of the state?

No, they do not need to be a citizen or even resident – it will be **sufficient that the person is present in the territory** of the state.

Can the procedure be used in conjunction with another system?

The Committee **cannot consider a complaint being dealt with at the same time** under another international procedure (this does not apply to the 1503 procedure [>B:2]).

BUT there is **nothing to prevent the victim from using another procedure first** and upon completion **then** applying under the ICCPR, **UNLESS** the state has entered **a reservation to the contrary**, which several have done [>C:3].

How should the complaint be set out?

The **model communication** on the following pages can be used as a guide. It has been produced by the Committee to assist complainants, but it does not have to be followed exactly.

The more information that can be provided the quicker the Committee will be able to examine it and the more seriously it will be taken. However, a rapid result should not be expected (it can take up to four years!) and, therefore, **this procedure should not be used if urgent action is required**. The Committee can request interim measures in the case of somebody under sentence of death [see below].

What if the complainant doesn't want his or her name to be revealed?

The communication must not be anonymous, but this does not mean that a request to the Committee cannot be made to **maintain the confidentiality** of the author and/or the victim when it makes its decision public.

How does the Committee consider the complaint?

Communication sent to the Human Rights Committee
c/o UN Human Rights Centre, Geneva

↓

Committee may request interim measures in cases of extreme urgency
(e.g. victim under sentence of death)

↓

If required, author contacted for further information

↓

Application registered and forwarded to Special Rapporteur on
New Applications

↓

Communication passes preliminary admissibility requirements
(not anonymous, an abuse or incompatible with ICCPR)

↓

continued . . .

Communication forwarded to state for its comments
on admissibility
↓
State must respond within two months
↓
Author able to comment on state's response
↓
Five-person Working Group meets prior to next Committee session to
consider admissibility and may declare communication admissible if
unanimous decisions
↓
All other communications considered by Committee
↓
If declared inadmissible, author may call for review based on new
evidence that domestic remedies have been exhausted/no longer being
considered by another body
↓
Admissible case allows state six months to submit written explanations
and information concerning any remedies
↓
State's statement forwarded to author who has 6 weeks to submit
additional information
↓
Committee arrives at decision usually by consensus based on
information received
(No provision for oral hearing or on-site investigation)
↓
Committee adopts its 'views', which are forwarded to both complainant
and state
↓
Views made public in communiqué at end of each Committee session
and published in Annual Report to General Assembly

Can the Committee's views have any effect?

They are **not legally binding** and until recently the Committee did not take any active measures to check whether states had taken action, apart from sending a letter inviting them to respond.

However, since 1990 the Committee gives **a state 180 days to respond** and if it fails to do so or does not provide a satisfactory remedy for a victim then its name will be listed in the Committee's Annual Report. Although this amounts to no more than international shame this should not be entirely discounted at the diplomatic level.

The Committee has also introduced a requirement for states to provide information about redress for violations in their periodic reports and appointed a 'Special Rapporteur for the Follow-Up of Views' to recommend appropriate action for those victims who remain without a remedy. He can communicate directly with both the government and victims.

Is this all the redress that is available?

Compared with the European or American systems clearly the redress is not as strong. However, the recent developments at least mean that the Committee will not be dispensing with the case at the end of its session, but, through its consideration of periodic reports and the Special Rapporteur, will be reminding the state regularly that it needs to provide redress to victims where there have been proven violations of the Covenant.

Moreover, **the Committee has not been afraid to demand that states take immediate action** to:

○ ensure strict observance of the Covenant
○ release someone wrongly detained
○ commute a death sentence imposed in circumstances which violates the Covenant
○ provide remedies to a victim – including compensation.

1.3 International Covenant on Economic, Social and Cultural Rights (ICESCR)

Does the Human Rights Committee monitor this Covenant as well?

No, the ICESCR has its own monitoring body called the **Committee on Economic, Social and Cultural Rights** which was created by ECOSOC in 1987. It is composed of 18 independent expert members.

Can the Committee receive complaints?

Unlike the Human Rights Committee, **the Committee** on Economic, Social and Cultural Rights **cannot receive individual complaints, but only monitors state reports**. Many governments and some human rights academics argue that it is almost impossible to judge cases alleging violations of economic and social rights because of the requirement only to 'progressively realize' the implementation of such rights [see ART 2(1)] and the lack of suitable benchmarks to assess whether abuses have actually occurred. It is also a fact that few international human rights NGOs campaign on economic and social rights and that little of the UN human rights budget is devoted to them.

However, it is becoming increasingly evident that such rights do need to be better protected under international human rights law. Once in force, the African Charter on the Rights and Welfare of the Child **[>B:5]** – although open to question as to how effective it will prove to be – will have an individual petition system for both civil and political and economic, social and cultural rights. This symbolic development should at least contribute to the increasing pressure to introduce such a system at the international level.

So what can be done in the meantime?

Reports can be submitted by NGOs to both the Committee on Economic, Social and Cultural Rights and the Committee on the Rights of the Child when a government is due to report.

The Committee meets **annually for one two-week session in November/ December** at the UN building in Geneva.

Although the rights under the Covenant generally require only progressive implementation, this is subject to two qualifications:

○ all the Covenant **rights** have to be exercised **without any form of discrimination**
○ states must adopt **measures** within a reasonably short period of time of ratifying the Covenant **which are 'deliberate, concrete and targeted** as clearly as possible towards meeting [their] obligations . . .'

[per the *Committee's General Comment No. 3* (1990) – emphasis added].

36

These measures should at least meet the basic essential levels required for each right to be enjoyed.

Hence, in the case of street children, it is justified to argue that basic levels of access to food, health care, education and shelter should be provided by the state for all its people without discrimination as a matter of urgency. The state may argue that it is not in a position to provide this, but will need to justify its failure to protect economic and social rights for street and working children before the Committee, showing that it has 'made every effort to use all the resources at its disposition'.

Non-discrimination clauses in human rights treaties show that street and working children have the same rights as everyone else.

Is the procedure much the same as for the Human Rights Committee and the Committee on the Rights of the Child?

Yes. States **submit an initial report within two years of ratification and thereafter every five years. [>C:3]** and the Committee follows essentially the same requirements for contents and assessment as do the other two Committees **[<1.1.1; 1.2.1]** with one main exception. In order to improve the effectiveness of Committee sessions for both initial and periodic reports the Committee on Economic, Social and Cultural Rights will use a five-member working group to draft and forward questions to the state in advance of the full meeting. The Human Rights Committee and the Committee on the Elimination of the Discrimination Against Women also carry out this procedure, but only for periodic reports.

The Committee has also taken the innovative step of examining the situations in countries that fail to submit reports, in order to ensure that they remain accountable to their treaty commitments.

The Human Rights Centre in Geneva has information on which countries are to be examined by the Committee, enabling NGOs still to submit reports.

What happens after the Committee has examined the report?

It forms part of the Committee's Annual Report that is forwarded to ECOSOC – not to the General Assembly. Again, this can be consulted and used as evidence of state failings.

The Committee is the only major international body dealing solely with economic, social and cultural rights. Although it is less well known than its civil and political counterpart, Section A demonstrated that many of the rights it examines are of fundamental importance for street and working children. Committee members are striving to obtain more resources for the Committee's work and to strengthen its monitoring mechanisms. NGOs can play their part by submitting reports to the Committee and using its reports in their own campaigns.

1.4 The Convention Against Torture and Other Forms of Cruel, Inhuman or Degrading Treatment (CAT)

1.4.1 Reporting
Does the Committee Against Torture work in a similar way to the other bodies?

The ten-member Committee of independent experts, which meets for **two two-week sessions in April and November in Geneva each year**, has adopted the same set of guidelines followed by the other treaty bodies.

Since its establishment in 1988 the Committee has been **particularly forceful in its questioning of states**, asking for information such as the specific numbers of people being held in detention and how they are being treated. If NGOs have detailed information on systematic torture being carried out against street children or instances of inhumane treatment while in custody, this should receive a sympathetic hearing.

However, because of the **Committee's narrow remit**, irrelevant information on the situation of street children generally (which may be of concern to the two Covenant Committees and/or the Child Rights Committee but which does not concern torture or cruel, inhuman or degrading treatment as defined by CAT) will not be well received and will only waste everybody's time.

Reconceptualizing certain abuses such as economic and sexual exploitation as inhumane and degrading treatment **[<A:2]** is less clear cut as it is still a relatively new concept. The Committee's Secretariat in Geneva and/or international NGOs such as Anti-Slavery International **[>C:5]** are able to provide further advice.
Does the Committee have any additional monitoring powers?

The Committee is the only supervisory body **expressly empowered to make comments** on individual state reports (ART 19 CAT) which can then be included in its Annual Report to the UN General Assembly; if it chooses to do so these can be a powerful indictment of a state's record. Any NGO reports submitted to the Committee will naturally help to inform this process.

1.4.2 Individual Complaints and Information on Systematic Torture Practices
Are there similar restrictions to the ICCPR?

Yes – only states that have accepted the Committee's standing to hear complaints can be made the subject of an individual complaint, except that the procedure is contained within the Convention (ART 22) rather than in a protocol.

Appendix **C:3** lists the parties to the Convention that have made such a declaration.
Who can apply?

If it is an individual complaint, the victim or his or her close representative can apply alleging a violation under the Convention.

However, the Committee **will also receive information from any concerned person**, or group of persons – including NGOs – **on the systematic practice of torture** being carried out within a state. They do not even need to be subject to the state's jurisdiction to submit such information.
Does the Committee therefore have a wider mandate than the Human Rights Committee?

Upon receiving such information relating to systematic torture the Committee can:

o invite the state to make appropriate observations on the information
o initiate its own **on-site investigation**.

These investigations and the receipt of information **can be carried out in relation to any state that has ratified the Convention, UNLESS** the state has made a declaration to the contrary under Article 28 **[>C:3]**.

These powers are unique to the Committee in the UN system, but the **practice must relate to torture** and not to any less severe forms of treatment.
Is it possible to use the same format as for an individual complaint under the ICCPR?

Yes. The model communication can be used as a guide **[<1.2.3]**, substituting the ICCPR articles with those relating to CAT and sending it c/o the UN Human Rights Centre in Geneva.

What about a communication on systematic torture?

In order to demonstrate that there has been a systematic practice carried out over a considerable period of time **it is necessary to provide more than one or two apparently isolated incidents**. For instance, it is important if street children are being tortured as a matter of routine while in custody to gather as much evidence as possible – witness statements, medical reports – with times, dates and locations, before submitting it to the Committee.

How will the Committee deal with an individual complaint?

See the admissibility criteria and procedure used by the Human Rights Committee [**<1.2.3**], which are very similar to that used by the Committee Against Torture. Again, as with the HRC, it may be possible to obtain a review of an inadmissible decision on the basis of non-exhaustion if it can be demonstrated that all domestic remedies have been exhausted.

After the Committee declares a case admissible it sends that decision – and any new submissions by the complainant – to the state, which then has six months to respond.

Unlike the HRC, **the Committee may invite the parties to attend an oral hearing** at which they may be questioned or required to clarify certain points in the case. UN and other specialized agencies may also be requested to provide additional information.

If the victim is in imminent danger the Committee can, at any stage during the proceedings, request the state to take some form of appropriate **interim measures** to protect them from any permanent harm.

All proceedings are **confidential**.

Once the Committee has made its views known both to the complainant and the state – and decisions are published in the Committee's Annual Report to the UN General Assembly – there is no other mechanism for ensuring that action is taken. In this sense it is weaker than the Human Rights Committee, but if the follow-up procedures of the latter prove to be successful it is likely that the CAT will introduce something similar.

And communications on systematic torture practices?

A Committee member will be appointed to conduct a confidential enquiry into the information received and produce a report with observations and suggestions. This report will then be sent to the state for its comments, with an invitation to inform the Committee of any action it proposes to take.

Again, there is no sanction available for a state that chooses to ignore the report and the Committee's conclusions, although a summary account can be published in the Committee's annual report after 'consultations' with the state.

1.5 International Convention on the Elimination of All Forms of Racial Discrimination (CERD)

1.5.1 Reporting
Isn't this treaty superfluous, given the non-discrimination clauses in other documents?

There might be less cause to use both this Convention and the following Convention on Discrimination Against Women than the other four systems we have looked at in this section.

BUT the Convention contains **a number of very important substantive provisions**, some of which are **fundamental to the protection of street and working children** and which they might not enjoy because of their racial or ethnic background including:

- the right to equal treatment before the law
- the right to security of person and protection by the state against violence or bodily harm, whether inflicted by government officials or others
- certain economic and social rights.

Countries have also been questioned about **non-citizens** even though ART 1 of the Convention expressly denies it is concerned with their different treatment.

As with many of the systems we are examining in this manual, there is some overlap with other bodies. However, if the violations suffered by a street or working child occur specifically because of their racial or ethnic origin it may be worth considering submitting a report or making a complaint (see below) under the CERD system.

So how does the Committee monitor state compliance?

The 18 independent-member Committee on the Elimination of Racial Discrimination – the oldest in the UN system – **examines state reports one year after ratification and then every four years**. It also requests brief interim update reports every two years.

The reports are again subject to the same guidelines as the other bodies **[<1.1.1]**.

1.5.2 Individual Complaints

Is this procedure used much?

To date only 21 of the state parties to CERD have made the required optional declaration under ART 14 of the Convention **[>C:3]** and the Committee has considered very few individual complaints.

BUT this low level of use compared with the Human Rights Committee does not imply it is less effective – rather that a lack of publicity about the Committee's work and the relatively small number of states accepting complaints against them has worked against it.

What requirements are there to submit a complaint?

Communications can be received from both **individuals and groups of individuals who come under the state's jurisdiction** and who claim to be victims of any violation of a right under the Convention.

Does groups include NGOs?

In this case (unlike the Human Rights Committee **[<1.2.3]**) – **no**. It must be a victim or a formal representative such as a relative or advocate. It may be possible in exceptional circumstances, but the NGO will need to justify why the victim cannot submit, and the need for the NGO to act on their behalf.

Can the complaint be submitted to another body as well?

In principle, yes.

BUT a number of states have made reservations **[>C:3]** that they will accept the Committee's competence to examine a complaint only when the matter in question is not being or has not been examined by another international body.

And all domestic remedies have to be exhausted?

As always, it will be necessary to show that these have been pursued through the relevant judicial and administrative bodies in the country unless they are in practice ineffective, subject to unreasonable delays, or access to them has been denied. Evidence will have to be provided to back up these arguments.

It is also important to remember the time limit – **six months** to submit the complaint **after all available remedies have been exhausted**. This can be waived only in exceptional circumstances.

When preparing the complaint should the same format as for the Human Rights Committee be used?

In the absence of any suggested format from the Committee this is the best idea, providing as much supporting evidence as possible.

It should be sent to the Committee on the Elimination of Racial Discrimination, c/o the Human Rights Centre, Geneva [>C:5].

Unless it is expressly permitted, the applicant's name will not be disclosed to the state.

How will the Committee investigate the complaint?

Communication received and declared admissible
↓
Communication and any other relevant material sent to state
↓
State has two months to submit observations
↓
Committee may transmit state observations to complainant – in practice it will do so
↓
Committee considers merits of complaint – may request state at this stage to take interim measures to protect victim from lasting harm
↓
Power to invite parties to oral hearing and to receive additional information from UN and other specialized agencies
↓
Committee reaches majority decision and makes appropriate recommendations and suggestions for attention of parties
↓
Decision publicized through communiqué and included in next Annual Report to General Assembly

1.6 Convention on the Elimination of All Forms of Discrimination Against Women (CEDAW)

How can this Convention benefit street and working girls?

The Convention contains a range of provisions designed to outlaw discrimination against women of any age and to achieve equality with men, including equal rights in:

○ education
○ employment
○ health care
○ treatment under the law

and to suppress the exploitation of women through trafficking and prostitution (ART 6). See Appendix C:2 for a complete copy of the treaty.

Because of their gender, street and working girls suffer discrimination and abuse in addition to the marginalization already experienced by street children generally. CEDAW provides NGOs and activists working in this field with a specific tool.

Are there any drawbacks?

○ There is no individual right of petition (although the Committee has been mandated to draft an optional protocol containing one) – only an overburdened reporting system.
○ The Committee is based in Vienna and meets there or in New York every year for two weeks in January/February and hence does not have the advantage of being able to use the UN human rights services in Geneva.
○ A number of states have weakened the effect of the Convention through making reservations to some of its provisions **[C:3]** (reflecting their attitude towards women).
○ Its workload is such that it has been unable to give adequate consideration to the state reports it does receive.

In the light of these problems, it is not surprising that NGOs have been reluctant to become involved in its work. Those wishing to submit reports should follow the same procedures as for the other Committees, but should contact the Committee through its Vienna office not through Geneva **[>C:5]**. States must submit an initial report within one year of ratification and then every four years **[>C:3]**.

B2: United Nations Non-Treaty Mechanisms

A NUMBER OF procedures have been established directly under the United Nations Charter to protect and promote human rights.

2.1 Why are they Important?

Unlike, for example, the Committee on the Rights of the Child, they have not been created as a result of a particular treaty. While some have their drawbacks in terms of their political nature or confidentiality, it is important to remember that **they can all be used regardless of whether a state has signed up to a particular human rights treaty or not**.

Although like their international treaty counterparts they are unable to enforce any of their decisions – unlike some regional mechanisms – their sanction lies in:

○ widespread, embarrassing international publicity for a criticized state
○ focusing attention of other governments and international organizations
○ the opportunity for international and local NGOs to coordinate their activities in conjunction with sympathetic governments to ensure that information about violations has the greatest possible impact, and to press for reforms – which sometimes does occur.

2.2 The Commission on Human Rights

This is the most important body established by the UN's Economic and Social Council (ECOSOC) **[>C:1]** and the one that receives the most attention in the international media.
When and where does it meet?
Annually at the UN's Palais des Nations **in Geneva for six weeks starting in late January or early February**.
Who are its members and what is their status?
Fifty-three members who are elected by ECOSOC and who vote and act as their government representatives – **they are not independent**. At the annual session they are joined by observer delegates from other governments who can make statements, but not vote on any Commission resolutions.

How much freedom Commission members have to vote on particular issues will naturally depend upon the sensitivity of the issue under discussion for their respective governments. (It is not surprising to find allies reluctant to condemn each other at such a public forum, although the divide between West and East has now been replaced by one between North and South).
What does it do?
It:

○ receives reports on and discusses the human rights situations in specific countries under Resolution 1235 **[>2.4]**
○ drafts international human rights law: e.g. the Convention on the Rights of the Child

○ appoints and receives reports from Special Rapporteurs **[>2.6]**
○ receives confidential communications on country situations under Resolution 1503 **[>2.5]**
○ reports to ECOSOC, which in turn reports to the UN General Assembly.

How can NGOs participate?

Although the Commission's meetings are open to the public, the level of participation of an NGO will depend upon whether it enjoys consultative status with ECOSOC (categories I or II) or is on the Roster **[>C:1]**.

Membership has to be applied for from the UN in New York, although the NGO Liaison Office in Geneva **[>C:5]** should be able to obtain the necessary papers for the NGO concerned. The three levels of category reflect the amount of expertise and information an NGO is able to bring to the concerns addressed by ECOSOC – of which human rights is one area. Experienced NGOs will enjoy category I status and be able to play a full role in Commission sessions as well as assist with drafting human rights law.

Applications are considered only every two years by ECOSOC in January, and the application process is quite demanding. If an NGO is relatively new, its chances of being accepted are slim. Instead, it should consider linking up with other NGOs which enjoy consultative status – the NGO Liaison Office can supply an up-to-date list – and lobby the Commission via them on issues of shared concern.

If an NGO has, or manages to obtain, consultative status it can:

○ submit oral and written communications
○ refer to specific countries without restriction.

BUT it cannot participate in any of the substantive debates on the final resolutions to be adopted by the Commission, even if it considers that certain countries are giving inaccurate and misleading information. Indeed, there are moves to further restrict the amount of NGO involvement, given the large number of oral interventions that now take place during the six-week session.

How should an NGO prepare?

A *provisional* agenda can be obtained from the NGO Liaison Office a few weeks in advance of the Commission meeting. The agenda items most relevant to the issue it wishes to raise should be considered and it should then be decided whether to make a written or oral statement, or both.

Written statements should be no longer than 2000 words (category I NGOs) or 1500 words (category II or Roster) and be submitted to the Commission Secretariat in Geneva **[>C:5]** well in advance of the Commission meeting. Addressing a particular theme of street and working children's rights, and using country examples to support its recommendations, is usually the preferred approach unless one country merits special attention because of systematic violations.

One of the most popular – and longest – agenda items is item 10 which concerns the 'question of the violation of human rights and fundamental freedoms in any part of the world'. Because it is so broad any subject could in theory be raised under it, although in practice certain issues and countries tend to dominate because of their political sensitivity.

The Rights of the Child has its own agenda item (currently item 20) which in 1996 followed item 10 and hence was delayed by several days before it could be discussed.

Anyone interested in attending should be prepared for sessions overrunning and the need to be flexible. If possible an extra one or two days should be booked after the concerned agenda item is due to finish, otherwise it may well be missed. Sessions continue until 9pm most nights and midnight during the final week.

The Commission examines the progress on implementation of the Convention on the Rights of the Child and also any current Special Rapporteurs' reports (e.g. in 1996 on the sale of children, child prostitution and pornography).

Before an NGO considers making an intervention it should take into account these general rules:

○ oral statements will have a greater impact than written ones
○ the more interventions an NGO makes on the same theme the less its impact will be
○ repetition/duplication of other NGOs should be avoided – activities should be coordinated – a joint statement may be more effective
○ a thematic approach – e.g. torture, child labour – using examples from several countries is often better than focusing on just one government
○ it should be considered how an intervention fits in with the overall purpose of the meeting – the temptation to use the occasion for self-promotion should be avoided
○ time will be short – five minutes is the current maximum for NGOs – so it should be well used.

What should an NGO representative do when he or she is there?

If the representative decides to make an oral intervention, he or she will need to ask the Commission secretariat to be placed on the list of NGOs due to speak under a chosen item and then **make sure he or she is present and available to speak when his or her turn comes**. NGOs have a space reserved at the back of the hall from where they make their interventions and it is usually advisable to be seated there at the beginning of the session.

The representative will have to weigh up whether he or she wishes to inform the country delegation(s) whom he or she will be mentioning in his or her statement in advance. On the one hand, this is only courtesy and gives the NGO representative an opportunity perhaps to discuss his or her concerns in person with delegates. On the other, it could give them an opportunity to instigate a procedural motion to block the NGO representative intervention, although this is rare given the number of NGOs and countries referred to in current Commission meetings. If there is any risk of this happening it is worth remembering that NGO representatives are under no obligation to inform states in advance, and they should deliver their statement without notification.

Finally, **a large number of copies of a statement** should be made available for distribution after an intervention. The secretariat will place copies on desks at the back of the hall immediately before or during the NGO's statement, but these invariably run out. Therefore, it is necessary to ensure that colleagues have sufficient copies available to hand out after an NGO representative's speech.

What else is worth doing while an NGO's representative is in Geneva?

As with most conferences, much of the real business is done outside of the main meeting. The opportunity to **lobby government delegates** – should be used, particularly those who are known to be sympathetic to a particular case – and to meet up with other NGOs. Although written materials cannot be left in official places they may be distributed in person. However, do not overwhelm delegates with paper – a brief statement of the NGO's aims and current concerns will suffice, together with a business card or letter head. In return, the delegates' card should be requested, in order that further materials may be sent at a later date.

Unless the representative of the NGO has personal contacts or is from a well-known NGO he or she may find it difficult to get any response from the large **press** contingent present at the Commission. If the NGO's press releases are being ignored, its representative should consider linking up with a larger NGO with experience of handling the press – a joint statement or news conference may give an NGO the necessary publicity.

If at any point an NGO representative needs help or advice, he or she should contact the **International Service for Human Rights** which is based in Geneva **[>C:5]** and which can help with anything from obtaining reasonably priced accommodation (it is possible in Geneva!) to linking up with other NGOs.

2.3 The Sub-Commission on Prevention of Discrimination and Protection of Minorities

When and where does it meet?

For **four weeks every year in late July or early August** at the same building **in Geneva**.

Membership?

Twenty-six individual experts who are nominated by their governments and elected by the Commission for four-year periods. They are there to act in their personal capacity and therefore **the Sub-Commission is seen as a less political body** than the Commission. Since 1989 members have voted in secret ballot on particular country issues.

How is it related to the Commission?

The Sub-Commission was created by the Commission to assist it with the various human rights functions it has to perform. The Commission regularly delegates tasks to the Sub-Commission, including examination of specific country situations under Resolution 1235. In turn, the Sub-Commission submits draft resolutions for consideration by the Commission.

What does it do?

It:

○ can also receive reports on, and discuss the human rights situations in, specific countries under Resolution 1235 **[>2.4]**
○ commissions and considers studies for setting new human rights standards
○ can adopt its own resolutions, although these are limited
○ establishes working groups to study particular human rights issues **[>2.6]**: e.g. Working Group on Slavery
○ reports annually to the Commission.

How can NGOs participate?

The Sub-Commission, apart from having a more limited agenda and being less political than its better-known counterpart, operates in a similar way. Therefore, **follow the guidance offered for the Commission in the last section [<2.2]**.

2.4 The '1235 Procedure': Public Examination of Specific Countries

Why is it called the '1235 procedure'?

This procedure was named after ECOSOC resolution 1235 (XLII) which was adopted in 1967 at the request of the Commission. It authorizes both the Commission and the Sub-Commission '**to examine information relevant to gross violations of human rights and fundamental freedoms**'.

Is it limited in any way?

In theory any country could be examined under this procedure, but there is a need to show '**a consistent pattern**' of violations.

Has it been used much in practice?

The procedure has been used widely, not only to permit scrutiny of governments at the annual sessions of the Commission and Sub-Commission in Geneva, but also to establish various groups or individuals – Special Rapporteurs or Representatives – to carry out fact-finding investigations into particular countries. These have included: Afghanistan, Chile, Cuba, El Salvador, Guatemala, Iran, Iraq, Romania and southern Africa.

How can contact be made with a fact-finding mission?

Information can be received from any individual, group or government in any format. However, in order to ensure that proper notice is taken, the NGO should:

○ address its concern to the correct group/rapporteur care of the Special Procedures Section of the UN Centre for Human Rights, Geneva [>C:5]
○ avoid any political statements but **concentrate on the facts**, putting in as much relevant and up-to-date detail as possible
○ provide **supporting documentary evidence**.

What happens then?

An NGO should not expect to receive a reply, but that does not mean that its evidence will not contribute to the report presented to the Commission. Furthermore, the evidence can lead to the rapporteur contacting state officials directly to discuss the situation.

What happens if the case is urgent?

It will probably be better to contact **the relevant thematic mechanism [>2.6]**, but it would still be useful to request that, if relevant, the country-specific procedure is made aware of the urgency of the matter (even though the Centre is supposed to forward the information in any event).

2.5 The '1503 Procedure': Confidential Examinations

Is this also named after a Resolution?

This procedure takes it name from ECOSOC Resolution 1503 (XLVIII) which was passed in 1970 to allow NGOs to make communications in restricted circumstances.

How is it restricted?

1503 is confidential. The Commission and Sub-Commission examine your communications in **closed sessions**.

Like 1235, it is not concerned with individual complaints, but country situations where there is '**a consistent pattern of gross and reliably attested violations of human rights**'.

If it is so secret is it worth using?

If there are other more public and quicker ways of having the matter considered either internationally or regionally, then it might not be worth sending a communication under 1503. Steps should be taken with the view to consulting with those NGOs such as Amnesty International, Human Rights Watch and the International Commission of Jurists, who have experience of using the procedure [>C:5].

An NGO or an individual should beware of using 1503 before it considers using a more public procedure for the same complaint – the Commission may block its use of 1235.

Despite these limitations, the mechanism does allow a formal direct channel for NGOs to communicate with the UN's main human rights bodies outside their plenary meetings. Furthermore, **it makes good sense to use 1503 if the NGO is *already* using 1235** as the former will be the only means whereby additional information may be submitted.

There is no restriction on who can be the author of a communication – it can be an individual, victim or NGO as long as they have 'reliable knowledge of the violations'.

How does it work?

Communication sent to UN Centre for Human Rights in Geneva [>**C5**]
↓
UN acknowledges receipt and forwards to government concerned
↓
Communication and government replied summarized by UN for inclusion in monthly confidential lists
↓
Five-member *Working Group on Communications* reviews lists in private two weeks prior to Sub-Commission meeting
↓
Three out of five agree that communication reveals consistent pattern of gross violations
↓
Communication forwarded to Sub-Commission which decides in closed session which situations should be forwarded to Commission
↓
Commission's *Working Group on Situations* examines country situation one week prior to Commission meeting and makes recommendations
↓
Commission considers country situation in closed session
↓
Commission may recommend:
↓
○ *thorough study (only two to date)*
○ *ad hoc committee (none to date)*
but will be more likely to:
○ *appoint independent expert/rapporteur*
○ *ask Secretary General to establish direct contact with government*
○ *ask government for further information*
○ *keep the situation under review*
↓
Situation reported on and considered next year or discontinued upon decision of Commission
↓
Commission's Chairman announces publicly names of countries that have been considered and those discontinued, but not the action taken
↓
Commission may recommend ECOSOC puts situation on public record (rare)

What official procedures need to be complied with?
  Sub-Commission Resolution 1 (XXIV) of 1971 states that:

o the communication **must not be anonymous**
o it **must not be manifestly politically motivated**
o it **must not appear to be based exclusively on mass media reports**
o it must explain how **domestic remedies have been exhausted**
o it must be submitted **within a reasonable time** after domestic remedies have been exhausted.

What about the contents?

o The communication must demonstrate that there has been a **consistent pattern** of **gross violations**. A pattern could be as few as six cases of a similar nature. 'Gross' will include *torture, extra judicial executions, disappearances, widespread arbitrary imprisonment*, but this is not an exhaustive list.
o **All relevant facts** must be included – names, places, dates – to illustrate a consistent pattern.
o It should be made clear **which specific articles** of the **Universal Declaration of Human Rights** have been **violated**.
o Claims should be supported with **clear evidence** – i.e. direct testimony of the victim and/or relatives if this is possible. This is particularly important if the complainant is not itself the victim, but an NGO/representative acting on its behalf.
o The complainant should clearly and simply **indicate what action it wants the UN to take**, but it must be realistic. Asking the Commission to demand internal investigations or sanctions against the alleged perpetrators or even compensation for victims has proved fruitless in the past. Instead, it is better to make a general request for the UN to take action to end the violations listed within the communication and let the 1503 procedure take its course.

Is there anything else that should be done?

o The **covering letter** must refer to ECOSOC resolution 1503 and should include a brief summary of the allegations, together with the purpose of the petition – the request for action by the UN.
o It is important to check that all relevant documents are included and that are correctly listed as **annexes** in the order they are cited in the communication.
o If required, all material should be translated into one of the six UN official languages – preferably **English, French or Spanish** (the others are Arabic, Chinese and Russian).
o **Six copies** of the communication should be forwarded to the Commission.
o **Supplementary communications** with updated facts should be sent, as required, if the case is still being considered by the Commission. These should read as stand-alone documents, containing complete details of the violations, as previously with the additional new facts.

2.6 Thematic Mechanisms: Special Rapporteurs and Working Groups

How do these differ from 1235 and 1503?
  They can receive information about individual cases of violations or threatened violations as part of a continuing examination of countries where there appears to be a widespread pattern of such abuses.

What form do they take?

They consist of specially appointed individual experts – Special Rapporteurs – and groups of experts – Working Groups – who have proven and respected track records as **impartial** promoters and protectors of human rights. To date their reports have continued this tradition of independent examination of countries, leaving aside political considerations – compare this with the Commission **[<2.2]**.

What human rights areas do they cover?

Working Groups:

○ Arbitrary detention
○ Enforced or involuntary disappearances
○ Slavery.

Special Rapporteurs:

○ Arbitrary executions
○ Child pornography and child prostitution
○ Freedom of opinion and expression
○ Racism
○ Religious intolerance
○ Torture.

These are the Working Groups and Rapporteurs that are most likely to be used. However, as the Commission expands its mandate, new appointments – such as the Special Rapporteur on Mercenaries and the Working Group of Government Experts on the Right to Development – have been made, so an NGO should not be surprised if other themes affecting its work, particularly in the economic and social rights field, are not examined in the future, and, if not, why not lobby for them? **[>B:6]**.

What do they do?

As their names suggest, the mechanisms analyse the particular human rights issue in question – how it happens, why it happens, how to prevent it happening again in the future, and to make suitable recommendations to governments to take necessary action.

As part of this process individual cases can be notified to governments for their comments, and requests made for internal investigations to be carried out.

Urgent communications regarding cases of summary or arbitrary executions or torture can be made the subject of **urgent action appeals** demanding a swifter government response.

Visits are made to countries where there appear to be serious human rights problems, providing a good opportunity for local NGOs and individuals to make their concerns known directly to UN officials.

Annual reports submitted to the Commission contain detailed information on all of the above activities. Despite the fact that they seek to present their findings without passing judgement on whether particular allegations have been proved or not, they do provide a significant and influential picture of a country's human rights record. In addition, a critical entry increases the likelihood of individual communications from that country being taken seriously (see below).

Can anyone contact them?

Practice has shown that both Working Groups and the Special Rapporteurs are willing to accept information from any source as long as the information appears to be credible. Credibility will naturally increase where the country concerned is already being considered under other UN procedures, or has previously been the subject of thematic reports.

However, **the more reliable the source** – a known and respected NGO, a family member or representative of a disappeared person – **the more likely that it will be taken seriously and acted upon.**

Moreover, each mechanism is technically constrained to a greater or lesser degree by the various Resolutions that established them:

○ WG on Disappearances – 'governments, intergovernmental organizations, humanitarian organizations and other reliable sources'
○ WG on Arbitrary Detention – no restrictions on NGOs + 'individuals concerned, their families or their representatives'
○ SR on Executions – only those NGOs in consultative status with ECOSOC
○ SR on Torture – no restrictions on NGOs – international + national
○ SR on Religious Intolerance – as for torture + 'communities of religion or belief'.

What should be included in an individual violation communication?

○ Name of the victim (and identity number if possible)
○ date and location of the incident or, in the case of a disappeared person, the time and place they were last seen
○ identity of the suspected perpetrator(s) and official status if known
○ any information of the local remedies that have been tried and exhausted or, if not, the reasons why
○ the steps taken to trace a disappeared person.

As for a 1503 communication, all relevant documentation must be included – witness statements, medical reports – as annexes. If the case is urgent there may be no time to assemble and include this information. A letter covering the points above – or all the available information that the NGO has – will then suffice. *NB: the covering letter should indicate clearly whether the petitioner's identity can be disclosed or not.*

The Rapporteur or Working Group should always be kept notified of any developments which either confirm (autopsy report) or lessen the applicant's concerns (person alive).

B3: The African System

What is the main governing document called?

The African Charter on Human and People's Rights, which came into force in 1981. It was initiated by the inter-governmental organisation, the Organisation of African Unity, and to date has been ratified by 49 members **[>C:3]**.

Does it cover the broad range of rights to be found in the two international covenants?

Yes. It includes the traditional individual civil and political rights, together with economic and social rights that need to be realized progressively by developing countries **[>C:2]**.

Specific provisions aim to eradicate discrimination against women and children:

The State shall ensure the elimination of every discrimination against women and also ensure the protection of the rights of the women and the child as stipulated in international declarations and conventions (ART 18(3)).

In addition, the Charter has introduced an innovative range of people's rights, including the right to:

o self-determination
o free disposition of natural resources
o development
o satisfactory environment.

Perhaps of more immediate relevance and interest for those concerned with child rights is **the duties of the individual to family and society** (see ARTS 27–29) reflecting these strong traditions in African culture.

And it has its own supervisory mechanism?

The African Commission on Human and People's Rights has 11 members who are meant to serve in a personal capacity, although many come straight from senior government positions. Elected by the OAU Assembly, they serve for up to six-year periods, although these can be renewed. The Commission's secretariat is in Banjul, The Gambia.

What functions does it have?

Under ARTICLE 45 of the Charter, the Commission's role may be divided into four main areas:

o promotion of the Charter
o protection of the rights under the Charter
o interpretation of the Charter at the request of states, OAU institutions or **any other African organisation**
o performance of other tasks stipulated by the OAU Assembly.

3.1 Promotion

This covers a similar range of tasks to those undertaken by other international human rights bodies, such as assembling resource materials, disseminating information, organizing conferences and encouraging and supporting national bodies.

It also includes providing assistance to state legislators through the formulation of relevant rules and principles to enable domestic legislation to be reformed and redrafted as required to better protect human rights.

Since 1991 it has produced a journal – *The African Review of Human Rights* – in addition to its annual reports and other information on the Charter.

Since the beginning of the Commission's promotional work **NGOs have played a pivotal role**, with over 30 being granted observer status. For anyone wishing to network with any of them – the majority are indigenous, with some large international organisations such as Amnesty International, Human Rights Watch and the International Commission of Jurists – the Commission's secretariat [**>C:5**] will be able to supply a current list.

3.2 Protection

The Commission has adopted the three traditional methods of monitoring states' protection of rights and receiving information about violations:

○ receiving regular reports
○ complaints from individuals or NGOs
○ inter-state complaints.

3.2.1 Reporting

States must submit **periodic reports every two years** on the legislative and other measures they have taken to give effect to the Charter's provisions.

The Commission has yet to receive a significant number of reports and has yet to introduce any monitoring system similar to the Human Rights Committee [**<B:1.2**] to check on whether its recommendations are being adopted.

3.2.2 Individual, NGO and Group Complaints

Permitted under the Commission's wide powers of investigation, this allows submissions to be made by:

○ the victim (or in the victim's name where the person is unable to submit themself) of individual violations
○ an individual or NGO alleging serious and/or violations on a massive scale.

To submit a complaint against a state the person **does not need to live there**.
Beyond these requirements it will be necessary to make sure that:

○ violations of rights under the Charter are being alleged
○ the language is not insulting
○ information is not based solely on media reports
○ it can be shown that all available domestic remedies have been exhausted
○ the complaint is submitted within a 'reasonable period of time' after the exhaustion of remedies.

Having the complaint considered by another international procedure (for example, the Human Rights Committee or 1503 procedure) does not bar the complainant from having it considered at the same time under the African Charter **UNLESS** the state has **already settled** the case under a UN or OAU procedure.

How does it work?

If the complaint is admissible the procedure is then:

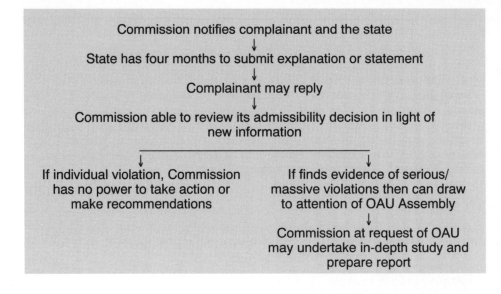

Commission notifies complainant and the state
↓
State has four months to submit explanation or statement
↓
Complainant may reply
↓
Commission able to review its admissibility decision in light of new information

If individual violation, Commission has no power to take action or make recommendations

If finds evidence of serious/ massive violations then can draw to attention of OAU Assembly
↓
Commission at request of OAU may undertake in-depth study and prepare report

All proceedings are **confidential** and only the OAU Assembly may decide to make public a Commission report.

The procedure shows that **there is effectively no remedy for individual violations** since the Commission can take no further action once it has considered a case, and there is no higher Court of Human Rights as under the American and European systems [>**B:4 and B:5**]. Even for more systematic violations the Commission is dependent on the decision of the political OAU Assembly as to whether it can make its findings known.

Despite this lack of formal procedures, the Commission may use the opportunity to persuade states to take action aided by the confidentiality the process enjoys. This, coupled with the ability of the Commission to take information from a wide range of sources, does mean that it is not totally pointless to use the existing system. However, it is understandable if individuals and NGOs have little confidence in a complaints procedure that lacks any mechanism for securing binding judgements against states or any redress for victims.

3.2.3 Inter-state Complaints
These may take two forms:

○ negotiation communications
○ complaint communications.

Under the first procedure one state may bring to the attention of another the fact that it believes the latter has violated the Charter. If a satisfactory conclusion cannot be reached, or the respondent state does not reply within three months, then the matter may be submitted to the Commission by either party for the second procedure to come into operation.

The Commission endeavours to reach a friendly settlement and only if this fails will it produce a report containing the facts of the case and its conclusions – this may draw on **information 'from other sources.'** Copies of this report, together with recommendations from the Commission, are sent to the states and the OAU Assembly, which can decide whether the matter should be made public or not. There is no capacity for monitoring whether the states concerned have acted upon the Commission's recommendations.

To date there have been no complaints under the Charter.

Are there any further developments that could strengthen the protection for African children?

An *African Charter on the Rights and Welfare of the Child* has been drafted which once in force (it still requires a number of ratifications) could bring many potential benefits. It has been described as 'the most progressive of the treaties on the rights of the child' [Van Bueren 1994 p 402]. Crucially, it not only significantly improves the substantive provisions relating to children's rights but more importantly the **mechanisms** for protecting them.

An 11-member Committee of Independent Experts will monitor state performance on children's rights, formulate new principles and interpret the new Charter not only at the behest of states and the OAU, but also any 'other person or institution' recognized by the OAU, i.e. **those NGOs that have observer status**.

States will have to **report every three years** (compared with five under the Convention on the Rights of the Child).

Will this new Committee also be able to receive complaints?

Yes, and not only from states but also from 'any person, group or non-governmental organization recognized by the Organization of African Unity... or the United Nations' [ART 44(1)]. Hence, **children will be able to petition** the Committee and on both civil and political rights, and also **economic, social and cultural rights**. Given the reluctance of the international community to enable individuals or their representatives to bring their governments to account for these types of rights, this is **a major step forward**.

Obviously it has great potential for the empowerment of street and working children since it is often these marginalized groups whose economic and social rights are most at risk and who have correspondingly been most excluded from the international human rights legal process.

If the system is to have any success, it will be crucial that NGOs and street and working children's advocates participate to the fullest extent of their ability even though the immediate benefits may appear to be minimal or non-existent. If economic and social rights are to be 'progressively realized' then both states and the international community must be pressured to act through every possible channel of this new mechanism when it comes into force.

Information on the progress of the new Charter can be obtained from the Secretariat in Banjul.

Will there be any point in using the original Charter once the new children's one comes into force?

Probably not, as both the range of rights and the procedures will be stronger under the new treaty and any issue that can be raised under the current mechanism should be able to be brought under the future one. However, in the interim the existing Charter can be used both to increase NGOs' experience and to highlight abuses of children's rights, which could continue to be progressed under the new body.

B4: The Inter-American System

What are the governing documents?

(i) ***Charter of the Organization of American States 1948***

This is the main constitutional text of the system **BUT** contains few references to human rights. The two most important are the American Declaration and the American Convention of Human Rights.

(ii) ***American Declaration of the Rights and Duties of Man 1948***

This established human rights standards for all OAS members and **significantly applies to those states which are not parties to the American Convention**.

It covers both civil and political rights and **economic, social and cultural rights [>C:2]** including rights to:

○ work
○ health
○ education
○ social security.

Per ARTICLE 7 '**all children have the right to special protection and aid**'

(iii) ***American Convention on Human Rights 1969***

This is the **main human rights instrument** of the system **[>C:2]**.

It focuses primarily on **civil and political rights**, although the new protocol described below will extend its protection to economic, social and cultural rights.

ARTICLE 19 specifically focuses on the **Rights of the Child**:

... every minor child has the right to the measures of protection required by his condition as a minor on the part of his family, society and the state.

(iv) ***Protocol of San Salvador 1995***

This is an additional protocol to the Convention, which covers **economic, social and cultural rights**. It is not yet in force.

As with the ICESCR, states will be required to take progressive action, according to their level of development, to protect the rights to:

○ work
○ just and equitable conditions of work
○ organize trade unions
○ strike
○ social security
○ health
○ food
○ education
○ formation and protection of families.

What special protection under the Protocol will there be for children?

Article 7(f) – prohibition on night work
– prohibition on unhealthy and dangerous work and working conditions for those aged under 18
– work should not prevent those under 16 from attending school.

Article 15(3) – guarantees adequate nutrition for children of nursery school and (primary) school age
– places a duty on states to undertake family training programmes.

Article 16 – establishes the principle that children should not be separated from their parents
– right to free and compulsory elementary education for all children.

(v) *The Inter-American Convention to Prevent and Punish Torture 1985*

How are all these different standards protected?
Two bodies have been created under the OAS Charter:

○ **The Inter-American Commission on Human Rights** in Washington DC, USA
○ **The Inter-American Court of Human Rights** in San José, Costa Rica.

The Commission carries out functions similar to its African and European counterparts, although it does have **greater investigatory powers**. It has seven independent experts elected for four-year terms by the OAS General Assembly. Most of the Commission's sessions are in Washington, but it also holds some in other member states during which it **can hear submissions from both individuals and NGOs**.

The Court is made up of seven elected judges sitting for six-year terms. States are subject to its jurisdiction only if they make a separate declaration after ratifying the Convention.

4.1 Petitioning the Commission

Can an action be brought against any American country?
Yes. For those states that have ratified the 1969 Convention an action can be brought under that treaty; for the remainder, the 1948 Declaration can be cited since it applies to all American states even if they have not signed up to any binding documents. The two procedures are virtually identical.
What requirements have to be satisfied to have the complaint admitted?
The Commission's rules are **not as strict** as many other human rights bodies, both in terms of who can petition it and the matters they can raise.
A petition may be submitted by:

○ an individual
○ a group of individuals
○ an NGO which has legal recognition in an OAS state.

The victim does not need to:

○ file the petition directly
○ authorize your submission
○ even have knowledge of the submission.

The submission may:

○ allege violations committed against an **individual**
○ be a **collective petition** alleging violations against several named victims committed as a result of a specific incident or practice
○ be a **general petition** involving allegations of widespread and systematic violations against named victims

o include violations of **economic, social or cultural rights** under the San Salvador Protocol.

When submitting collective and general petitions, the victims have to be identified even though they may not be able to authorize the action themselves.

What details have to be included?
Whoever submits the petition has to provide their:

o name
o nationality
o profession or occupation
o postal or current address
o signature.

Anyone acting on behalf of an NGO must make sure that they give its full name and address in addition to their own name and signature. The identity will not be disclosed to the state unless it is expressly authorized in writing.

A **statement** about the alleged violations should include information on:

o times, dates and locations of the incidents
o names, ranks or positions of any officials either directly involved in committing the violations or indirectly implicated
o names and ranks/positions of any officials who were notified, and when and where the specific rights under the Convention/Declaration have been violated.

Any witness statements, medical and media reports can be attached as annexes – **the more evidence there is to link the government to the alleged violations the better**, even if it is a question of failing to take action to prevent the commission of abuses by non-governmental forces.

The aim is to show that it is the government that has failed in its duty adequately to protect human rights.

What if the government has decided to suspend some of these rights?
Governments can suspend only certain rights under the Convention. The most important fundamental rights are **non-derogable** (see ARTS 8, 25 AND 27(2)) including:

o right to life
o right to be protected against torture and other inhumane treatment
o right not to be enslaved
o rights of the family and the child
o right to due process under the law.

If it is believed that a government has acted wrongly in suspending any of these rights then it may be raised in the petition citing the Convention and any relevant case law from the Inter-American Court.

What other requirements must be fulfilled?
As with other supranational procedures, it is necessary to demonstrate that **all available domestic remedies have been exhausted** or be able to show why they are not effective.

If it is not possible to do this because of the legal situation in the country, then the Commission may ask the government to show which remedies are still left to be tried and then ask the complainant, in turn, whether they are exempt from using them for one of the following reasons:

- there is no provision for obtaining due process under the current legal system
- access to the system has been restricted or denied
- inordinate time delays
- denial of adequate legal representation because of the complainant's financial situation or because of a climate of fear within the country.

This last reason was formulated by the Inter-American Court and is valuable to cite even where the legal system in theory provides a remedy, but where the practical circumstances dictate that it is not possible to take advantage of it. Ultimately it is up to the complainant to show that legal help was needed, but that it was impracticable to obtain it. The complainant must also:

- **file the petition within** a reasonable period of time – in this case **six months** after the date that the victim was notified of the last available judgement and
- ensure that the matter **is not being considered, or has been considered by another international procedure, UNLESS** it relates to a general complaint about the country's human rights situation (such as under the 1503 procedure [<B:2.5]) **AND** no decision has been reached on the facts in question **OR** the other procedure will not be able to provide an effective settlement.

The general rule is that the UN bodies should only be used once there is no further scope for proceeding under the Inter-American Commission system.

What happens next?

Commission Secretariat receives petition and, if necessary, requests additional information from author

↓

Case appears to satisfy admissibility criteria (otherwise petitioner informed and case closed)

↓

File opened and case number allocated. Petitioner notified

↓

Case (excluding information identifying petitioner) communicated to government with request for information on alleged facts and exhaustion of remedies

↓

Government replies within 90 days (although, in practice, time extensions of up to 180 days may be granted)

↓

Relevant parts of government reply and other documents are forwarded to petitioner

↓

Petitioner comments and submits any further information within 30 days (extensions should be requested if needed)
May ask for Commission to carry out oral hearing indicating evidence to be presented and witnesses to be called

↓

continued . . .

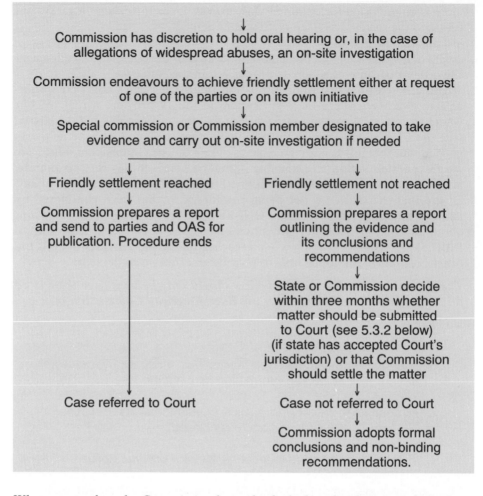

Commission has discretion to hold oral hearing or, in the case of
allegations of widespread abuses, an on-site investigation
↓
Commission endeavours to achieve friendly settlement either at request
of one of the parties or on its own initiative
↓
Special commission or Commission member designated to take
evidence and carry out on-site investigation if needed

Friendly settlement reached	Friendly settlement not reached
Commission prepares a report and send to parties and OAS for publication. Procedure ends	Commission prepares a report outlining the evidence and its conclusions and recommendations
	State or Commission decide within three months whether matter should be submitted to Court (see 5.3.2 below) (if state has accepted Court's jurisdiction) or that Commission should settle the matter
Case referred to Court	Case not referred to Court
	Commission adopts formal conclusions and non-binding recommendations.

What powers does the Commission have if it finds there has been a violation?

The Commission is not a court of law – it cannot make binding judgements. All it can do is **make recommendations for a state to take action** to remedy the fault. This may include awarding compensation, but usually consists of a declaration that a violation has occurred and that something should be done to correct it.

The whole process can be quite slow – what if the victim is in imminent danger?

The Commission can at the petitioner's request ask for prompt replies from the government and/or at any stage ask the Court to take interim measures to prevent the petitioner or others suffering permanent harm.

It is up to the petitioner to monitor both the situation of the victim(s) and the progress of the case through the Commission and to alert them to any changes that require action.

Each member of the Commission's legal team has responsibility for particular countries and the cases within them. It is advisable to find out who the relevant contact person is and to keep in regular touch. Because of its own limited resources the Commission will appreciate **any assistance the petitioner is able to give** in terms of complete and up-to-date information and the quality of the material submitted with the petition. By reducing the investigatory burden on the Commission to obtain relevant documents the process will be expedited and make the system more effective.

The petitioner retains considerable power and responsibility to manage the case through the system [Hurst Hannum (ed.) *Guide to International Rights Practice*, 1992 p.127].

4.2 Proceedings before the Court

The Commission's powers appear to be rather limited. Is it possible to invoke the Court's jurisdiction?

No. Only state parties to the Convention who have accepted the court's jurisdiction and the Commission itself can exercise this power within the three-month period after the latter's initial report is sent to the parties. Petitioners have no right to approach the Court directly.

If either of them decides to put the case before the Court, what happens then?

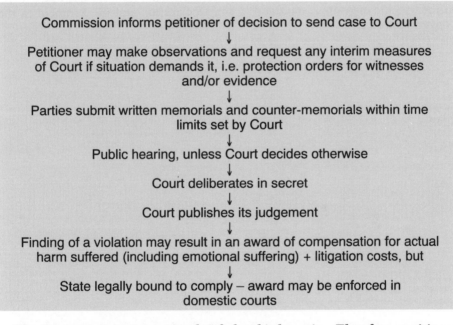

Commission informs petitioner of decision to send case to Court
↓
Petitioner may make observations and request any interim measures of Court if situation demands it, i.e. protection orders for witnesses and/or evidence
↓
Parties submit written memorials and counter-memorials within time limits set by Court
↓
Public hearing, unless Court decides otherwise
↓
Court deliberates in secret
↓
Court publishes its judgement
↓
Finding of a violation may result in an award of compensation for actual harm suffered (including emotional suffering) + litigation costs, but
↓
State legally bound to comply – award may be enforced in domestic courts

The Court accepts supporting briefs by third parties. Therefore, petitioners should consider asking for help if the issues are particularly complex.

Where is it possible to read about previous judgements?

The Court's case law is contained in the Inter-American Court of Human Rights Reports, which are arranged by Series and then by number (e.g. Ser. C No.4).

4.3 Submitting Reports to the Commission

Does the Commission receive periodic state reports?

No, but it does have the **power to prepare its own reports** on the human rights situation in OAS countries – hence it has the opportunity to be far more pro-active than many of its counterparts.

Can NGOs play a part in this process?

Despite the fact that there is no formal recognition of the need to draw on information supplied by individuals or NGOs, it is mainly by receiving such material that the Commission can decide to carry out its own study.

Reports may be submitted directly to the Commission [>C:5] after first ascertaining what areas are of particular concern and what action, if any, the Commission is considering taking in relation to certain countries.

It is also a good idea to provide material to inform the Commission's preparation of its annual reports to the OAS General Assembly. This can be an opportunity to highlight further domestic measures that need to be taken to provide better guarantees of human rights protection.

Has the OAS made any specific progress on children's rights?

In 1927 an **American Children's Institute** was founded and is governed by the Pan American Child Congress and Directing Council.

However, despite the fact that the Institute continues to collect information on the situation of children throughout the OAS region there is **still no regional children's treaty** as under the African system. Instead, reliance has to be made on the specific measures contained in the Declaration and the Protocol to the Convention.

B5: The European System

What features about the European system are worth noting?

The European human rights system is the oldest and most established procedure in the world, dating back over 40 years. It has developed a large amount of case law and a complex and strict series of requirements for people wishing to use it.

But why is it included in a manual about street and working children?

It is true that the scale of the problem, and the issues surrounding street and working children, is very different in most parts of Europe compared with other regions of the world. However, it is also true that:

○ street and working children do exist even in the most affluent Western European countries and face denial of both their civil and economic and social rights
○ the European Convention on Human Rights now extends to many Central and Eastern European countries where violations against street children is a significant problem
○ the main governing body, the Council of Europe continues to grow, bringing with it new human rights issues and challenges which the Convention machinery can be used to address
○ the Convention machinery is arguably the most effective system for securing redress beyond domestic courts and may provide useful precedents for developments in other systems.

So the Convention is what we are concerned with?

The European Convention for the Protection of Human Rights and Fundamental Freedoms (1950) to give it its full title, is the document we shall be focusing on here. Its two bodies – **the European Commission of Human Rights** and **the European Court of Human Rights** are the only European institutions (apart from the European Court of Justice – which deals with European Community law and only occasionally addresses human rights issues) that can receive complaints from individuals.

However, it is worth being aware of the following other instruments and bodies that can be made use of to a greater or lesser extent, depending upon your priorities:

(i) *The European Social Charter*

○ designed to protect economic and social rights – including right to work, social security and trade union rights
○ limited ratification **[>C:3]**
○ examines state reports biennially
○ employers and trade unions comment but no formal role for NGOs – use trade union contacts if you want to raise specific points
○ no right of individual complaint, but trade unions, employers and appropriate NGOs can make collective complaints.

(ii) *The European Convention for the Prevention of Torture and Inhuman or Degrading Treatment or Punishment*

63

o concentrates on preventive work – detention centres and prison visits
o no right of individual complaint or reporting system
o NGOs can supply Secretariat with relevant information [>C:5].

(iii) *Organisation for Security and Co-operation in Europe* (OSCE)

o diplomatic body which includes Europe, North America and Russia
o evolving 'human dimension' (i.e. human rights) mechanism based in Warsaw
o particularly concerned with minority rights and preventive work
o regular review conferences may provide opportunity for lobbying governments – contact Warsaw office for more details [>C:5].

But is there nothing specific to children?

In 1979, as part of the Council of Europe's support for the International Year of the Child, it was recommended that a separate European Charter on the Rights of the Child be drawn up. This was subsequently modified to become an additional Protocol of the Existing Convention which would cover both the child's economic and social rights as well as the more traditional civil and political rights favoured by the Convention. This latter development would have the advantage of enabling children and their representatives to use the existing Convention machinery without the confusion and expense of creating new mechanisms.

Despite these promising developments it was decided that another Protocol (to add to the 11 already in existence) was not required and that a separate treaty would be drafted after all. However, this **European Convention on the Exercise of Children's Rights [>C:2]** has been criticized both for its lack of new substantive provisions and for its potentially weak implementation machinery.

The progress of the new children's treaty should be monitored – updates can be obtained from the Council of Europe.

Thus the future for child rights remains uncertain even if the new treaty is eventually ratified, leaving two existing problems.

o The Convention is by its very nature outdated and many of its provisions too narrow. Economic and social rights are excluded altogether.
o The Commission and the Court have not enjoyed a strong tradition for applying a child-centred approach to rights. The child rights cases they have dealt with have usually concerned children living within families or those who are not on the margins of society – they may not be prepared to deal with the different type of case that could be introduced from Eastern European countries on behalf of street and working children.

However, as with all the systems covered in this manual, the European one, despite its imperfections, is there to be used and it is only by bringing more challenging cases (provided they can be accommodated within the existing substantive framework) that the jurisprudence can be progressively developed.
I can see the point in using the current system, so tell me more about the Commission and the Court.

There are actually three bodies (soon to be two) which play a part in consideration of individual complaints – one legal, one semi-legal and one political – all of which are based in Strasbourg, France [>C:5]. They are part of the intergovernmental organization called the **Council of Europe** which was set up by West European states in 1949 and adopted the European Convention on Human Rights in 1950. As stated above, since the end of the Cold War the Council has expanded rapidly to encompass the new democracies of Central and Eastern Europe in addition to its existing membership, which also includes Turkey.

The **Commission** is made up of one member from each party to the Convention who serve in their personal capacity. It acts as a quasi-judicial body and it is the first port of call when an application under the Convention is made. Even if the Commission decides that a case is admissible, as with its African and American counterparts, any **decisions** it reaches **are not legally binding**. Instead it endeavours to reach friendly settlements or refers the case to the Court. [From September 1998 its work will be taken over by the Court.]

The **Court** is composed of judges who again represent each of the Convention parties (but who are also independent of their governments) and decides cases referred to it by the Commission. It can make final and legally binding judgments and, although it cannot overturn national decisions, it does have the **power to award compensation** to victims where it has found their rights have been violated.

While the **Committee of Ministers** is a political body, composed of government representatives from the various Council states, it retains important powers under the European human rights system. Cases not referred to the Court will be considered in private by the Committee, and if it decides a violation has occurred it can publicly request states to provide a remedy. Ultimately, if the state fails to act it can suspend or expel the state from the Council. Needless to say, this has never happened (although Greece did leave before it was pushed in 1969). Clearly, the presence of such a political body in a human rights mechanism has the same potential to undermine the validity of the system as similar organizations within the UN **[<B:1.2]**.

5.1 Making an Individual Complaint

It was mentioned that the admissibility requirements are quite strict.

Less than 10 per cent of applications make it over the first hurdle of admissibility before the merits of their case can be considered. It is therefore crucial that the applicant or his or her representative adhere to the following rules closely. In any event it will naturally be advisable to seek legal advice both before submission and during the procedure.

The items in the following **checklist** should be examined to see whether the applicant's case could be declared admissible by the Commission.

(i) The primary requirement is to establish whether an applicant can bring a complaint against the state in question, and for what rights:

○ Has the **state** against which the applicant wishes to proceed, **agreed to accept the Commission's right to examine individual complaints** under Article 25 of the Convention? **[>C:3]** (NB All recent new state parties have accepted it automatically upon ratification, and this practice should continue.)

○ What **reservations** has the relevant state made which may exclude the applicability of certain rights? **[>C:3]**

○ Has the relevant state **ratified all of the additional Protocols** (e.g. Protocol 2 on the use of the death penalty) and, if so, extended the **right of individual complaint** to them? **[>C:3]**

○ Has the relevant state **derogated from any of the rights** under Art 15 because of war or public emergency? (NB certain rights remain non-derogable in any event – life, freedom from torture and slavery – see ART 15)

○ Did the **violation occur as a result of acts or omissions** by the relevant state and/or its employees?

(ii) Next, it is necessary to establish whether the applicant is qualified to make the application:

○ Is the applicant the victim or does he or she have a **sufficiently close link to the victim** (e.g. a relative)?
○ If the victim is an NGO or group of people, is the applicant an **appropriately designated person** to represent you?
○ Was the victim **subject to the jurisdiction of the state** at the time of the violation? The violation does not need to occur on the state's territory.
○ Does the case concern **direct violations of the Convention?** A general or abstract complaint without identifiable victims will not be accepted.
○ **What Convention rights have actually been violated?** Many applications are rejected because the rights in question are not covered by the Convention's sometimes narrow focus.

(iii) As with all other international mechanisms:

○ **Have *all* available domestic remedies been exhausted?** Again, many applications are refused because of this. The case law should be carefully studied in order to ascertain what the Commission and Court define as a remedy, at what stage is it exhausted and when the applicant can be excused from its applicability because it has either been inadequate or ineffective.

The general rule is that unless there is a good reason to the contrary, the applicant should ensure that he or she has used all the judicial and administrative appeals available before bringing the application.

Having fulfilled all the requirements, how should one apply?

An **application form** from the Commission's Secretariat *must be obtained* in which it requests you to supply:

○ applicant's name, age, occupation and address
○ the same details for the applicant's representative
○ the name of the state party concerned
○ the purpose of the application, and the Convention provisions that the applicant alleges to have been violated
○ a statement of the facts and initial legal argument, using Convention case law and domestic decisions where applicable
○ a confirmation as to whether the applicant is seeking damages, although the amount does not need to be specified at this stage
○ written authorisation/power of attorney for the applicant's legal representative to act
○ any relevant documents attached as annexes, such as witness statements, medical and forensic reports, details of domestic judicial decisions to demonstrate exhaustion (include transcripts where available)
○ signature of the applicant or that of the representative – confidentiality can be requested and will be respected by the Commission.

The more detail and evidence the applicant and his or her legal representative can include the better. It should be remembered that on average an applicant has only a one-in-ten chance of success.

It is possible to use the official language of the state party, but most applications are submitted in English or French and it will be in one of these languages that the proceedings will be conducted.

The application should be addressed to the Secretary General of the Council of Europe. All subsequent correspondence will be with the Commission Secretariat.

The applicant will have **six months from the date of the last domestic decision** concerning his or her case to file the application, **BUT**:

o a full application may not have to be filed by this date (although it is wise to do so) – a summary of the complaint may suffice as long as it is communicated to the Commission
o the Commission allows submission of applications **prior** to the exhaustion of all domestic remedies where these remain speculative
o the rule does not apply to on-going violations.

Is there anything else that should be remembered?

o **Insulting, abusive or political language should not be used, otherwise there is a risk that the application will be thrown out as an 'abuse of the right of petition' (see ART 27(2)).**
o **Once the proceedings have begun they are confidential – if the press does try to contact the applicant, he or she should refer them to Strasbourg.**

Is it necessary to have a lawyer?

It should be clear both from the requirements of the application process and the length of the subsequent legal proceedings described below that it is preferable to have access to legal advice. Some applicants do represent themselves, but obviously in the case of most children dealing with sometimes quite complex legal issues this is not a viable option.

What happens if the applicant cannot afford a lawyer?

Legal aid is provided either at the applicant's request or on the initiative of the Commission. The respondent government concerned will be asked to comment upon the request and whether the applicant's means justify awarding legal aid.

Note that the aid covers not only the legal fees of hiring a professional lawyer or law professor to draft all written pleadings and attend oral hearings, but also his and the applicant's other necessary expenses, including travel. However, the applicant will not be entitled to receive it at the initial application stage, but only after the details have been communicated to the government party.

Can the Commission take some action in urgent cases?

Yes, but the Commission has only limited powers and the case must be one of genuine urgency, for example, threats to life, preventing continuing ill-treatment or deportation. A covering letter with the application will suffice, setting out the situation, the reasons why action is needed urgently and requesting the Commission to assist.

In such circumstances the Commission may circumvent its normal procedures, which can take up to three years, and both consider the case more rapidly and request the state to take appropriate interim measures to prevent further harm to the victim pending the outcome of the application. This request has no legal force, but in practice, given the Commission's well-established position in the field of human rights, it is usually heeded.

What happens after the Commission has received the application?

Initial Admissibility Consideration

Provisional file opened by the Secretariat. Any obvious grounds of admissibility and/or requests for further information communicated to applicant. Clearly inadmissible applications discouraged from proceeding → END
↓
Complaint registered as formal application
↓
Case assigned to member of Commission who as rapporteur formally examines admissibility
↓
Rapporteur, after requesting further information from applicant and government as required, presents report to full Commission

Preliminary consideration by full Commission

Commission considers Rapporteur's report and either declares application inadmissible → END
↓
OR communicates case to government for its observations on facts (unless not in dispute), admissibility and merits of case
↓
Government must reply within six weeks
↓
Government's observations forwarded to applicant who may respond
↓
Rapporteur prepares new report on admissibility for consideration by Commission, whichh may choose to dismiss the case → END
↓
OR invite parties to attend oral hearing on admissibility and the merits

Examination of Admissibility and the Merits by Commission

Oral hearing in closed session – both parties address the Commission and then reply to each other's submissions
↓
Communicates immediately afterwards whether inadmissible → END
↓
OR admissible and then, if able to, gives preliminary views on merits
↓
Admissibility decision published
↓
Commission seeks to establish the facts and to obtain friendly settlement between the parties
↓
Commission may conduct further oral hearings (rare) or carry out on-site visits
↓
Friendly settlement reached and Commission prepares public report for Committee of Ministers and parties. State agrees to amend legislation or pay compensation → END
↓
OR settlement cannot be agreed and Commission prepares report for Committee of Ministers on whether there has been breach
↓
Report forwarded to state, but not to applicant who is informed that it has been adopted
↓
Three-month interval

Consideration by Committee of Ministers and Court

Committee decides whether breach has occurred and to publish Commission's report within three months
↓
Respondent state, national state of applicant or (increasingly) Commission may refer case to Court for final decision (applicant will also have power to refer after Protocol 9 comes into force)
↓
Commission member chosen by peers to prepare and present oral submission to Court
↓
Applicant and government invited to submit written memorials
↓
Court hears case in public and reaches decision by majority vote
↓
Committee supervises implementation of legally binding judgement

B6: Taking Further Action: Lobbying for Change at the National and International Level

READING THIS MANUAL and awareness of your own domestic legal and administrative system should indicate that the systems at both international and national level for protecting children's human rights are far from perfect.

Many of the changes that have occurred during the past 50 years to better protect human rights have come about through the concerted pressure of individuals, groups and NGOs upon governments and the international community. If you want to take further action to strengthen the legal protection of street and working children you might consider campaigning on the following issues.

○ Introduce a **right of individual petition** under the Convention on the Rights of the Child to allow children to bring complaints themselves against violating governments.
○ The United Nations to create a post of **High Commissioner for Children's Rights** to ensure that children's rights issues are not neglected by any of the UN bodies and to co-ordinate their work effectively.
○ Introduce **international class actions**. This mechanism would allow those unable to bring complaints directly themselves – such as the marginalized and dispossessed – to be represented as a group before a court or tribunal. It could be particularly useful where large numbers of street and working children are being denied their economic and social rights, but have no means of redress.
○ **Expand the existing set of children's rights** to introduce more that have particular relevance for street children, for example the right not to be labelled; the right to have their own support systems respected.
○ At a national level, introduce **independent Children's Ombudsmen or Commissioners** (as they have done in a number of countries such as Costa Rica and New Zealand) to champion the cause of children's rights.
○ Consider adopting a similar measure to the **Brazilian Child and Adolescent Statute of 1990** which granted specific new rights to street children and placed responsibility for their care and protection at a local level. Although it has not ended the abuse of street children and the record of progress is mixed across the country the statute did represent a radical departure in terms of public policy and the attitude of society.
○ Finally, encourage other activists and and NGOs to **make more use of existing regional and international mechanisms** – particularly the new ones when they come into force, such as the African Charter on the Rights and Welfare of the Child – since it is only by doing so that their effectiveness will be strengthened.

SECTION C
Information Appendices

C1: Glossary of Terms

covenant/convention
Other names that are used for the word treaty.

customary international law
A principle (e.g. freedom from slavery) or set of principles (e.g. the Universal Declaration of Human Rights) which, although not necessarily treaty law, have become binding upon all states because of their widespread acceptance over a long period of time.

derogation
A state may decide to opt out of certain obligations under a treaty after notifying the supervisory body and other state parties. This usually occurs during a period of war or public emergency and should last only as long as the exceptional circumstances do – although this can be years in the case of some countries. Some fundamental rights – e.g. the right to life, freedom from torture – cannot be derogated from in any circumstances.

indivisibility of rights
Most often applied to the relationship of economic, social and cultural rights with civil and political rights to show how rights are interrelated and interdependant and that one set should not take precedence over another.

justiciable
A matter which is sufficiently well defined so as to enable determination by a legal body – usually a court of law.

petition
The right of an individual in international or regional human rights law to bring a case against a state alleging violations. Under most systems the right is not automatic, but has to be agreed by the state through ratification of an optional protocol.

procedural law
That part of a treaty which describes the system for enforcing the substantive law of the document.

protocol
An additional section(s) to a treaty which contains new substantive or procedural clauses. A state will be bound by these new clauses only if it chooses to ratify the protocol separately – hence they are often called optional protocols.

ratification
Final acceptance by a state's legislature or executive of its commitment to an international treaty. From the date of ratification the treaty's terms are binding upon a state.

reservation
A state party upon ratifying a treaty may make certain reservations regarding its unwillingness to accept certain obligations for cultural or political reasons. Reservations will not always be accepted if they fundamentally undermine the purpose of the treaty.

resolution

A non-binding recommendation passed by the United Nations General Assembly.

state party

Those states that have ratified a particular treaty and have become bound by it.

street children

'those for whom the street (in the widest sense of the word, i.e. unoccupied dwellings, waste land etc.) more than their family has become their real home, a situation in which there is no protection, supervision or direction from responsible adults'

(International Catholic Child Bureau at UNICEF Ideas Forum 1982)

substantive law

That part of an international or regional treaty which lists and describes the rights to be protected.

treaty

An international agreement which, when ratified by states, becomes binding upon them. Treaty law takes precedence over other forms of international and national law.

The U.N. Convention on the Rights of the Child: A Summary Guide

Fundamental Principles

Definition of a Child
Article 1

Non-Discrimination

Article 2 –	General principle
Article 17(d) –	Media's regard for linguistic minorities
Article 23 –	Provision for children with disabilities
Article 28 –	Equal opportunities in education
Article 30 –	Rights of children of minorities and indigenous populations
Article 31 –	Equal opportunities to culture

Best Interests of the Child
Article 3

Identity

Article 7 –	Child's right to a name and nationality, to know and be cared for by parents
Article 8 –	Right to preserve name, nationality and family relations
Article 9 –	Rights when separated from parents
Article 10 –	Family reunification
Article 17 –	Access to appropriate information
Article 22 –	Refugees

Civil and Political Rights

Article 12 –	Right to express views freely
Article 13 –	Freedom of expression
Article 14 –	Freedom of thought, conscience and religion
Article 15 –	Freedom of association
Article 16 –	Protection of privacy
Article 17 –	Access to information including media
Article 19 –	Protection from all forms of physical and mental violence
Article 37 –	Protection from inhuman or degrading treatment and from arbitrary or unlawful restriction of liberty

Economic and Social Rights

Survival and Health

Article 3(3) –	Proper standards for all health care services and institutions
Article 6 –	Right to life and maximum survival and development
Article 17 –	Information to promote mental health
Article 23 –	Rights of children with disabilities and learning difficulties
Article 24 –	Provision of health services
Article 25 –	Right to periodic review of treatment

Article 36 –   Protection from exploitation in medical research

Protection against poverty –Standard of living
Article 26 –   Right to social security
Article 27 –   Right to an adequate standard of living

Protection from violence, abuse and exploitation
Article 11 –   Illicit transfer and non-return of children
Article 19 –   Legal and educational action to protect a child from all forms of physical or mental violence
Article 24(3) –   Protection from traditional practices
Article 32 –   Protection against economic exploitation
Article 33 –   Protection from drugs
Article 34 –   Protection from sexual exploitation
Article 35 –   Sale, traffic and abduction of children
Article 36 –   Protection from social and all other forms of exploitation
Article 38 –   Protection of children involved in armed conflicts
Article 39 –   Right to rehabilitation for victims

Education
Article 28 –   Right to education
Article 30 –   Rights of children of minorities and indigenous populations

Non-family care of children
Article 3(3) –   Standards for institutions
Article 20 –   Protection of children not in a family environment
Article 21 –   Adoption including inter-country adoption
Article 25 –   Right to periodic review of care and treatment

2.1: The Convention on the Rights of the Child (1989)

PREAMBLE

The States Parties to the Present Convention,

Considering that, in accordance with the principles proclaimed in the Charter of the United Nations, recognition of the inherent dignity and of the equal and inalienable rights of all members of the human family is the foundation of freedom, justice and peace in the world,

Bearing in mind that the peoples of the United Nations have, in the Charter, reaffirmed their faith in fundamental human rights and in the dignity and worth of the human person, and have determined to promote social progress and better standards of life in larger freedom,

Recognising that the United Nations has, in the Universal Declaration of Human Rights and in the International Covenants on Human Rights, proclaimed and agreed that everyone is entitled to all the rights and freedoms set forth therein, without distinction of any kind, such as race, colour, sex, language, religion, political or other opinion, national or social origin, property, birth or other status,

Recalling that, in the Universal Declaration of Human Rights, the United Nations has proclaimed that childhood is entitled to special care and assistance,

Convinced that the family, as the fundamental group of society and the natural environment for the growth and well-being of all its members and particularly children, should be afforded the necessary protection and assistance so that it can fully assume its responsibilities within the community,

Recognising that the child, for the full and harmonious development of his or her personality, should grow up in a family environment, in an atmosphere of happiness, love and understanding,

Considering that the child should be fully prepared to live an individual life in society, and brought up in the spirit of the ideals proclaimed in the Charter of the United Nations, and in particular in the spirit of peace, dignity, tolerance, freedom, equality and solidarity,

Bearing in mind that the need to extend particular care to the child has been stated in the Geneva Declaration on the Rights of the Child of 1924 and in the Declaration of the Rights of the Child adopted by the United Nations in 1959 and recognised in the Universal Declaration of Human Rights, in the International Covenant on Civil and Political Rights (in particular in Articles 23 and 24), in the International Covenant on Economic, Social and Cultural Rights (in particular in its article 10) and in the statutes and relevant instruments of specialised agencies and international organisations concerned with the welfare of children,

Bearing in mind that, as indicated in the Declaration of the Rights of the Child adopted by the General Assembly on 20 November 1959, 'the child, by reason of his physical and mental immaturity, needs special safeguards and care, including appropriate legal protection, before as well as after birth',

Recalling the provisions of the Declaration on Social and Legal Principles relating to the Protection and Welfare of Children, with Special Reference to the Foster Placement and Adoption Nationally and Internationally; the United Nations Standard Minimum Rules for the Administration of Juvenile Justice (The Beijing Rules); and the Declaration on the Protection of Women and Children in Emergency and Armed Conflict,

Recognising that, in all countries in the world, there are children living in exceptionally difficult conditions, and that such children need special consideration,

Taking due account of the importance of the traditions and cultural values of each people for the protection and harmonious development of the child,

Recognising the importance of international co-operation for improving the living conditions of children in every country, in particular in developing countries,

Have agreed as follows:

Article 1

For the purpose of the present Convention, a child means every human being below the age of eighteen years, unless, under the law applicable to the child, majority is attained earlier.

Article 2

1. The States Parties shall respect and ensure the rights set forth in the Convention to each child within their respective jurisdiction without discrimination of any kind, irrespective of the child's or his or her parent's or legal guardian's race, colour, sex, language, religion, political or other opinion, national, ethnic or social origin, property, disability, birth or other status.
2. States Parties shall take all appropriate measures to ensure that the child is protected against all forms of discrimination or punishment on the basis of the status, activities, expressed opinions, or beliefs of the child's parents, legal guardians, or family members.

Article 3

1. In all actions concerning children, whether undertaken by public or private social welfare institutions, courts of law, administrative authorities or legislative bodies, the best interests of the child shall be a primary consideration.
2. States Parties undertake to ensure the child such protection and care as is necessary for his or her well-being, taking into account the rights and duties of his or her parents, legal guardians, or other individuals legally responsible for him or her, and, to this end, shall take all appropriate legislative and administrative measures.
3. States Parties shall ensure that the institutions, services and facilities responsible for the care or protection of children shall conform with the standards established by competent authorities, particularly in the areas of safety, health, in the number and suitability of their staff, as well as competent supervision.

Article 4

States Parties shall undertake all appropriate legislative, administrative, and other measures for the implementation of the rights recognised in this Convention. With regard to economic, social and cultural rights, States Parties shall undertake such measures to the maximum extent of their available resources and, where needed, within the framework of international co-operation.

Article 5

States Parties shall respect the responsibilities, rights and duties of parents or, where applicable, the members of the extended family or community as provided for by local custom, legal guardians or other persons legally responsible for the child, to provide, in a manner consistent with the evolving capacities of the child, appropriate direction and guidance in the exercise by the child of the rights recognised in the present Convention.

Article 6

1. States Parties recognise that every child has the inherent right to life.
2. States Parties shall ensure to the maximum extent possible the survival and development of the child.

Article 7

1. The child shall be registered immediately after birth and shall have the right from birth to a name, the right to acquire a nationality and, as far as possible, the right to know and be cared for by his or her parents.

2. States Parties shall ensure the implementation of these rights in accordance with their national law and their obligations under the relevant international instruments in this field, in particular where the child would otherwise be stateless.

Article 8

1. States Parties undertake to respect the right of the child to preserve his or her identity, including nationality; name and family relations as recognised by law without unlawful interference.
2. Where a child is illegally deprived of some or all of the elements of his or her identity, States Parties shall provide appropriate assistance and protection, with a view to speedily re-establishing his or her identity.

Article 9

1. States Parties shall ensure that the child shall not be separated from his or her parents against their will, except when competent authorities subject to judicial review determine, in accordance with applicable law and procedures, that such separation is necessary for the best interests of the child. Such determination may be necessary in a particular case such as one involving abuse or neglect of the child by the parents, or one where the parents are living separately and a decision must be made as to the child's place of residence.
2. In any proceedings pursuant to paragraph 1, all interested parties shall be given an opportunity to participate in the proceedings and make their views known.
3. States Parties shall respect the right of the child who is separated from one or both parents to maintain personal relations and direct contact with both parents on a regular basis, except if it is contrary to the child's best interests.
4. Where such separation results from any action initiated by a State Party, such as the detention, imprisonment, exile, deportation or death (including death arising from any cause while the person is in the custody of the State) of one or both parents or of the child, that State Party shall, upon request, provide the parents, the child or, if appropriate, another member of the family with the essential information concerning the whereabouts of the absent family member(s) of the family unless the provision of the information would be detrimental to the well-being of the child. States Parties shall further ensure that the submission of such a request shall of itself entail no adverse consequences for the person(s) concerned.

Article 10

1. In accordance with the obligation of States Parties under article 9, paragraph 1, applications by a child or his or her parents to enter or leave a State Party for the purpose of family reunification shall be dealt with by States Parties in a positive, humane and expeditious manner. States Parties shall further ensure that the submission of such a request shall entail no adverse consequences for the applicants and for the members of their family.
2. A child whose parents reside in different States shall have the right to maintain on a regular basis save in exceptional circumstances personal relations and direct contacts with both parents. Towards that end and in accordance with the obligation of States Parties under article 9, paragraph 2, States Parties shall respect the right of the child and his or her parents to leave any country, including their own, and to enter their own country. The right to leave any country shall be subject only to such restrictions as are prescribed by law and which are necessary to protect the national security, public order (*ordre public*), public health or morals or the rights and freedoms of others and are consistent with the other rights recognised in the present Convention.

Article 11

1. States Parties shall take measures to combat the illicit transfer and non-return of children abroad.

2. To this end, States Parties shall promote the conclusion of bilateral or multilateral agreements or accession to existing agreements.

Article 12

1. States Parties shall assure to the child who is capable of forming his or her own views the right to express those views freely in all matters affecting the child, the views of the child being given due weight in accordance with the age and maturity of the child.
2. For this purpose, the child shall in particular be provided the opportunity to be heard in any judicial and administrative proceedings affecting the child, either directly, or through a representative or an appropriate body, in a manner consistent with the procedural rules of national law.

Article 13

1. The child shall have the right to freedom of expression; this right shall include freedom to seek, receive and impart information and ideas of all kinds, regardless of frontiers, either orally or in writing or in print, in the form of art, or through any other media of the child's choice.
2. The exercise of this right may be subject to certain restrictions, but these shall only be such as are provided by law and are necessary:
   (a) For respect of the rights or reputations of others; or
   (b) For the protection of national security or of public order (*ordre public*), or of public health or morals.

Article 14

1. States Parties shall respect the right of the child to freedom of thought, conscience and religion.
2. States Parties shall respect the rights and duties of the parents and, when applicable, legal guardians, to provide direction to the child in the exercise of his or her right in a manner consistent with the evolving capacities of the child.
3. Freedom to manifest one's religion or beliefs may be subject only to such limitations as are prescribed by law and are necessary to protect public safety, order, health or morals, or the fundamental rights and freedoms of others.

Article 15

1. States Parties recognise the rights of the child to freedom of association and to freedom of peaceful assembly.
2. No restrictions may be placed on the exercise of these rights other than those imposed in conformity with the law and which are necessary in a democratic society in the interests of national security or public order (*ordre public*), the protection of public health or morals or the protection of the rights and freedoms of others.

Article 16

1. No child shall be subjected to arbitrary or unlawful interference with his or her privacy, family, home or correspondence, nor to unlawful attacks on his or her honour and reputation.
2. The child has the right to the protection of the law against such interference or attacks.

Article 17

States Parties recognise the important function performed by the mass media and shall ensure that the child has access to information and material from a diversity of national and international sources, especially those aimed at the promotion of his or her social, spiritual and moral well-being and physical and mental health. To this end, States Parties shall:

(a) Encourage the mass media to disseminate information and material of social and cultural benefit to the child and in accordance with the spirit of article 29;

(b) Encourage international co-operation in the production, exchange and dissemination of such information and material from a diversity of cultural, national and international sources;

(c) Encourage the production and dissemination of children's books;

(d) Encourage the mass media to have particular regard to the linguistic needs of the child who belongs to a minority group or who is indigenous;

(e) Encourage the development of appropriate guidelines for the protection of the child from information and material injurious to his or her well-being, bearing in mind the provisions of articles 13 and 18.

Article 18

1. States Parties shall use their best efforts to ensure recognition of the principle that both parents have common responsibilities for the upbringing and development of the child. Parents or, as the case may be, legal guardians, have the primary responsibility for the upbringing and development of the child. The best interests of the child will be their basic concern.

2. For the purpose of guaranteeing and promoting the right set forth in the present Convention, States Parties shall render appropriate assistance to parents and legal guardians in the performance of their child-rearing responsibilities and shall ensure the development of institutions, facilities and services for the care of children.

3. States Parties shall take all appropriate measures to ensure that children of working parents have the right to benefit from child-care services and facilities for which they are eligible.

Article 19

1. States Parties shall take all appropriate legislative, administrative, social and educational measures to protect the child from all forms of physical or mental violence, injury or abuse, neglect or negligent treatment, maltreatment or exploitation, including sexual abuse, while in the care of parent(s), legal guardian(s) or any other person who has the care of the child.

2. Such protective measures should, as appropriate, include effective procedures for the establishment of social programmes to provide necessary support for the child and for those who have the care of the child, as well as for other forms of prevention and for identification, reporting, referral, investigation, treatment, and follow-up of instances of child maltreatment described heretofore, and, as appropriate, for judicial involvement.

Article 20

1. A child temporarily or permanently deprived of his or her family environment, or in whose own best interests cannot be allowed to remain in that environment, shall be entitled to special protection and assistance provided by the State.

2. States Parties shall in accordance with their national laws ensure alternative care for such a child.

3. Such care could include, *inter alia*, foster placement, *kafalah* of Islamic law, adoption, or if necessary placement in suitable institutions for the care of children. When considering solutions, due regard shall be paid to the desirability of continuity in a child's upbringing and to the child's ethnic, religious, cultural and linguistic background.

Article 21

States Parties that recognise and/or permit the system of adoption shall ensure that the best interests of the child shall be the paramount consideration and they shall:

(a) Ensure that the adoption of a child is authorised only by competent authorities who determine, in accordance with applicable law and procedures and on the basis of all pertinent and reliable information, that the adoption is permissible in view of the child's status concerning parents, relatives and legal guardians and that, if required, the persons concerned have given their informed consent to the adoption on the basis of such counselling as may be necessary;

(b) Recognise that inter-country adoption may not be considered as an alternative means of child's care, if the child cannot be placed in a foster or an adoptive family or cannot in any suitable manner be cared for in the child's country of origin;

(c) Ensure that the child concerned by inter-country adoption enjoys safeguards and standards equivalent to those existing in the case of national adoption;

(d) Take all appropriate measures to ensure that, in inter-country adoption, the placement does not result in improper financial gain for those involved in it;

(e) Promote, where appropriate, the objectives of the present article by concluding bilateral or multilateral arrangements or agreements, and endeavour, within this framework, to ensure that the placement of the child in another country is carried out by competent authorities or organs.

Article 22

1. States Parties shall take appropriate measures to ensure that a child who is seeking refugee status or who is considered a refugee in accordance with applicable international or domestic law and procedures shall, whether unaccompanied or accompanied by his parents or by any other person, receive appropriate protection and humanitarian assistance in the enjoyment of applicable rights set forth in the present Convention and in other international instruments to which the said States are Parties.

Article 23

1. States Parties recognise that a mentally or physically disabled child should enjoy a full and decent life, in conditions which ensure dignity, promote self-reliance and facilitate the child's active participation in the community.

2. States Parties recognise the right of the disabled child to special care and shall encourage and ensure the extension, subject to available resources to the eligible child and those responsible for his or her care, of assistance for which application is made and which is appropriate to the child's condition and to the circumstances of the parents or others caring for the child.

3. Recognising the special needs of a disabled child, assistance extended in accordance with paragraph 2 shall be provided free of charge, whenever possible, taking into account the financial resources of the parents or others caring for the child, and shall be designed to ensure that the disabled child has effective access to and receives education, training and health care services, rehabilitation services, preparation for employment and recreation opportunities in a manner conducive to the child's achieving the fullest possible social integration and individual development, including his or her cultural and spiritual development.

4. States Parties shall promote, in the spirit of international co-operation, the exchange of appropriate information in the field of preventative health care and of medical, psychological and functional treatment of disabled children, including dissemination of and access to information concerning methods of rehabilitation education and vocational services, with the aim of enabling States Parties to improve their capabilities and skills and to widen their experience in these areas. In this regard, particular account shall be taken of the needs of developing countries.

Article 24

1. States Parties recognise the right of the child to the enjoyment of the highest attainable standard of health and to facilities for the treatment of illness and rehabilitation of health. States Parties shall strive to ensure that no child is deprived of his or her right of access to such health care services.

2. States Parties shall pursue full implementation of this right and, in particular, shall take appropriate measures:

(a) To diminish infant and child mortality;

(b) To ensure the provision of necessary medical assistance and health care to all children with emphasis on the development of primary health care;

(c) To combat disease and malnutrition, including within the framework of primary health care, through, *inter alia*, the application of readily available technology and through the provision of adequate nutritious foods and clean drinking-water, taking into consideration the dangers and risks of environmental pollution;

(d) To ensure appropriate pre- and post-natal health care for mothers;

(e) To ensure that all segments of society, in particular parents and children, are informed, have access to education and are supported in the use of basic knowledge of child health and nutrition, the advantages of breast-feeding, hygiene and environmental sanitation and the prevention of accidents;

(f) To develop preventative health care, guidance for parents and family planning education and services.

3. States Parties shall take all effective and appropriate measures with a view to abolishing traditional practices prejudicial to the health of children.

4. States Parties undertake to promote and encourage international co-operation with a view to achieving progressively the full realisation of the right recognised in the present article. In this regard, particular account shall be taken of the needs of developing countries.

Article 25

States Parties recognise the right of a child who has been placed by the competent authorities for the purposes of care, protection or treatment of his or her physical or mental health, to a periodic review of the treatment provided to the child and all other circumstances relevant to his or her placement.

Article 26

1. States Parties shall recognise for every child the right to benefit from social security, including social insurance, and shall take the necessary measures to achieve the full realisation of this right in accordance with their national law.

2. The benefits should, where appropriate, be granted, taking into account the resources and the circumstances of the child and persons having responsibility for the maintenance of the child, as well as any other consideration relevant to an application for benefits made by or on behalf of the child.

Article 27

1. The States Parties recognise the right of every child to a standard of living adequate for the child's physical, mental, spiritual, moral and social development.

2. The parent(s) or others responsible for the child have the primary responsibility to secure, within their abilities and financial capacities, the conditions of living necessary for the child's development.

3. States Parties, in accordance with national conditions and within their means, shall take appropriate measures to assist parents and others responsible for the child to implement this right and shall in case of need provide material assistance and support programmes, particularly with regard to nutrition, clothing and housing.

4. States Parties shall take all appropriate measures to secure the recovery of maintenance for the child from the parents or other persons having financial responsibility for the child, both within the State Party and from abroad. In particular, where the person having financial responsibility for the child lives in a State different from that of the child, States Parties shall promote the accession to international agreements, as well as the making of other appropriate arrangements.

Article 28

1. States Parties recognise the right of the child to education, and with a view to achieving this right progressively and on the basis of equal opportunity, they shall, in particular:

(a) Make primary education compulsory and available free to all;

(b) Encourage the development of different forms of secondary education, including general and vocational education, make them available and accessible to every child, and take appropriate measures such as the introduction of free education and offering financial assistance in case of need;

(c) Make higher education accessible to all on the basis of capacity by every appropriate means;

(d) Make educational and vocational information and guidance available and accessible to all children;

(e) Take measures to encourage regular attendance at schools and the reduction of drop-out rates.

2. States Parties shall take all appropriate measures to ensure that school discipline is administered in a manner consistent with the child's human dignity and in conformity with the present Convention.

3. States Parties shall promote and encourage international co-operation in matters relating to education, in particular with a view to contributing to the elimination of ignorance and illiteracy throughout the world and facilitating access to scientific and technical knowledge and modern teaching methods. In this regard, particular account shall be taken of the needs of developing countries.

Article 29

1. States Parties agree that the education of the child shall be directed to:

(a) The development of the child's personality, talents and mental and physical abilities to their fullest potential;

(b) The development of respect for human rights and fundamental freedoms, and for the principles enshrined in the Charter of the United Nations;

(c) The development of respect for the child's parents, his or her own cultural identity, language and values, for the national values of the country in which the child is living, the country from which he or she may originate, and for civilisations different from his or her own;

(d) The preparation of the child for responsible life in a free society, in the spirit of understanding, peace, tolerance, equality of sexes, and friendship among all peoples, ethnic, national and religious groups and persons of indigenous origin;

(e) The development of respect for the natural environment.

2. No part of the present article or article 28 shall be construed so as to interfere with the liberty of individuals and bodies to establish and direct educational institutions, subject always to the observance of the principles set forth in paragraph 1 of the present article and to the requirements that the education given in such institutions shall conform to such minimum standards as may be laid down by the State.

Article 30

In those States in which ethnic, religious or linguistic minorities or persons of indigenous origin exist, a child belonging to such a minority or who is indigenous shall not be denied the right, in community with other members of his or her group, to enjoy his or her own culture, to profess and practice his or her own religion, or to use his or her own language.

Article 31

1. States Parties recognise the right of the child to rest and leisure, to engage in play and recreational activities appropriate to the age of the child and to participate freely in cultural life and the arts.

2. States Parties shall respect and promote the right of the child to participate fully in cultural and artistic life and shall encourage the provision of appropriate and equal opportunities for cultural, artistic, recreational and leisure activity.

Article 32

1. States Parties recognise the right of the child to be protected from economic exploitation and from performing any work that is likely to be hazardous or to interfere with the child's education, or to be harmful to the child's health or physical, mental, spiritual, moral or social development.
2. States Parties shall take legislative, administrative, social and educational measures to ensure the implementation of the present article. To this end, and having regard to the relevant provisions of other international instruments, States Parties shall in particular:
   (a) Provide for a minimum age or minimum ages for admissions to employment;
   (b) Provide for appropriate regulation of the hours and conditions of employment; and
   (c) Provide for appropriate penalties or other sanctions to ensure the effective enforcement of the present article.

Article 33

States Parties shall take all appropriate measures, including legislative, administrative, social and educational measures, to protect children from the illicit use of narcotic drugs and psychotropic substances as defined in the relevant international treaties, and to prevent the use of children in the illicit production and trafficking of such substances.

Article 34

States Parties undertake to protect the child from all forms of sexual exploitation and sexual abuse. For these purposes, States Parties shall in particular take all appropriate national, bilateral and multilateral measures to prevent:
   (a) The inducement or coercion of a child to engage in any unlawful sexual activity;
   (b) The exploitative use of children in prostitution or other unlawful sexual practices;
   (c) The exploitative use of children in pornographic performances and materials.

Article 35

States Parties shall take all appropriate national, bilateral and multilateral measures to prevent the abduction, the sale of or traffic in children for any purpose or in any form.

Article 36

States Parties shall protect the child against all other forms of exploitation prejudicial to any aspect of the child's welfare.

Article 37

States Parties shall ensure that:
   (a) No child shall be subjected to torture or other cruel, inhuman or degrading treatment or punishment. Neither capital punishment nor life imprisonment without possibility of release shall be imposed for offences committed by persons below eighteen years of age;
   (b) No child shall be deprived of his or her liberty unlawfully or arbitrarily. The arrest, detention or imprisonment of a child shall be in conformity with the law and shall be used only as a measure of last resort and for the shortest appropriate periods of time;
   (c) Every child deprived of liberty shall be treated with humanity and respect for the inherent dignity of the human person, and in a manner which takes into account the needs of persons of their age. In particular, every child deprived of liberty shall be separated from adults unless it is considered in the child's best interest not to do so and shall have the right to maintain contact with his or her family through correspondence and visits, save in exceptional circumstances;
   (d) Every child deprived of his or her liberty shall have the right to prompt access to legal and other appropriate assistance, as well as the right to challenge the legality of the deprivation of his or her liberty before a court or other competent, independent and impartial authority, and to a prompt decision on any such action.

Article 38

1. States Parties undertake to respect and to ensure respect for rules of international humanitarian law applicable to them in armed conflicts which are relevant to the child.
2. States Parties shall take all feasible measures to ensure that persons who have not attained the age of fifteen years do not take a direct part in hostilities.
3. States Parties shall refrain from recruiting any person who has not attained the age of fifteen years into the armed forces. In recruiting among those persons who have attained the age of fifteen years but who have not attained the age of eighteen years, States Parties shall endeavour to give priority to those who are oldest.
4. In accordance with their obligations under international humanitarian law to protect the civilian population in armed conflicts, States Parties shall take all feasible measures to ensure protection and care of children who are affected by an armed conflict.

Article 39

States Parties shall take all appropriate measures to promote physical and psychological recovery and social reintegration of a child victim of any form of neglect, exploitation, or abuse; torture or any other form of cruel, inhuman or degrading treatment or punishment; or armed conflicts. Such recovery and reintegration shall take place in an environment which fosters the health, self-respect and dignity of the child.

Article 40

1. States Parties recognise the right of every child alleged as, accused of, or recognised as having infringed the penal law to be treated in a manner consistent with the promotion of the child's sense of dignity and worth, which reinforces the child's respect for the human rights and fundamental freedoms of others and which takes into account the child's age and the desirability of promoting the child's reintegration and the child's assuming a constructive role in society.
2. To this end, and having regard to the relevant provisions of international instruments, States Parties shall, in particular, ensure that:
   (a) No child shall be alleged as, be accused of, or recognised as having infringed the penal law by reason of acts or omissions that were not prohibited by national or international law at the time they were committed;
   (b) Every child alleged as or accused of having infringed the penal law has at least the following guarantees:
   (i) To be presumed innocent until proven guilty according to law;
   (ii) To be informed promptly and directly of the charges against him or her, and, if appropriate, through his or her parents or legal guardian, and to have legal or other appropriate assistance in the preparation and presentation of his or her defence;
   (iii) To have the matter determined without delay by a competent, independent and impartial authority or judicial body in a fair hearing according to law, in the presence of legal or other appropriate assistance and, unless it is considered not to be in the best interest of the child, in particular, taking into account his or her age or situation, his or her parents or legal guardians;
   (iv) Not to be compelled to give testimony or to confess guilt; to examine or have examined adverse witnesses and to obtain the participation and examination of witnesses on his or her behalf under conditions of equality;
   (v) If considered to have infringed the penal law, to have this decision and any measures imposed in consequence thereof reviewed by a higher competent, independent and impartial authority or judicial body according to law;
   (vi) To have the free assistance of an interpreter if the child cannot understand or speak the language used;
   (vii) To have his or her privacy fully respected at all stages of the proceedings.
3. States Parties shall seek to promote the establishment of laws, procedures, authorities and institutions specifically applicable to children alleged as, accused of, or recognised as having infringed the penal law, and, in particular:

(a) The establishment of a minimum age below which children shall be presumed not to have the capacity to infringe the penal law;

(b) Whenever appropriate and desirable, measures for dealing with such children without resorting to judicial proceedings, providing that human rights and legal safeguards are fully respected.

4. A variety of dispositions, such as care; education and vocational training programmes and other alternatives to institutional care shall be available to ensure that children are dealt with in a manner appropriate to their well-being and proportionate both to their circumstances and the offence.

Article 41

Nothing in the present Convention shall affect any provisions which are more conducive to the realisation of the rights of the child and which may be contained in:

(a) The law of a State Party; or

(b) International law in force for that State.

2.2: International Covenant on Civil and Political Rights

[Adopted and opened for signature, ratification, and accession by United Nations General Assembly resolution 2200 A (XXI) on 16 December 1966.

Entered into force on 23 March 1976 in accordance with article 49.]

PREAMBLE

The States Parties to the present Covenant

Considering that, in accordance with the principles proclaimed in the Charter of the United Nations, recognition of the inherent dignity and of the equal and inalienable rights of all members of the human family is the foundation of freedom, justice and peace in the world.

Recognizing that these rights derive from the inherent dignity of the human person.

Recognizing that, in accordance with the Universal Declaration of Human Rights, the ideal of free human beings enjoying civil and political freedom and freedom from fear and want can only be achieved if conditions are created whereby everyone may enjoy his civil and political rights, as well as his economic, social and cultural rights.

Considering the obligation of States under the Charter of the United Nations to promote universal respect for, and observance of, human rights and freedoms.

Realizing that the individual, having duties to other individuals and to the community to which he belongs, is under a responsibility to strive for the promotion and observance of the rights recognized in the present Covenant,

Agree upon the following articles:

PART I

Article 1

1. All peoples have the right of self-determination. By virtue of that right they freely determine their political status and freely pursue their economic, social and cultural development.

2. All peoples may, for their own ends, freely dispose of their natural wealth and resources without prejudice to any obligations arising out of international economic co-operation, based upon the principle of mutual benefit, and international law. In no case may a people be deprived of its own means of subsistence.

3. The States Parties to the present Covenant, including those having responsibility for the administration of Non-Self-Governing and Trust Territories, shall promote the realization of the right of self-determination, and shall respect that right, in conformity with the provisions of the Charter of the United Nations.

PART II

Article 2

1. Each State Party to the present Covenant undertakes to respect and to ensure to all individuals within its territory and subject to its jurisdiction the rights recognized in the present Covenant, without distinction of any kind, such as race, colour, sex, language, religion, political or other opinion, national of social origin, property, birth or other status.

2. Where not already provided for by existing legislative or other measures, each State Party to the present Covenant undertakes to take the necessary steps, in accordance with its constitutional processes and with the provisions of the present Covenant, to adopt such other measures as may be necessary to negate effect to the rights recognized in the present Covenant.

3. Each State Party to the present Covenant undertakes:

(a) To ensure that any person whose rights or freedoms as herein recognized are violated shall have an effective remedy, notwithstanding that the violation has been committed by persons acting in an official capacity;

(b) To ensure that any person claiming such a remedy shall have his right thereto determined by competent judicial, administrative or legislative authorities, or by any other competent authority provided for by the legal system of the State, and to develop the possibilities of judicial remedy;

(c) To ensure that the competent authorities shall enforce such remedies when granted.

Article 3

The States Parties to the present Covenant undertake to ensure the equal right of men and women to the enjoyment of all civil and political rights set forth in the present Covenant.

Article 4

1 . In time of public emergency which threatens the life of the nation and the existence of which is officially proclaimed, the States Parties to the present Covenant may take measures derogating from their obligations under the present Covenant to the extent strictly required by the exigencies of the situation, provided that such measures are not inconsistent with their other obligations under international law and do not involve discrimination solely on the ground of race, colour, sex, language, religion or social origin.

2. No derogation from articles 6, 7, 8 (paragraphs I and 2), 11, 15, 16 and 18 may be made under this provision.

3. Any State Party to the present Covenant availing itself of the right of derogation shall immediately inform the other States Parties to the present Covenant, through the intermediary of the Secretary-General of the United Nations, of the provisions from which it has derogated and of the reasons by which it was actuated. A further communication shall be made, through the same intermediary, on the date on which it terminates such derogation.

Article 5

1. Nothing in the present Covenant may be interpreted as implying for any State, group or person any right to engage in any activity or perform any act aimed at the destruction of any of the rights and freedoms recognized herein or at their limitation to a greater extent than is provided for in the present Covenant.

2. There shall be no restriction upon or derogation from any of the fundamental human rights recognized or existing in any State Party to the present Covenant pursuant to law, conventions, regulations or custom on the pretext that the present Covenant, does not recognize such rights or that it recognizes them to a lesser extent.

PART III

Article 6

1. Every human being has the inherent right to life. This right shall be protected by law. No one shall be arbitrarily deprived of his life.

2. In countries which have not abolished the death penalty, sentence of death may be imposed only for the most serious crimes in accordance with the law in force at the time of the commission of the crime and not contrary to the provisions of the present Covenant and to the Convention on the Prevention and Punishment of the Crime of Genocide. This penalty can only be carried out pursuant to a final judgement rendered by a competent court.

3. When deprivation of life constitutes the crime of genocide, it is understood that nothing in this article shall authorize any State Party to the present Covenant to derogate in any way from any obligation assumed under the provisions of the Convention on the Prevention and Punishment of the Crime of Genocide.

4. Anyone sentenced to death shall have the right to seek pardon or commutation of the sentence. Amnesty, pardon or commutation of the sentence of death may be granted in all cases.

5. Sentence of death shall not be imposed for crimes committed by persons below eighteen years of age and shall not be carried out on pregnant women.

6. Nothing in this article shall be invoked to delay or to prevent the abolition of capital punishment by any State Party to the present Covenant.

Article 7

No one shall be subjected to torture or to cruel, inhuman or degrading treatment or punishment. In particular, no one shall be subjected without his free consent to medical or scientific experimentation.

Article 8

1. No one shall be held in slavery; slavery and the slave-trade in all their forms shall be prohibited.

2. No one shall be held in servitude.

3. (a) No one shall be required to perform forced or compulsory labour;

(b) Paragraph 3 (a) shall not be held to preclude, in countries where imprisonment with hard labour may be imposed as a punishment for a crime, the performance of hard labour in pursuance of a sentence to such punishment by a competent court;

(c) For the purpose of this paragraph the term 'forced or compulsory labour' shall not include:

(i) Any work or service, not referred to in subparagraph (b), normally required of a person who is under detention in consequence of a lawful order of a court, or of a person during conditional release from such detention;

(ii) Any service of a military character and, in countries where conscientious objection is recognized, any national service required by law of conscientious objectors;

(iii) Any service exacted in cases of emergency or calamity threatening the life or well-being of the community;

(iv) Any work or service which forms part of normal civil obligations.

Article 9

1. Everyone has the right to liberty and security of person. No one shall be subjected to arbitrary arrest or detention. No one shall be deprived of his liberty except on such grounds and in accordance with such procedure as are established by law.

2. Anyone who is arrested shall be informed, at the time of arrest, of the reasons for his arrest and shall be promptly informed of any charges against him.

3. Anyone arrested or detained on a criminal charge shall be brought promptly before a judge or other officer authorized by law to exercise judicial power and shall be entitled to trial within a reasonable time or to release. It shall not be the general rule that persons awaiting trial shall be detained in custody, but release may be subject to guarantees to appear for trial, at any other stage of the judicial proceedings, and, should occasion arise, for execution of the judgement.

4. Anyone who is deprived of his liberty by arrest or detention shall be entitled to take proceedings before a court, in order that court may decide without delay on the lawfulness of his detention and order his release if the detention is not lawful.

5. Anyone who has been the victim of unlawful arrest or detention shall have an enforceable right to compensation.

Article 10

1. All persons deprived of their liberty shall be treated with humanity and with respect for the inherent dignity of the human person.

2. (a) Accused persons shall, save in exceptional circumstances, be segregated from convicted persons and shall be subject to separate treatment appropriate to their status as unconvicted persons;

(b) Accused juvenile persons shall be separated from adults and brought as speedily as possible for adjudication.

3. The penitentiary system shall comprise treatment of prisoners the essential aim of which shall be their reformation and social rehabilitation. Juvenile offenders shall be segregated from adults and be accorded treatment appropriate to their age and legal status.

Article 11

No one shall be imprisoned merely on the ground of inability to fulfil a contractual obligation.

Article 12

1. Everyone lawfully within the territory of a State shall, within that territory, have the right to liberty of movement and freedom to choose his residence.

2. Everyone shall be free to leave any country, including his own.

3. The above-mentioned rights shall not be subject to any restrictions except those which are provided by law, are necessary to protect national security, public order (*ordre public*), public health or morals or the rights and freedoms of others, and are consistent with the other rights recognized in the present Covenant.

4. No one shall be arbitrarily deprived of the right to enter his own country.

Article 13

An alien lawfully in the territory of a State Party to the present Covenant may be expelled therefrom only in pursuance of a decision reached in accordance with law and shall, except where compelling reasons of national security otherwise require, be allowed to submit the reasons against his expulsion and to have his case reviewed by, and be represented for the purpose before, the competent authority or a person or persons especially designated by the competent authority.

Article 14

1. All persons shall be equal before the courts and tribunals. In the determination of any criminal charge against him, or of his rights and obligations in a suit at law, everyone shall be entitled to a fair and public hearing by a competent, independent and impartial tribunal established by law. The press and the public may be excluded from all or part of a trial for reasons of morals, public order (*ordre public*) or national security in a democratic society, or when the interest of the private lives of the parties so requires, or to the extent strictly necessary in the opinion of the court in special circumstances where publicity would prejudice the interests of justice; but any judgement rendered in a criminal case or in a suit at law shall be made public except where the interest of juvenile persons otherwise requires or the proceedings concern matrimonial disputes or the guardianship of children.

2. Everyone charged with a criminal offence shall have the right to be presumed innocent until proved guilty according to law.

3. In the determination of any criminal charge against him, everyone shall be entitled to the following minimum guarantees, in full equality:

(a) To be informed promptly and in detail in a language which he understands of the nature and cause of the charge against him;

(b) To have adequate time and facilities for the preparation of his defence and to communicate with counsel of his own choosing;

(c) To be tried without undue delay;

(d) To be tried in his presence, and to defend himself in person or through legal assistance of his own choosing; to be informed, if he does not have legal assistance, of this right; and to have legal assistance assigned to him, in any case where the interests of justice so require, and without payment by him in any such case if he does not have sufficient means to pay for it;

(e) To examine, or have examined, the witnesses against him and to obtain the attendance and examination of witnesses on his behalf under the same conditions as witnesses against him;

(f) To have the free assistance of an interpreter if he cannot understand or speak the language used in court;

(g) Not to be compelled to testify against himself or to confess guilt.

4. In the case of juvenile persons, the procedure shall be such as will take account of their age and the desirability of promoting their rehabilitation.

5. Everyone convicted of a crime shall have the right to his conviction and sentence being reviewed by a higher tribunal according to law.

6. When a person has by a final decision been convicted of a criminal offence and when subsequently his conviction has been reversed or he has been pardoned on the ground that a new or newly discovered fact shows conclusively that there has been a miscarriage of justice, the person who has suffered punishment as a result of such conviction shall be compensated according to law, unless it is proved that the non-disclosure of the unknown fact in time is wholly or partly attributable to him.

7. No one shall be liable to be tried or punished again for an offence for which he has already been finally convicted or acquitted in accordance with the law and penal procedure of each country.

Article 15

1 . No one shall be held guilty of any criminal offence on account of any act or omission which did not constitute a criminal offence, under national or international law, at the time when it was committed. Nor shall a heavier penalty be imposed than the one that was applicable at the time when the criminal offence was committed. If, subsequent to the commission of the offence, provision is made by law for the imposition of the lighter penalty, the offender shall benefit thereby.

2. Nothing in this article shall prejudice the trial and punishment of any person for any act or omission which, at the time when it was committed, was criminal according to the general principles of law recognized by the community of nations.

Article 16

Everyone shall have the right to recognition everywhere as a person before the law.

Article 17

1. No one shall be subjected to arbitrary or unlawful interference with his privacy, family, home or correspondence, nor to unlawful attacks on his honour and reputation.

2. Everyone has the right to the protection of the law against such interference or attacks.

Article 18

1. Everyone shall have the right to freedom of thought, conscience and religion. This right shall include freedom to have or to adopt a religion or belief of his choice, and freedom, either individually or in community with others and in public or private, to manifest his religion or belief in worship, observance, practice and teaching.

2. No one shall be subject to coercion which would impair his freedom to have or to adopt a religion or belief of his choice.

3. Freedom to manifest one's religion or beliefs may be subject only to such limitations as are prescribed by law and are necessary to protect public safety, order, health, or morals or the fundamental rights and freedoms of others.

4. The States Parties to the present Covenant undertake to have respect for the liberty of parents and, when applicable, legal guardians to ensure the religious and moral education of their children in conformity with their own convictions.

Article 19

1. Everyone shall have the right to hold opinions without interference.

2. Everyone shall have the right to freedom of expression; this right shall include freedom to seek, receive and impart information and ideas of all kinds, regardless of frontiers, either orally, in writing or in print, in the form of art, or through any other media of his choice.

3. The exercise of the rights provided for in paragraph 2 of this article carries with it special duties and responsibilities. It may therefore be subject to certain restrictions, but these shall only be such as are provided by law and are necessary:

(a) For respect of the rights or reputations of others;

(b) For the protection of national security or of public order (*ordre public*), or of public health or morals.

Article 20

1. Any propaganda for war shall be prohibited by law.

2. Any advocacy of national, racial or religious hatred that constitutes incitement to discrimination, hostility or violence shall be prohibited by law.

Article 21

The right of peaceful assembly shall be recognized. No restrictions may be placed on the exercise of this right other than those imposed in conformity with the law and which are necessary in a democratic society in the interests of national security or public safety, public order (*ordre public*), the protection of public health or morals or the protection of the rights and freedoms of others.

Article 22

1. Everyone shall have the right to freedom of association with others, including the right to form and join trade unions for the protection of his interests.

2. No restrictions may be placed on the exercise of this right other than those which are prescribed by law and which are necessary in a democratic society in the interests of national security or public safety, public order (*ordre public*), the protection of public health or morals or the protection of the rights and freedoms of others. This article shall not prevent the imposition of lawful restrictions on members of the armed forces and of the police in their exercise of this right.

3. Nothing in this article shall authorize States Parties to the International Labour Organisation Convention of 1948 concerning Freedom of Association and Protection of the Right to Organize to take legislative measures which would prejudice, or to apply the law in such a manner as to prejudice, the guarantees provided for in that Convention.

Article 23

1. The family is the natural and fundamental group unit of society and is entitled to protection by society and the State.

2. The right of men and women of marriageable age to marry and to found a family shall be recognized.

3. No marriage shall be entered into without the free and full consent of the intending spouses.

4. States Parties to the present Covenant shall take appropriate steps to ensure equality of rights and responsibilities of spouses as to marriage, during marriage and at its dissolution. In the case of dissolution, provision shall be made for the necessary protection of any children.

Article 24

1. Every child shall have, without any discrimination as to race, colour, sex, language, religion, national or social origin, property or birth, the right to such measures of protection as are required by his status as a minor, on the part of his family, society and the State.

2. Every child shall be registered immediately after birth and shall have a name.

3. Every child has the right to acquire a nationality.

Article 25

Every citizen shall have the right and the opportunity, without any of the distinctions mentioned in article 2 and without unreasonable restrictions:

(a) To take part in the conduct of public affairs, directly or through freely chosen representatives

(b) To vote and to be elected at genuine periodic elections which shall be by universal and equal suffrage and shall be held by secret ballot, guaranteeing the free expression of the will of the electors;

(c) To have access, on general terms of equality, to public service in his country.

Article 26

All persons are equal before the law and are entitled without any discrimination to the equal protection of the law. In this respect, the law shall prohibit any discrimination and guarantee to all persons equal and effective protection against discrimination on any ground such as race, colour, sex, language, religion, political or other opinion, national or social origin, property, birth or other status.

Article 27

In those States in which ethnic, religious or linguistic minorities exist, persons belonging to such minorities shall not be denied the right, in community with the other members of their group, to enjoy their own culture, to profess and practise their own religion, or to use their own language.

PART IV

Article 28

1. There shall be established a Human Rights Committee (hereafter referred to in the present Covenant as the Committee). It shall consist of eighteen members and shall carry out the functions hereinafter provided.

2. The Committee shall be composed of nationals of the States Parties to the present Covenant who shall be persons of high moral character and recognized competence in the field of human rights, consideration being given to the usefulness of the participation of some persons having legal experience.

3. The members of the Committee shall be elected and shall serve in their personal capacity.

Article 29

1 . The members of the Committee shall be elected by secret ballot from a list of persons possessing the qualifications prescribed in article 28 and nominated for the purpose by the States Parties to the present Covenant.

2. Each State Party to the present Covenant may nominate not more than two persons. These persons shall be nationals of the nominating State.

3. A person shall be eligible for renomination.

Article 30

1. The initial election shall be held no later than six months after the date of the entry into force of the present Covenant.

2. At least four months before the date of each election to the Committee, other than an election to fill a vacancy declared in accordance with article 34, the Secretary-General of the United Nations shall address a written invitation to the States Parties to the present Covenant to submit their nominations for membership of the Committee within three months.

3. The Secretary-General of the United Nations shall prepare a list in alphabetical order of all the persons thus nominated, with an indication of the States Parties which have

nominated them, and shall submit it to the States Parties to the present Covenant no later than one month before the date of each election.

4. Elections of the members of the Committee shall be held at a meeting of the States Parties to the present Covenant convened by the Secretary General of the United Nations at the Headquarters of the United Nations. At that meeting, for which two thirds of the States Parties to the present Covenant shall constitute a quorum, the persons elected to the Committee shall be those nominees who obtain the largest number of votes and an absolute majority of the votes of the representatives of States Parties present and voting.

Article 31

1. The Committee may not include more than one national of the same State.

2. In the election of the Committee, consideration shall be given to equitable geographical distribution of membership and to the representation of the different forms of civilization and of the principal legal systems.

Article 32

1. The members of the Committee shall be elected for a term of four years. They shall be eligible for re-election if renominated. However, the terms of nine of the members elected at the first election shall expire at the end of two years; immediately after the first election, the names of these nine members shall be chosen by lot by the Chairman of the meeting referred to in article 30, paragraph 4.

2. Elections at the expiry of office shall be held in accordance with the preceding articles of this part of the present Covenant.

Article 33

1. If, in the unanimous opinion of the other members, a member of the Committee has ceased to carry out his functions for any cause other than absence of a temporary character, the Chairman of the Committee shall notify the Secretary-General of the United Nations, who shall then declare the seat of that member to be vacant.

2. In the event of the death or the resignation of a member of the Committee, the Chairman shall immediately notify the Secretary-General of the United Nations, who shall declare the seat vacant from the date of death or the date on which the resignation takes effect.

Article 34

1. When a vacancy is declared in accordance with article 33 and if the term of office of the member to be replaced does not expire within six months of the declaration of the vacancy, the Secretary-General of the United Nations shall notify each of the States Parties to the present Covenant, which may within two months submit nominations in accordance with article 29 for the purpose of filling the vacancy.

2. The Secretary-General of the United Nations shall prepare a list in alphabetical order of the persons thus nominated and shall submit it to the States Parties to the present Covenant. The election to fill the vacancy shall then take place in accordance with the relevant provisions of this part of the present Covenant.

3. A member of the Committee elected to fill a vacancy declared in accordance with article 33 shall hold office for the remainder of the term of the member who vacated the seat on the Committee under the provisions of that article.

Article 35

The members of the Committee shall, with the approval of the General Assembly of the United Nations, receive emoluments from United Nations resources on such terms and conditions as the General Assembly may decide, having regard to the importance of the Committee's responsibilities.

Article 36

The Secretary-General of the United Nations shall provide the necessary staff and facilities for the effective performance of the functions of the Committee under the present Covenant.

Article 37

1. The Secretary-General of the United Nations shall convene the initial meeting of the Committee at the Headquarters of the United Nations.
2. After its initial meeting, the Committee shall meet at such times as shall be provided in its rules of procedure.
3. The Committee shall normally meet at the Headquarters of the United Nations or at the United Nations Office at Geneva.

Article 38

Every member of the Committee shall, before taking up his duties, make a solemn declaration in open committee that he will perform his functions impartially and conscientiously.

Article 39

1. The Committee shall elect its officers for a term of two years. They may be re-elected.
2. The Committee shall establish its own rules of procedure, but these rules shall provide, *inter alia*, that:
   (a) Twelve members shall constitute a quorum;
   (b) Decisions of the Committee shall be made by a majority vote of the members present.

Article 40

1. The States Parties to the present Covenant undertake to submit reports on the measures they have adopted which give effect to the rights recognized herein and on the progress made in the enjoyment of those rights:
   (a) Within one year of the entry into force of the present Covenant for the States Parties concerned;
   (b) Thereafter whenever the Committee so requests.
2. All reports shall be submitted to the Secretary-General of the United Nations, who shall transmit them to the Committee for consideration. Reports shall indicate the factors and difficulties, if any, affecting the implementation of the present Covenant.
3. The Secretary-General of the United Nations may, after consultation with the Committee, transmit to the specialized agencies concerned copies of such parts of the reports as may fall within their field of competence.
4. The Committee shall study the reports submitted by the States Parties to the present Covenant. It shall transmit its reports, and such general comments as it may consider appropriate, to the States Parties. The Committee may also transmit to the Economic and Social Council these comments along with the copies of the reports it has received from States Parties to the present Covenant.
5. The States Parties to the present Covenant may submit to the Committee observations on any comments that may be made in accordance with paragraph 4 of this article.

Article 41

1. A State Party to the present Covenant may at any time declare under this article that it recognizes the competence of the Committee to receive and consider communications to the effect that a State Party claims that another State Party is not fulfilling its obligations under the present Covenant. Communications under this article may be received and considered only if submitted by a State Party which has made a declaration recognizing in regard to itself the competence of the Committee. No communication shall be received by

the Committee if it concerns a State Party which has not made such a declaration. Communications received under this article shall be dealt with in accordance with the following procedure:

(a) If a State Party to the present Covenant considers that another State Party is not giving effect to the provisions of the present Covenant, it may, by written communication, bring the matter to the attention of that State Party. Within three months after the receipt of the communication the receiving State shall afford the State which sent the communication an explanation, of any other statement in writing clarifying the matter which should include, to the extent possible and pertinent, reference to domestic procedures and remedies taken, pending, or available in the matter;

(b) If the matter is not adjusted to the satisfaction of both States Parties concerned within six months after the receipt by the receiving State of the initial communication, either State shall have the right to refer the matter to the Committee, by notice given to the Committee and to the other State;

(c) The Committee shall deal with a matter referred to it only after it has ascertained that all available domestic remedies have been invoked and exhausted in the matter, in conformity with the generally recognized principles of international law. This shall not be the rule where the application of the remedies is unreasonably prolonged;

(d) The Committee shall hold closed meetings when examining communications under this article;

(e) Subject to the provisions of subparagraph (c), the Committee shall make available its good offices to the States Parties concerned with a view to a friendly solution of the matter on the basis of respect for human rights and fundamental freedoms as recognized in the present Covenant;

(f) In any matter referred to it, the Committee may call upon the States Parties concerned, referred to in subparagraph (b), to supply any relevant information;

(g) The States Parties concerned, referred to in subparagraph (b), shall have the right to be represented when the matter is being considered in the Committee and to make submissions orally and/or in writing;

(h) The Committee shall, within twelve months after the date of receipt of notice under subparagraph (b), submit a report:

(i) If a solution within the terms of subparagraph (e) is reached, the Committee shall confine its report to a brief statement of the facts and of the solution reached;

(ii) If a solution within the terms of subparagraph (e) is not reached, the Committee shall confine its report to a brief statement of the facts; the written submissions and record of the oral submissions made by the States Parties concerned shall be attached to the report. In every matter, the report shall be communicated to the States Parties concerned.

2. The provisions of this article shall come into force when ten States Parties to the present Covenant have made declarations under paragraph I of this article. Such declarations shall be deposited by the States Parties with the Secretary-General of the United Nations, who shall transmit copies thereof to the other States Parties. A declaration may be withdrawn at any time by notification to the Secretary-General. Such a withdrawal shall not prejudice the consideration of any matter which is the subject of a communication already transmitted under this article; no further communication by any State Party shall be received after the notification of withdrawal of the declaration has been received by the Secretary-General, unless the State Party concerned has made a new declaration.

Article 42

1. (a) If a matter referred to the Committee in accordance with article 41 is not resolved to the satisfaction of the States Parties concerned, the Committee may, with the prior consent of the States Parties concerned, appoint an *ad hoc* Conciliation Commission (hereinafter referred to as the Commission). The good offices of the Commission shall be made available to the States Parties concerned with a view to an amicable solution of the matter on the basis of respect for the present Covenant;

(b) The Commission shall consist of five persons acceptable to the States Parties concerned. If the States Parties concerned fail to reach agreement within three months on all or part of the composition of the Commission, the members of the Commission concerning whom no agreement has been reached shall be elected by secret ballot by a two-thirds majority vote of the Committee from among its members.

2. The members of the Commission shall serve in their personal capacity. They shall not be nationals of the States Parties concerned, or of a State not Party to the present Covenant, or of a State Party which has not made a declaration under article 41.

3. The Commission shall elect its own Chairman and adopt its own rules of procedure.

4. The meetings of the Commission shall normally be held at the Headquarters of the United Nations or at the United Nations Office at Geneva. However, they may be held at such other convenient places as the Commission may determine in consultation with the Secretary-General of the United Nations and the States Parties concerned.

5. The secretariat provided in accordance with article 36 shall also service the commissions appointed under this article.

6. The information received and collated by the Committee shall be made available to the Commission and the Commission may call upon the States Parties concerned to supply any other relevant information.

7. When the Commission has fully considered the matter, but in any event not later than twelve months after having been seized of the matter, it shall submit to the Chairman of the Committee a report for communication to the States Parties concerned:

(a) If the Commission is unable to complete its consideration of the matter within twelve months, it shall confine its report to a brief statement of the status of its consideration of the matter;

(b) If an amicable solution to the matter on the basis of respect for human rights as recognized in the present Covenant is reached, the Commission shall confine its report to a brief statement of the facts and of the solution reached;

(c) If a solution within the terms of subparagraph (b) is not reached, the Commission's report shall embody its findings on all questions of fact relevant to the issues between the States Parties concerned, and its views on the possibilities of an amicable solution of the matter. This report shall also contain the written submissions and a record of the oral submissions made by the States Parties concerned;

(d) If the Commission's report is submitted under subparagraph (c), the States Parties concerned shall, within three months of the receipt of the report, notify the Chairman of the Committee whether or not they accept the contents of the report of the Commission.

8. The provisions of this article are without prejudice to the responsibilities of the Committee under article 41.

9. The States Parties concerned shall share equally all the expenses of the members of the Commission in accordance with estimates to be provided by the Secretary-General of the United Nations.

10. The Secretary-General of the United Nations shall be empowered to pay the expenses of the members of the Commission, if necessary, before reimbursement by the States Parties concerned, in accordance with paragraph 9 of this article.

Article 43

The members of the Committee, and of the *ad hoc* conciliation commissions which may be appointed under article 42, shall be entitled to the facilities, privileges and immunities of experts on mission for the United Nations as laid down in the relevant sections of the Convention on the Privileges and Immunities of the United Nations.

Article 44

The provisions for the implementation of the present Covenant shall apply without prejudice to the procedures prescribed in the field of human rights by or under the constituent instruments and the conventions of the United Nations and of the specialized agencies and shall not prevent the States Parties to the present Covenant from having recourse to other procedures for settling a dispute in accordance with general or special international agreements in force between them.

Article 45

The Committee shall submit to the General Assembly of the United Nations, through the Economic and Social Council, an annual report on its activities.

PART V

Article 46

Nothing in the present Covenant shall be interpreted as impairing the provisions of the Charter of the United Nations and of the constitutions of the specialized agencies which define the respective responsibilities of the various organs of the United Nations and of the specialized agencies in regard to the matters dealt with in the present Covenant.

Article 47

Nothing in the present Covenant shall be interpreted as impairing the inherent right of all peoples to enjoy and utilize fully and freely their natural wealth and resources.

PART VI

Article 48

1. The present Covenant is open for signature by any State Member of the United Nations or member of any of its specialized agencies, by any State Party to the Statute of the International Court of Justice, and by any other State which has been invited by the General Assembly of the United Nations to become a Party to the present Covenant.
2. The present Covenant is subject to ratification. Instruments of ratification shall be deposited with the Secretary-General of the United Nations.
3. The present Covenant shall be open to accession by any State referred to in paragraph 1 of this article.
4. Accession shall be effected by the deposit of an instrument of accession with the Secretary-General of the United Nations.
5. The Secretary-General of the United Nations shall inform all States which have signed this Covenant or acceded to it of the deposit of each instrument of ratification or accession.

Article 49

1. The present Covenant shall enter into force three months after the date of the deposit with the Secretary-General of the United Nations of the thirty-fifth instrument of ratification or instrument of accession.
2. For each State ratifying the present Covenant or acceding to it after the deposit of the thirty-fifth instrument of ratification or instrument of accession, the present Covenant shall enter into force three months after the date of the deposit of its own instrument of ratification or instrument of accession.

Article 50

The provisions of the present Covenant shall extend to all parts of federal States without any limitations or exceptions.

Article 51

1. Any State Party to the present Covenant may propose an amendment and file it with the Secretary-General of the United Nations. The Secretary-General of the United Nations shall thereupon communicate any proposed amendments to the States Parties to the present Covenant with a request that they notify him whether they favour a conference of States Parties for the purpose of considering and voting upon the proposals. In the event that at least one third of the States Parties favours such a conference, the Secretary-General shall convene the conference under the auspices of the United Nations.

Any amendment adopted by a majority of the States Parties present and voting at the conference shall be submitted to the General Assembly of the United Nations for approval.

2. Amendments shall come into force when they have been approved by the General Assembly of the United Nations and accepted by a two-thirds majority of the States Parties to the present Covenant in accordance with their respective constitutional processes.

3. When amendments come into force, they shall be binding on those States Parties which have accepted them, other States Parties still being bound by the provisions of the present Covenant and any earlier amendment which they have accepted.

Article 52

Irrespective of the notifications made under article 48, paragraph 5, the Secretary-General of the United Nations shall inform all States referred to in paragraph I of the same article of the following particulars:

(a) Signatures, ratifications and accessions under article 48;

(b) The date of the entry into force of the present Covenant under article 49 and the date of the entry into force of any amendments under article 51.

Article 53

1. The present Covenant, of which the Chinese, English, French, Russian and Spanish texts are equally authentic, shall be deposited in the archives of the United Nations.

2. The Secretary-General of the United Nations shall transmit certified copies of the present Covenant to all States referred to in article 48.

Protocols to the International Covenant on Civil and Political Rights

(First) Optional Protocol,

The States Parties to the present Protocol

Considering that in order further to achieve the purpose of the International Covenant on Civil and Political Rights (hereinafter referred to as the Covenant) and the implementation of its provisions it would be appropriate to enable the Human Rights Committee set up in part IV of the Covenant (hereinafter referred to as the Committee) to receive and consider, as provided in the present Protocol, communications from individuals claiming to be victims of violations of any of the rights set forth in the Covenant.

Have agreed as follows:

Article 1

A State Party to the Covenant that becomes a Party to the present Protocol recognizes the competence of the Committee to receive and consider communications from individuals subject to its jurisdiction who claim to be victims of a violation by that State Party of any of the rights set forth in the Covenant. No communication shall be received by the Committee if it concerns a State Party to the Covenant which is not a Party to the present Protocol.

Article 2

Subject to the provisions of article 1, individuals who claim that any of their rights enumerated in the Covenant have been violated and who have exhausted all available domestic remedies may submit a written communication to the Committee for consideration.

Article 3

The Committee shall consider inadmissible any communication under the present Protocol which is anonymous, or which it considers to be an abuse of the right of submission of such communications or to be incompatible with the provisions of the Covenant.

Article 4

1. Subject to the provisions of article 3, the Committee shall bring any communications submitted to it under the present Protocol to the attention of the State Party to the present Protocol alleged to be violating any provision of the Covenant.
2. Within six months, the receiving State shall submit to the Committee written explanations or statements clarifying the matter and the remedy, if any, that may have been taken by that State.

Article 5

1. The Committee shall consider communications received under the present Protocol in the light of all written information made available to it by the individual and by the State Party concerned.
2. The Committee shall not consider any communication from an individual unless it has ascertained that:
   (a) The same matter is not being examined under another procedure of international investigation or settlement;
   (b) The individual has exhausted all available domestic remedies. This shall not be the rule where the application of the remedies is unreasonably prolonged.

3. The Committee shall hold closed meetings when examining communications under the present Protocol.

4. The Committee shall forward its views to the State Party concerned and to the individual.

Article 6

The Committee shall include in its annual report under article 45 of the Covenant a summary of its activities under the present Protocol.

SECOND OPTIONAL PROTOCOL

The States Parties to the present Protocol

Believing that abolition of the death penalty contributes to enhancement of dignity and progressive development of human rights,

Recalling article 3 of the Universal Declaration of Human Rights, adopted on 10 December 1948, and article 6 of the International Covenant on Civil and Political Rights, adopted on 16 December 1966,

Noting that article 6 of the International Covenant on Civil and Political Rights refers to abolition of the death penalty in terms that strongly suggest that abolition is desirable,

Convinced that all measures of abolition of the death penalty should be considered as progress in the enjoyment of the right to life,

Desirous to undertake hereby an international commitment to abolish the death penalty,

Have agreed as follows:

Article 1

1. No one within the jurisdiction of a State Party to the present Protocol shall be executed.

2. Each State Party shall take all necessary measures to abolish the death penalty within its jurisdiction.

Article 2

No reservation is admissible to the present Protocol, except for a reservation made at the time of ratification or accession that provides for the application of the death penalty in time of war pursuant to a conviction for a most serious crime of a military nature committed during wartime.

Article 3

The States Parties to the present Protocol shall include in the reports they submit to the Human Rights Committee, in accordance with article 40 of the Covenant, information on the measures that they have adopted to give effect to the present Protocol.

2.3: International Covenant on Economic, Social, and Cultural Rights

[Adopted and opened for signature, ratification, and accession by United Nations General Assembly resolution 2200 A (XXI) on 16 December 1966.

Entered into force on 3 January 1976 in accordance with article 27.]

[Adopted and opened for signature, ratification, and accession by United Nations General Assembly resolution 2200 A (XXI) on 16 December 1966. Entered into force on 3 January 1976 in accordance with article 27.]

PREAMBLE

The States Parties to the present Covenant

Considering that, in accordance with the principles proclaimed in the Charter of the United Nations, recognition of the inherent dignity and of the equal and inalienable rights of all members of the human family is the foundation of freedom, justice and peace in the world.

Recognizing that these rights derive from the inherent dignity of the human person.

Recognizing that, in accordance with the Universal Declaration of Human Rights, the ideal of free human beings enjoying freedom from fear and want can only be achieved if conditions are created whereby everyone may enjoy his economic, social and cultural rights, as well as his civil and political rights.

Considering the obligation of States under the Charter of the United Nations to promote universal respect for, and observance of, human rights and freedoms.

Realizing that the individual, having duties to other individuals and to the community to which he belongs, is under a responsibility to strive for the promotion and observance of the rights recognized in the present Covenant.

Agree upon the following articles:

PART I

Article 1

1. All peoples have the right of self-determination. By virtue of that right they freely determine their political status and freely pursue their economic, social and cultural development.

2. All peoples may, for their own ends, freely dispose of their natural wealth and resources without prejudice to any obligations arising out of international economic co-operation, based upon the principle of mutual benefit, and international law. In no case may a people be deprived of its own means of subsistence.

3. The States Parties to the present Covenant, including those having responsibility for the administration of Non-Self-Governing and Trust Territories, shall promote the realization of the right of self-determination, and shall respect that right, in conformity with the provisions of the Charter of the United Nations.

PART II

Article 2

1. Each State Party to the present Covenant undertakes to take steps, individually and through international assistance and co-operation, especially economic and technical, to the maximum of its available resources, with a view to achieving progressively the full realization of the rights recognized in the present Covenant by all appropriate means, including particularly the adoption of legislative measures.

2. The States Parties to the present Covenant undertake to guarantee that the rights enunciated in the present Covenant will be exercised without discrimination of any kind as to race, colour, sex, language, religion, political or other opinion, national or social origin, property, birth or other status.

3. Developing countries, with due regard to human rights and their national economy, may determine to what extent they would guarantee the economic rights recognized in the present Covenant to non-nationals.

Article 3

The States Parties to the present Covenant undertake to ensure the equal right of men and women to the enjoyment of all economic, social and cultural rights set forth in the present Covenant.

Article 4

The States Parties to the present Covenant recognizes that, in the enjoyment of those rights provided by the State in conformity with the present Covenant, the State may subject such rights only to such limitations as are determined by law only in so far as this may be compatible with the nature of these rights and solely for the purpose of promoting the general welfare in a democratic society.

Article 5

1. Nothing in the present Covenant may be interpreted as implying for any State, group or person any right to engage in any activity or to perform any act aimed at the destruction of any of the rights or freedoms recognized herein, or at their limitation to a greater extent than is provided for in the present Covenant.
2. No restriction upon or derogation from any of the fundamental human rights recognized or existing in any country in virtue of law, conventions, regulations or custom shall be admitted on the pretext that the present Covenant does not recognize such rights or that it recognizes them to a lesser extent.

PART III
Article 6

1. The States Parties to the present Covenant recognize the right to work, which includes the right of everyone to the opportunity to gain his living by work which he freely chooses or accepts, and will take appropriate steps to safeguard this right.
2. The steps to be taken by a State Party to the present Covenant to achieve the full realization of this right shall include technical and vocational guidance and training programmes, policies and techniques to achieve steady economic, social and cultural development and full and productive employment under conditions safeguarding fundamental political and economic freedoms to the individual.

Article 7

The States Parties to the present Covenant recognize the right of everyone to the enjoyment of just and favourable conditions of work which ensure, in particular:
    (a) Remuneration which provides all workers, as a minimum, with:
        (i) Fair wages and equal remuneration for work of equal value without distinction of any kind, in particular women being guaranteed conditions of work not inferior to those enjoyed by men, with equal pay for equal work;
        (ii) A decent living for themselves and their families in accordance with the provisions of the present Covenant;
    (b) Safe and healthy working conditions;
    (c) Equal opportunity for everyone to be promoted in his employment to an appropriate higher level, subject to no considerations other than those of seniority and competence;
    (d) Rest, leisure and reasonable limitation of working hours and periodic holidays with pay, as well as remuneration for public holidays.

Article 8

1. The States Parties to the present Covenant undertake to ensure:

(a) The right of everyone to form trade unions and join the trade union of his choice, subject only to the rules of the organization concerned, for the promotion and protection of his economic and social interests. No restrictions may be placed on the exercise of this right other than those prescribed by law and which are necessary in a democratic society in the interests of national security or public order or for the protection of the rights and freedoms of others;

(b) The right of trade unions to establish national federations or confederations and the right of the latter to form or join international trade-union organizations;

(c) The right of trade unions to function freely subject to no limitations other than those prescribed by law and which are necessary in a democratic society in the interests of national security or public order or for the protection of the rights and freedoms of others;

(d) The right to strike, provide that it is exercised in conformity with the laws of the particular country.

2. This article shall not prevent the imposition of lawful restrictions on the exercise of these rights by members of the armed forces or of the police or of the administration of the State.

3. Nothing in this article shall authorize States Parties to the International Labour Organisation Convention of 1948 concerning Freedom of Association and Protection of the Right to Organize to take legislative measures which would prejudice, or apply the law in such a manner as would prejudice, the guarantees provided for in that Convention.

Article 9

The States Parties to the present Covenant recognize the right of everyone to social security, including social insurance.

Article 10

The States Parties to the present Covenant recognizes that:

1. The widest possible protection and assistance should be accorded to the family, which is the natural and fundamental group unit of society, particularly for its establishment and whilst it is responsible for the care and education of dependent children. Marriage must be entered into with the free consent of the intending spouses.

2. Special protection should be accorded to mothers during a reasonable period before and after childbirth. During such period working mothers should be accorded paid leave or leave with adequate social security benefits.

3. Special measures of protection and assistance should be taken on behalf of all children and young persons without any discrimination for reasons of parentage or other conditions. Children and young persons should be protected from economic and social exploitation. Their employment in work harmful to their morals or health or dangerous to life or likely to hamper their normal development should be punishable by law. States should also set age limits below which the paid employment of child labour should be prohibited and punishable by law.

Article 11

1. The States Parties to the present Covenant recognizes the right of everyone to an adequate standard of living for himself and his family, including adequate food, clothing and housing, and to the continuous improvement of living conditions. The States Parties will take appropriate steps to ensure the realization of this right, recognizing to this effect the essential importance of international co-operation based on free consent.

2. The States Parties to the present Covenant, recognizing the fundamental right of everyone to be free from hunger, shall take, individually and through international co-operation, the measures, including specific programmes, which are needed:

(a) To improve methods of production, conservation and distribution of food by making full use of technical and scientific knowledge, by disseminating knowledge of the principles of nutrition and by developing or reforming agrarian systems in such a way as to achieve the most efficient development and utilization of natural resources;

(b) Taking into account the problems of both food-importing and food-exporting countries, to ensure an equitable distribution of world food supplies in relation to need.

Article 12

1. The States Parties to the present Covenant recognizes the right of everyone to the enjoyment of the highest attainable standard of physical and mental health.

2. The steps to be taken by the States Parties to the present Covenant to achieve the full realization of this right shall include those necessary for:

(a) The provision for the reduction of the stillbirth-rate and of infant mortality and for the healthy development of the child;

(b) The improvement of all aspects of environmental and industrial hygiene;

(c) The prevention, treatment and control of epidemic, endemic, occupational and other diseases;

(d) The creation of conditions which would assure to all medical service and medical attention in the event of sickness.

Article 13

1. The States Parties to the present Covenant recognize the right of everyone to education. They agree that education shall be directed to the full development of the human personality and the sense of its dignity, and shall strengthen the respect for human rights and fundamental freedoms. They further agree that education shall enable all persons to participate effectively in a free society, promote understanding, tolerance and friendship among all nations and all racial, ethnic or religious groups, and further the activities of the United Nations for the maintenance of peace.

2. The States Parties to the present Covenant recognize that, with a view to achieving the full realization of this right:

(a) Primary education shall be compulsory and available free to all;

(b) Secondary education in its different forms, including technical and vocational secondary education, shall be made generally available and accessible to all by every appropriate means, and in particular by the progressive introduction of free education;

(c) Higher education shall be made equally accessible to all, on the basis of capacity, by every appropriate means, and in particular by the progressive introduction of free education;

(d) Fundamental education shall be encouraged or intensified as far as possible for those persons who have not received or completed the whole period of their primary education;

(e) The development of a system of schools at all levels shall be actively pursued, an adequate fellowship system shall be established, and the material conditions of teaching staff shall be continuously improved.

3. The States Parties to the present Covenant undertake to have respect for the liberty of parents and, when applicable, legal guardians to choose for their children schools, other than those established by the public authorities, which conform to such minimum educational standards as may be laid down or approved by the State and to ensure the religious and moral education of their children in conformity with their own convictions.

4. No part of this article shall be construed so as to interfere with the liberty of individuals and bodies to establish and direct educational institutions, subject always to the observance of the principles set forth in paragraph 1 of this article and to the requirement that the education given in such institutions shall conform to such minimum standards as may be laid down by the State.

Article 14

Each State Party to the present Covenant which, at the time of becoming a Party, has not been able to secure in its metropolitan territory or other territories under its jurisdiction compulsory primary education, free of charge, undertakes within two years, to work out and adopt a detailed plan of action for the progressive implementation, within a reasonable number of years, to be fixed in the plan, of the principle of compulsory education free of charge for all.

Article 15

1. The States Parties to the present Covenant recognize the right of everyone:
    (a) To take part in cultural life;
    (b) To enjoy the benefits of scientific progress and its applications;
    (c) To benefit from the protection of the moral and material interests resulting from any scientific, literary or artistic production of which he is the author.
2. The steps to be taken by the States Parties to the present Covenant to achieve the full realization of this right shall include those necessary for the conservation, the development and the diffusion of science and culture.
3. The States Parties to the present Covenant undertake to respect the freedom indispensable for scientific research and creative activity.
4. The States Parties to the present Covenant recognize the benefits to be derived from the encouragement and development of international contacts and co-operation in the scientific and cultural fields.

PART IV
Article 16

1. The States Parties to the present Covenant undertake to submit in conformity with this part of the Covenant reports on the measures which they have adopted and the progress made in achieving the observance of the rights recognized herein.
2 (a) All reports shall be submitted to the Secretary-General of the United Nations, who shall transmit copies to the Economic and Social Council for consideration in accordance with the provisions of the present Covenant;
    (b) The Secretary-General of the United Nations shall also transmit to the specialized agencies copies of the reports, or any relevant parts therefrom, from States Parties to the present Covenant which are also members of these specialized agencies in so far as these reports, or parts therefrom, relate to any matters which fall within the responsibilities of the said agencies in accordance with their constitutional instruments.

Article 17

1. The States Parties to the present Covenant shall furnish their reports in stages, in accordance with a programme to be established by the Economic and Social Council within one year of the entry into force of the present Covenant after consultation with the States Parties and the specialized agencies concerned.
2. Reports may indicate factors and difficulties affecting the degree of fulfilment of obligations under the present Covenant.
3. Where relevant information has previously been furnished to the United Nations or to any specialized agency by any State Party to the present Covenant, it will not be necessary to reproduce that information, but a precise reference to the information so furnished will suffice.

Article 18

Pursuant to its responsibilities under the Charter of the United Nations in the field of human rights and fundamental freedoms, the Economic and Social Council may make arrangements with the specialized agencies in respect of their reporting to it on the progress made in achieving the observance of the provision of the present Covenant falling within the scope of their activities. These reports may include particulars of decisions and recommendations on such implementation adopted by their competent organs.

Article 19

The Economic and Social Council may transmit to the Commission on Human Rights for study and general recommendations or, as appropriate, for information the reports concerning human rights submitted by States in accordance with articles 16 and 17, and those concerning human rights submitted by the specialized agencies in accordance with article 18.

Article 20

The States Parties to the present Covenant and the specialized agencies concerned may submit comments to the Economic and Social Council on any general recommendation under article 19 or reference to such general recommendation in any report of the Commission on Human Rights or any documentation referred to therein.

Article 21

The Economic and Social Council may submit from time to time to the General Assembly reports with recommendations of a general nature and a summary of the information received from the States Parties to the present Covenant and the specialized agencies on the measures taken and the progress made in achieving general observance of the rights recognized in the present Covenant.

Article 22

The Economic and Social Council may bring to the attention of other organs of the United Nations, their subsidiary organs and specialized agencies concerned with furnishing technical assistance any matters arising out of the reports referred to in this part of the present Covenant which may assist such bodies in deciding, each within its field of competence, on the advisability of international measures likely to contribute to the effective progressive implementation of the present Covenant.

Article 23

The States Parties to the present Covenant agree that international action for the achievement of the rights recognized in the present Covenant includes such methods as the conclusion of conventions, the adoption of recommendations, the furnishing of technical assistance and the holding of regional meetings and technical meetings for the purpose of consultation and study organized in conjunction with the Governments concerned.

Article 24

Nothing in the present Covenant shall be interpreted as impairing the provisions of the Charter of the United Nations and of the constitutions of the specialized agencies which define the respective responsibilities of the various organs of the United Nations and of the specialized agencies in regard to the matters dealt with in the present Covenant.

Article 25

Nothing in the present Covenant shall be interpreted as impairing the inherent right of all peoples to enjoy and utilize fully and freely their natural wealth and resources.

PART V

Article 26

1. The present Covenant is open for signature by any State Member of the United Nations or member of any of its specialized agencies, by any State Party to the Statute of the international Court of Justice, and by any other State which has been invited by the General Assembly of the United Nations to become a party to the present Covenant.
2. The present Covenant is subject to ratification. Instruments of ratification shall be deposited with the Secretary-General of the United Nations.

3. The present Covenant shall be open to accession by any State referred to in paragraph 1 of this article.

4. Accession shall be effected by the deposit of an instrument of accession with the Secretary-General of the United Nations.

5. The Secretary-General of the United Nations shall inform all States which have signed the present Covenant or acceded to it of the deposit of each instrument of ratification or accession.

Article 27

1. The present Covenant shall enter into force three months after the date of the deposit with the Secretary-General of the United Nations of the thirty-fifth instrument of ratification or instrument of accession.

2. For each State ratifying the present Covenant or acceding to it after the deposit of the thirty-fifth instrument of ratification or instrument of accession, the present Covenant shall enter into force three months after the date of the deposit of its own instrument of ratification or instrument of accession.

Article 28

The provision of the present Covenant shall extend to all parts of federal States without any limitations or exceptions.

Article 29

1. Any State Party to the present Covenant may propose an amendment and file it with the Secretary-General of the United Nations. The Secretary-General shall thereupon communicate any proposed amendments to the States Parties to the present Covenant with a request that they notify him whether they favour a conference of States Parties for the purpose of considering and voting upon the proposals. In the event that at least one third of the States Parties favours such a conference, the Secretary-General shall convene the conference under the auspices of the United Nations. Any amendment adopted by a majority of the States Parties present and voting at the conference shall be submitted to the General Assembly of the United Nations for approval.

2. Amendments shall come into force when they have been approved by the General Assembly of the United Nations and accepted by a two-thirds majority of the States Parties to the present Covenant in accordance with their respective constitutional processes.

3. When amendments come into force they shall be binding on those States Parties which have accepted them, other States Parties still being bound by the provisions of the present Covenant and any earlier amendment which they have accepted.

2.4: Convention against Torture and Other Cruel, Inhuman or Degrading Treatment or Punishment

Annex to GA Res. 39/46 of 10 December 1984.
Approved by consensus on 10 December 1984 and opened for signature on 4 February 1984.
Entered into force 26 June 1987.

The States Parties to this Convention,
  Considering that, in accordance with the principles proclaimed in the Charter of the United Nations, recognition of the equal and inalienable rights of all members of the human family is the foundation of freedom, justice and peace in the world,
  Recognizing that those rights derive from the inherent dignity of the human person,
  Considering the obligation of States under the Charter, in particular Article 55, to promote universal respect for, and observance of, human rights and fundamental freedoms,
  Having regard to article 5 of the Universal Declaration of Human Rights and article 7 of the International Covenant on Civil and Political Rights, both of which provide that no one shall be subjected to torture or to cruel, inhuman or degrading treatment or punishment,
  Having regard also to the Declaration on the Protection of All Persons from Being Subjected to Torture and Other Cruel, Inhuman or Degrading Treatment or Punishment, adopted by the General Assembly on 9 December 1975,
  Desiring to make more effective the struggle against torture and other cruel, inhuman or degrading treatment or punishment throughout the world,
Have agreed as follows:

PART I

Article 1

1. For the purposes of this Convention, the term 'torture' means any act by which severe pain or suffering, whether physical or mental, is intentionally inflicted on a person for such purposes as obtaining from him or a third person information or a confession, punishing him for an act he or a third person has committed or is suspected of having committed, or intimidating or coercing him or a third person, or for any reason based on discrimination of any kind, when such pain or suffering is inflicted by or at the instigation of or with the consent or acquiescence of a public official or other person acting in an official capacity. It does not include pain or suffering arising only from, inherent in or incidental to lawful sanctions.
2. This article is without prejudice to any international instrument or national legislation which does or may contain provisions of wider application.

Article 2

1. Each State Party shall take effective legislative, administrative, judicial or other measures to prevent acts of torture in any territory under its jurisdiction.
2. No exceptional circumstances whatsoever, whether a state of war or a threat of war, internal political instability or any other public emergency, may be invoked as a justification of torture.
3. An order from a superior officer or a public authority may not be invoked as a justification of torture.

Article 3

1. No State Party shall expel, return (*'refouler'*) or extradite a person to another State where there are substantial grounds for believing that he would be in danger of being subjected to torture.

2. For the purpose of determining whether there are such grounds, the competent authorities shall take into account all relevant considerations including, where applicable, the existence in the State concerned of a consistent pattern of gross, flagrant or mass violations of human rights.

Article 4

1. Each State Party shall ensure that all acts of torture are offences under its criminal law. The same shall apply to an attempt to commit torture and to an act by any person which constitutes complicity or participation in torture.
2. Each State Party shall make these offences punishable by appropriate penalties which take into account their grave nature.

Article 5

1. Each State Party shall take such measures as may be necessary to establish its jurisdiction over the offences referred to in article 4 in the following cases:
   (a) When the offences are committed in any territory under its jurisdiction or on board a ship or aircraft registered in that State;
   (b) When the alleged offender is a national of that State;
   (c) When the victim is a national of that State if that State considers it appropriate.
2. Each State Party shall likewise take such measures as may be necessary to establish its jurisdiction over such offences in cases where the alleged offender is present in any territory under its jurisdiction and it does not extradite him pursuant to article 8 to any of the States mentioned in paragraph 1 of this article.
3. This Convention does not exclude any criminal jurisdiction exercised in accordance with internal law.

Article 6

1. Upon being satisfied, after an examination of information available to it, that the circumstances so warrant, any State Party in whose territory a person alleged to have committed any offence referred to in article 4 is present shall take him into custody or take other legal measures to ensure his presence. The custody and other legal measures shall be as provided in the law of that State but may be continued only for such time as is necessary to enable any criminal or extradition proceedings to be instituted.
2. Such State shall immediately make a preliminary inquiry into the facts.
3. Any person in custody pursuant to paragraph 1 of this article shall be assisted in communicating immediately with the nearest appropriate representative of the State of which he is a national, or, if he is a stateless person, with the representative of the State where he usually resides.
4. When a State, pursuant to this article, has taken a person into custody, it shall immediately notify the States referred to in article 5, paragraph 1, of the fact that such person is in custody and of the circumstances which warrant his detention. The State which makes the preliminary inquiry contemplated in paragraph 2 of this article shall promptly report its findings to the said States and shall indicate whether it intends to exercise jurisdiction.

Article 7

1. The State Party in the territory under whose jurisdiction a person alleged to have committed any offence referred to in article 4 is found shall in the cases contemplated in article 5, if it does not extradite him, submit the case to its competent authorities for the purpose of prosecution.
2. These authorities shall take their decision in the same manner as in the case of any ordinary offence of a serious nature under the law of that State. In the cases referred to in article 5, paragraph 2, the standards of evidence required for prosecution and conviction shall in no way be less stringent than those which apply in the cases referred to in article 5, paragraph 1.

3. Any person regarding whom proceedings are brought in connection with any of the offences referred to in article 4 shall be guaranteed fair treatment at all stages of the proceedings.

Article 8

1. The offences referred to in article 4 shall be deemed to be included as extraditable offences in any extradition treaty existing between States Parties. States Parties undertake to include such offences as extraditable offences in every extradition treaty to be concluded between them.
2. If a State Party which makes extradition conditional on the existence of a treaty receives a request for extradition from another. State Party with which it has no extradition treaty, it may consider this Convention as the legal basis for extradition in respect of such offences. Extradition shall be subject to the other conditions provided by the law of the requested State.
3. States Parties which do not make extradition conditional on the existence of a treaty shall recognize such offences as extraditable offences between themselves subject to the conditions provided by the law of the requested State.
4. Such offences shall be treated, for the purpose of extradition between States Parties, as if they had been committed not only in the place in which they occurred but also in the territories of the States required to establish their jurisdiction in accordance with article 5, paragraph 1.

Article 9

1. States Parties shall afford one another the greatest measure of assistance in connection with criminal proceedings brought in respect of any of the offences referred to in article 4, including the supply of all evidence at their disposal necessary for the proceedings.
2. States Parties shall carry out their obligations under paragraph 1 of this article in conformity with any treaties on mutual judicial assistance that may exist between them.

Article 10

1. Each State Party shall ensure that education and information regarding the prohibition against torture are fully included in the training of law enforcement personnel, civil or military, medical personnel, public officials and other persons who may be involved in the custody, interrogation or treatment of any individual subjected to any form of arrest, detention or imprisonment.
2. Each State Party shall include this prohibition in the rules or instructions issued in regard to the duties and functions of any such person.

Article 11

Each State Party shall keep under systematic review interrogation rules, instructions, methods and practices as well as arrangements for the custody and treatment of persons subjected to any form of arrest, detention or imprisonment in any territory under its jurisdiction, with a view to preventing any cases of torture.

Article 12

Each State Party shall ensure that its competent authorities proceed to a prompt and impartial investigation, wherever there is reasonable ground to believe that an act of torture has been committed in any territory under its jurisdiction.

Article 13

Each State Party shall ensure that any individual who alleges he has been subjected to torture in any territory under its jurisdiction has the right to complain to, and to have his case promptly and impartially examined by, its competent authorities. Steps shall be taken to ensure that the complainant and witnesses are protected against all ill-treatment or intimidation as a consequence of his complaint or any evidence given.

Article 14

1. Each State Party shall ensure in its legal system that the victim of an act of torture obtains redress and has an enforceable right to fair and adequate compensation, including the means for as full rehabilitation as possible. In the event of the death of the victim as a result of an act of torture, his dependants shall be entitled to compensation.
2. Nothing in this article shall affect any right of the victim or other persons to compensation which may exist under national law.

Article 15

Each State Party shall ensure that any statement which is established to have been made as a result of torture shall not be invoked as evidence in any proceedings, except against a person accused of torture as evidence that the statement was made.

Article 16

1. Each State Party shall undertake to prevent in any territory under its jurisdiction other acts of cruel, inhuman or degrading treatment or punishment which do not amount to torture as defined in article 1, when such acts are committed by or at the instigation of or with the consent or acquiescence of a public official or other person acting in an official capacity. In particular, the obligations contained in articles 10, 11, 12 and 13 shall apply with the substitution for references to torture or references to other forms of cruel, inhuman or degrading treatment or punishment.
2. The provisions of this Convention are without prejudice to the provisions of any other international instrument or national law which prohibits cruel, inhuman or degrading treatment or punishment or which relates to extradition or expulsion.

PART II

Article 17

1. There shall be established a Committee against Torture (hereinafter referred to as the Committee) which shall carry out the functions hereinafter provided. The Committee shall consist of ten experts of high moral standing and recognized competence in the field of human rights, who shall serve in their personal capacity. The experts shall be elected by the States Parties, considering being given to equitable geographical distribution and to the usefulness of the participation of some persons having legal experience.
2. The members of the Committee shall be elected by secret ballot from a list of persons nominated by States Parties. Each State Party may nominate one person from among its own nationals. States Parties shall bear in mind the usefulness of nominating persons who are also members of the Human Rights Committee established under the International Covenant on Civil and Political Rights and who are willing to serve on the Committee against Torture.
3. Elections of the members of the Committee shall be held at biennial meetings of States Parties convened by the Secretary-General of the United Nations. At those meetings, for which two thirds of the States Parties shall constitute a quorum, the persons elected to the Committee shall be those who obtain the largest number of votes and an absolute majority of the votes of the representatives of States Parties present and voting.
4. The initial election shall be held no later than six months after the date of the entry into force of this Convention. At least four months before the date of each election, the Secretary-General of the United Nations shall address a letter to the States Parties inviting them to submit their nominations within three months. The Secretary-General shall prepare a list in alphabetical order of all persons thus nominated, indicating the States Parties which have nominated them, and shall submit it to the States Parties.
5. The members of the Committee shall be elected for a term of four years. They shall be eligible for re-election if renominated. However, the term of five of the members elected

at the first election shall expire at the end of two years; immediately after the first election the names of these five members shall be chosen by lot by the chairman of the meeting referred to in paragraph 3 of this article.

6. If a member of the Committee dies or resigns or for any other cause can no longer perform his Committee duties, the State Party which nominated him shall appoint another expert from among its nationals to serve for the remainder of his term, subject to the approval of the majority of the States Parties. The approval shall be considered given unless half or more of the States Parties respond negatively within six weeks after having been informed by the Secretary-General of the United Nations of the proposed appointment.

7. States Parties shall be responsible for the expenses of the members of the Committee while they are in performance of Committee duties.

Article 18

1. The Committee shall elect its officers for a term of two years. They may be re-elected.
2. The Committee shall establish its own rules of procedure, but these rules shall provide, *inter alia*, that:
    (a) Six members shall constitute a quorum;
    (b) Decisions of the Committee shall be made by a majority vote of the members present.
3. The Secretary-General of the United Nations shall provide the necessary staff and facilities for the effective performance of the functions of the Committee under this Convention.
4. The Secretary-General of the United Nations shall convene the initial meeting of the Committee. After its initial meeting, the Committee shall meet at such times as shall be provided in its rules of procedure.
5. The States Parties shall be responsible for expenses incurred in connection with the holding of meetings of the States Parties and of the Committee, including reimbursement to the United Nations for any expenses, such as the cost of staff and facilities, incurred by the United Nations pursuant to paragraph 3 of this article.

Article 19

1. The States Parties shall submit to the Committee, through the Secretary-General of the United Nations, reports on the measures they have taken to give effect to their undertakings under this Convention, within one year after the entry into force of the Convention for the State Party concerned. Thereafter the States Parties shall submit supplementary reports every four years on any new measures taken and such other reports as the Committee may request.
2. The Secretary-General of the United Nations shall transmit the reports to all States Parties.
3. Each report shall be considered by the Committee which may make such general comments on the report as it may consider appropriate and shall forward these to the State Party concerned. That State Party may respond with any observations it chooses to the Committee.
4. The Committee may, at its discretion, decide to include any comments made by it in accordance with paragraph 3 of this article, together with the observations thereon received from the State Party concerned, in its annual report made in accordance with article 24. If so requested by the State Party concerned, the Committee may also include a copy of the report submitted under paragraph 1 of this article.

Article 20

1. If the Committee receives reliable information which appears to it to contain well-founded indications that torture is being systematically practised in the territory of a State Party, the Committee shall invite that State Party to co-operate in the examination of the information and to this end to submit observations with regard to the information concerned.

2. Taking into account any observations which may have been submitted by the State Party concerned, as well as any other relevant information available to it, the Committee may, if it decides that this is warranted, designate one or more of its members to make a confidential inquiry and to report to the Committee urgently.

3. If an inquiry is made in accordance with paragraph 2 of this article, the Committee shall seek the co-operation of the State Party concerned. In agreement with that State Party, such an inquiry may include a visit to its territory.

4. After examining the findings of its member or members submitted in accordance with paragraph 2 of this article, the Commission shall transmit these findings to the State Party concerned together with any comments or suggestions which seem appropriate in view of the situation.

5. All the proceedings of the Committee referred to in paragraphs 1 to 4 of this article shall be confidential, and at all stages of the proceedings the co-operation of the State Party shall be sought. After such proceedings have been completed with regard to an inquiry made in accordance with paragraph 2, the Committee may, after consultations with the State Party concerned, decide to include a summary account of the results of the proceedings in its annual report made in accordance with article 24.

Article 21

1. A State Party to this Convention may at any time declare under this article that it recognizes the competence of the Committee to receive and consider communications to the effect that a State Party claims that another State Party is not fulfilling its obligations under this Convention. Such communications may be received and considered according to the procedures laid down in this article only if submitted by a State Party which has made a declaration recognizing in regard to itself the competence of the Committee. No communication shall be dealt with by the Committee under this article if it concerns a State Party which has not made such a declaration. Communications received under this article shall be dealt with in accordance with the following procedure:

   (a) If a State Party considers that another State Party is not giving effect to the provisions of this Convention, it may, by written communication, bring the matter to the attention of that State Party. Within three months after the receipt of the communication the receiving State shall afford the State which sent the communication an explanation or any other statement in writing clarifying the matter, which should include, to the extent possible and pertinent, reference to domestic procedures and remedies taken, pending or available in the matter;

   (b) If the matter is not adjusted to the satisfaction of both States Parties concerned within six months after the receipt by the receiving State of the initial communication, either State shall have the right to refer the matter to the Committee, by notice given to the Committee and to the other State;

   (c) The Committee shall deal with a matter referred to it under this article only after it has ascertained that all domestic remedies have been invoked and exhausted in the matter, in conformity with the generally recognized principles of international law. This shall not be the rule where the application of the remedies is unreasonably prolonged or is unlikely to bring effective relief to the person who is the victim of the violation of this Convention;

   (d) The Committee shall hold closed meetings when examining communications under this article;

   (e) Subject to the provisions of subparagraph (c), the Committee shall make available its good offices to the States Parties concerned with a view to a friendly solution of the matter on the basis of respect for the obligations provided for in this Convention. For this purpose, the Committee may, when appropriate, set up an *ad hoc* conciliation commission;

   (f) In any matter referred to it under this article, the Committee may call upon the States Parties concerned, referred to in subparagraph (b), to supply any relevant information;

   (g) The States Parties concerned, referred to in subparagraph (b), shall have the right to be represented when the matter is being considered by the Committee and to make submissions orally and/or in writing;

(h) The Committee shall, within twelve months after the date of receipt of notice under subparagraph (b), submit a report:

(i) If a solution within the terms of subparagraph (e) is reached, the Committee shall confine its report to a brief statement of the facts and of the solution reached;

(ii) If a solution within the terms of subparagraph (e) is not reached, the Committee shall confine its report to a brief statement of the facts; the written submissions and record of the oral submissions made by the States Parties concerned shall be attached to the report.

In every matter, the report shall be communicated to the States Parties concerned.

2. The provisions of this article shall come into force when five States Parties to this Convention have made declarations under paragraph 1 of this article. Such declarations shall be deposited by the States Parties with the Secretary-General of the United Nations, who shall transmit copies thereof to the other States Parties. A declaration may be withdrawn at any time by notification to the Secretary-General. Such a withdrawal shall not prejudice the consideration of any matter which is the subject of a communication already transmitted under this article; no further communication by any State Party shall be received under this article after the notification of withdrawal of the declaration has been received by the Secretary-General, unless the State Party concerned has made a new declaration.

Article 22

1. A State Party to this Convention may at any time declare under this article that it recognizes the competence of the Committee to receive and consider communications from or on behalf of individuals subject to its jurisdiction who claim to be victims of a violation by a State Party of the provisions of the Convention. No communication shall be received by the Committee if it concerns a State Party which has not made such a declaration.

2. The Committee shall consider inadmissible any communication under this article which is anonymous or which it considers to be an abuse of the right of submission of such communications or to be incompatible with the provisions of this Convention.

3. Subject to the provisions of paragraph 2, the Committee shall bring any communications submitted to it under this article to the attention of the State Party to this Convention which has made a declaration under paragraph 1 and is alleged to be violating any provisions of the Convention. Within six months, the receiving State shall submit to the Committee written explanations or statements clarifying the matter and the remedy, if any, that may have been taken by that State.

4. The Committee shall consider communications received under this article in the light of all information made available to it by or on behalf of the individual and by the State Party concerned.

5. The Committee shall not consider any communications from an individual under this article unless it has ascertained that:

(a) The same matter has not been, and is not being, examined under another procedure of international investigation or settlement;

(b) The individual has exhausted all available domestic remedies; this shall not be the rule where the application of the remedies is unreasonably prolonged or is unlikely to bring effective relief to the person who is the victim of the violation of this Convention.

6. The Committee shall hold closed meetings when examining communications under this article.

7. The Committee shall forward its views to the State Party concerned and to the individual.

8. The provisions of this article shall come into force when five States Parties to this Convention have made declarations under paragraph 1 of this article. Such declarations shall be deposited by the States Parties with the Secretary-General of the United Nations, who shall transmit copies thereof to the other States Parties. A declaration may be withdrawn at any time by notification to the Secretary-General. Such a withdrawal shall not prejudice the consideration of any matter which is the subject of a communication already transmitted under this article; no further communication by or on behalf of an

individual shall be received under this article after the notification of withdrawal of the declaration has been received by the Secretary-General, unless the State Party has made a new declaration.

Article 23

The members of the Committee and of the *ad hoc* conciliation commissions which may be appointed under article 21, paragraph 1 (e), shall be entitled to the facilities, privileges and immunities of experts on mission for the United Nations as laid down in the relevant sections of the Convention on the Privileges and Immunities of the United Nations.

For the Convention on the Privileges and Immunities of the United Nations, see GA Res. 22A(1) of 13 February 1946, *I.O.I., I.A.3.4.c.*

Article 24

The Committee shall submit an annual report on its activities under this Convention to the States Parties and to the General Assembly of the United Nations.

PART III

Article 25

1. This Convention is open for signature by all States.
2. This Convention is subject to ratification. Instruments of ratification shall be deposited with the Secretary-General of the United Nations.

Article 26

This Convention is open to accession by all States. Accession shall be effected by the deposit of an instrument of accession with the Secretary-General of the United Nations.

Article 27

1. This Convention shall enter into force on the thirtieth day after the date of the deposit with the Secretary-General of the United Nations of the twentieth instrument of ratification or accession.
2. For each State ratifying this Convention or acceding to it after the deposit of the twentieth instrument of ratification or accession, the Convention shall enter into force on the thirtieth day after the date of the deposit of its own instrument of ratification or accession.

Article 28

1. Each State may, at the time of signature or ratification of this Convention or accession thereto, declare that it does not recognize the competence of the Committee provided for in article 20.
2. Any State Party having made a reservation in accordance with paragraph 1 of this article may, at any time, withdraw this reservation by notification to the Secretary-General of the United Nations.

Article 29

1. Any State Party to this Convention may propose an amendment and file it with the Secretary-General of the United Nations. The Secretary-General shall thereupon communicate the proposed amendment to the States Parties with a request that they notify him whether they favour a conference of States Parties for the purpose of considering and voting upon the proposal. In the event that within four months from the date of such communication at least one third of the States Parties favours such a conference, the Secretary-General shall convene the conference under the auspices of the United Nations. Any amendment adopted by a majority of the States Parties present and voting at the

conference shall be submitted by the Secretary-General to all the States Parties for acceptance.

2. An amendment adopted in accordance with paragraph 1 of this article shall enter into force when two thirds of the States Parties to this Convention have notified the Secretary-General of the United Nations that they have accepted it in accordance with their respective constitutional processes.

3. When amendments enter into force, they shall be binding on those States Parties which have accepted them, other States Parties still being bound by the provisions of this Convention and any earlier amendments which they have accepted.

Article 30

1. Any dispute between two or more States Parties concerning the interpretation or application of this Convention which cannot be settled through negotiation shall, at the request of one of them, be submitted to arbitration. If within six months from the date of the request for arbitration the Parties are unable to agree on the organization of the arbitration, any one of those Parties may refer the dispute to the International Court of Justice by request in conformity with the Statute of the Court.

2. Each State may, at the time of signature or ratification of this Convention or accession thereto, declare that it does not consider itself bound by paragraph 1 of this article. The other States Parties shall not be bound by paragraph 1 of this article with respect to any State Party having made such a reservation.

3. Any State Party having made a reservation in accordance with paragraph 2 of this article may at any time withdraw this reservation by notification to the Secretary-General of the United Nations.

Article 31

1. A State Party may denounce this Convention by written notification to the Secretary-General of the United Nations. Denunciation becomes effective one year after the date of receipt of the notification by the Secretary-General.

2. Such a denunciation shall not have the effect of releasing the State Party from its obligations under this Convention in regard to any act or omission which occurs prior to the date at which the denunciation becomes effective, nor shall denunciation prejudice in any way the continued consideration of any matter which is already under consideration by the Committee prior to the date at which the denunciation becomes effective.

3. Following the date at which the denunciation of a State Party becomes effective, the Committee shall not commence consideration of any new matter regarding that State.

Article 32

The Secretary-General of the United Nations shall inform all States Members of the United Nations and all States which have signed this Convention or acceded to it of the following:

(a) Signatures, ratifications and accessions under articles 25 and 26;
(b) The date of entry into force of this Convention under article 27 and the date of the entry into force of any amendments under article 29;
(c) Denunciations under article 31.

Article 33

1. This Convention, of which the Arabic, Chinese, English, French, Russian and Spanish texts are equally authentic, shall be deposited with the Secretary-General of the United Nations.

2. The Secretary-General of the United Nations shall transmit certified copies of this Convention to all States.

2.5: International Convention on the Elimination of All Forms of Racial Discrimination

Entered into force 4 January 1969.

The States Parties to this Convention,

Considering that the Charter of the United Nations is based on the principles of the dignity and equality inherent in all human beings, and that all Member States have pledged themselves to take joint and separate action, in co-operation with the Organization, for the achievement of one of the purposes of the United Nations which is to promote and encourage universal respect for and observance of human rights and fundamental freedoms for all, without distinction as to race, sex, language or religion,

Considering that the Universal Declaration of Human Rights proclaims that all human beings are born free and equal in dignity and rights and that everyone is entitled to all the rights and freedoms set out therein, without distinction of any kind, in particular as to race, colour or national origin,

Considering that all human beings are equal before the law and are entitled to equal protection of the law against any discrimination and against any incitement to discrimination,

Considering that the United Nations has condemned colonialism and all practices of segregation and discrimination associated therewith, in whatever form and wherever they exist, and that the Declaration on the Granting of Independence to Colonial Countries and Peoples of 14 December 1960 (General Assembly resolution 1514 (XV)) has affirmed and solemnly proclaimed the necessity of bringing them to a speedy and unconditional end,

Considering that the United Nations Declaration on the Elimination of All Forms of Racial Discrimination of 20 November 1963 (General Assembly resolution 1904 (XVIII)) solemnly affirms the necessity of speedily eliminating racial discrimination throughout the world in all its forms and manifestations and of securing understanding of and respect for the dignity of the human person,

Convinced that any doctrine of superiority based on racial differentiation is scientifically false, morally condemnable, socially unjust and dangerous, and that there is no justification for racial discrimination, in theory or in practice, anywhere,

Reaffirming that discrimination between human beings on the grounds of race, colour or ethnic origin is an obstacle to friendly and peaceful relations among nations and is capable of disturbing peace and security among peoples and the harmony of persons living side by side even within one and the same State,

Convinced that the existence of racial barriers is repugnant to the ideals of any human society,

Alarmed by manifestations of racial discrimination still in evidence in some areas of the world and by governmental policies based on racial superiority or hatred, such as policies of *apartheid*, segregation or separation,

Resolved to adopt all necessary measures for speedily eliminating racial discrimination in all its forms and manifestations, and to prevent and combat racist doctrines and practices in order to promote understanding between races and to build an international community free from all forms of racial segregation and racial discrimination,

Bearing in mind the Convention concerning Discrimination in respect of Employment and Occupation adopted by the International Labour Organisation in 1958, and the Convention against Discrimination in Education adopted by the United Nations Educational, Scientific and Cultural Organization in 1960,

Desiring to implement the principles embodied in the United Nations Declaration on the Elimination of All Forms of Racial Discrimination and to secure the earliest adoption of practical measures to that end,

Have agreed as follows:

PART I

Article 1

1. In this Convention, the term 'racial discrimination' shall mean any distinction, exclusion, restriction or preference based on race, colour, descent, or national or ethnic origin which has the purpose or effect of nullifying or impairing the recognition, enjoyment or exercise, on an equal footing, of human rights and fundamental freedoms in the political, economic, social, cultural or any other field of public life.

2. This Convention shall not apply to distinctions, exclusions, restrictions or preferences made by a State Party to this Convention between citizens and non-citizens.

3. Nothing in this Convention may be interpreted as affecting in any way the legal provisions of States Parties concerning nationality, citizenship or naturalization, provided that such provisions do not discriminate against any particular nationality.

4. Special measures taken for the sole purpose of securing adequate advancement of certain racial or ethnic groups or individuals requiring such protection as may be necessary in order to ensure such groups or individuals equal enjoyment or exercise of human rights and fundamental freedoms shall not be deemed racial discrimination, provided, however, that such measures do not, as a consequence, lead to the maintenance of separate rights for different racial groups and that they shall not be continued after the objectives for which they were taken have been achieved.

Article 2

1. States Parties condemn racial discrimination and undertake to pursue by all appropriate means and without delay a policy of eliminating racial discrimination in all its forms and promoting understanding among all races, and, to this end:

(a) Each State Party undertakes to engage in no act or practice of racial discrimination against persons, groups of persons or institutions and to ensure that all public authorities and public institutions, national and local, shall act in conformity with this obligation;

(b) Each State Party undertakes not to sponsor, defend or support racial discrimination by any persons or organizations;

(c) Each State Party shall take effective measures to review governmental, national and local policies, and to amend, rescind or nullify any laws and regulations which have the effect of creating or perpetuating racial discrimination wherever it exists;

(d) Each State Party shall prohibit and bring to an end, by all appropriate means, including legislation as required by circumstances, racial discrimination by any persons, group or organization;

(e) Each State Party undertakes to encourage, where appropriate, integrationist multiracial organizations and movements and other means of eliminating barriers between races, and to discourage anything which tends to strengthen racial division.

2. States Parties shall, when the circumstances so warrant, take, in the social, economic, cultural and other fields, special and concrete measures to ensure the adequate development and protection of certain racial groups or individuals belonging to them, for the purpose of guaranteeing them the full and equal enjoyment of human rights and fundamental freedoms. These measures shall in no case entail as a consequence the maintenance of unequal or separate rights for different racial groups after the objectives for which they were taken have been achieved.

Article 3

States Parties particularly condemn racial segregation and *apartheid* and undertake to prevent, prohibit and eradicate all practices of this nature in territories under their jurisdiction.

Article 4

States Parties condemn all propaganda and all organizations which are based on ideas or theories of superiority of one race or group of persons of one colour or ethnic origin, or which attempt to justify or promote racial hatred and discrimination in any form, and undertake to adopt immediate and positive measures designed to eradicate all incitement to, or acts of, such discrimination and, to this end, with due regard to the principles embodied in the Universal Declaration of Human Rights and the rights expressly set forth in article 5 of this Convention, *inter alia*:

(a) Shall declare an offence punishable by law all dissemination of ideas based on racial superiority or hatred, incitement to racial discrimination, as well as all acts of violence or incitement to such acts against any race or group of persons of another colour or ethnic origin, and also the provision of any assistance to racist activities, including the financing thereof;

(b) Shall declare illegal and prohibit organizations, and also organized and all other propaganda activities, which promote and incite racial discrimination, and shall recognize participation in such organizations or activities as an offence punishable by law;

(c) Shall not permit public authorities or public institutions, national or local, to promote or incite racial discrimination.

Article 5

In compliance with the fundamental obligations laid down in article 2 of this Convention, States Parties undertake to prohibit and to eliminate racial discrimination in all its forms and to guarantee the right of everyone, without distinction as to race, colour, or national or ethnic origin, to equality before the law, notably in the enjoyment of the following rights:

(a) The right to equal treatment before the tribunals and all other organs administering justice;

(b) The right to security of person and protection by the State against violence or bodily harm, whether inflicted by government officials or by any individual group or institution;

(c) Political rights, in particular the right to participate in elections to vote and to stand – for election – on the basis of universal and equal suffrage, to take part in the Government as well as in the conduct of public affairs at any level and to have equal access to public service;

(d) Other civil rights, in particular:

(i) The right to freedom of movement and residence within the border of the State;

(ii) The right to leave any country, including one's own, and to return to one's country;

(iii) The right to nationality;

(iv) The right to marriage and choice of spouse;

(v) The right to own property alone as well as in association with others;

(vi) The right to inherit;

(vii) The right to freedom of thought, conscience and religion;

(viii) The right to freedom of opinion and expression;

(ix) The right to freedom of peaceful assembly and association;

(e) Economic, social and cultural rights, in particular:

(i) The rights to work, to free choice of employment, to just and favourable conditions of work, to protection against unemployment, to equal pay for equal work, to just and favourable remuneration;

(ii) The right to form and join trade unions;

(iii) The right to housing;

(iv) The right to public health, medical care, social security and social services;

(v) The right to education and training;

(vi) The right to equal participation in cultural activities;

(f) The right of access to any place or service intended for use by the general public, such as transport hotels, restaurants, cafes, theatres and parks.

Article 6

States Parties shall assure to everyone within their jurisdiction effective protection and remedies, through the competent national tribunals and other State institutions, against any acts of racial discrimination which violate his human rights and fundamental freedoms contrary to this Convention, as well as the right to seek from such tribunals just and adequate reparation or satisfaction for any damage suffered as a result of such discrimination.

Article 7

States Parties undertake to adopt immediate and effective measures, particularly in the fields of teaching, education, culture and information, with a view to combating prejudices which lead to racial discrimination and to promoting understanding, tolerance and friendship among nations and racial or ethnical groups, as well as to propagating the purposes and principles of the Charter of the United Nations, the Universal Declaration of Human Rights, the United Nations Declaration on the Elimination of All Forms of Racial Discrimination, and this Convention.

PART II

Article 8

1. There shall be established a Committee on the Elimination of Racial Discrimination (hereinafter referred to as the Committee) consisting of eighteen experts of high moral standing and acknowledged impartiality elected by States Parties from among their nationals, who shall serve in their personal capacity, consideration being given to equitable geographical distribution and to the representation of the different forms of civilization as well as of the principal legal systems.
2. The members of the Committee shall be elected by secret ballot from a list of persons nominated by the States Parties. Each State Party may nominate one person from among its own nationals.
3. The initial election shall be held six months after the date of the entry into force of this Convention. At least three months before the date of each election the Secretary-General of the United Nations shall address a letter to the States Parties inviting them to submit their nominations within two months. The Secretary-General shall prepare a list in alphabetical order of all persons thus nominated, indicating the States Parties which have nominated them, and shall submit it to the States Parties.
4. Elections of the members of the Committee shall be held at a meeting of States Parties convened by the Secretary-General at United Nations Headquarters. At that meeting, for which two thirds of the States Parties shall constitute a quorum, the persons elected to the Committee shall be nominees who obtain the largest number of votes and an absolute majority of the votes of the representatives of States Parties present and voting.
5. (a) The members of the Committee shall be elected for a term of four years. However, the terms of nine of the members elected at the first election shall expire at the end of two years; immediately after the first election the names of these nine members shall be chosen by lot by the Chairman of the Committee;
(b) For the filling of casual vacancies, the State Party whose expert has ceased to function as a member of the Committee shall appoint another expert from among its nationals, subject to the approval of the Committee.
6. States Parties shall be responsible for the expenses of the members of the Committee while they are in performance of Committee duties.

Article 9

1. States Parties undertake to submit to the Secretary-General of the United Nations, for consideration by the Committee, a report on the legislative, judicial, administrative or other measures which they have adopted and which give effect to the provisions of this Convention:
(a) within one year after the entry into force of the Convention for the State concerned; and
(b) thereafter every two years and whenever the Committee so requests. The Committee may request further information from the States Parties.

122

2. The Committee shall report annually, through the Secretary General, to the General Assembly of the United Nations on its activities and may make suggestions and general recommendations based on the examination of the reports and information received from the States Parties. Such suggestions and general recommendations shall be reported to the General Assembly together with comments, if any, from States Parties.

Article 10

1. The Committee shall adopt its own rules of procedure.
2. The Committee shall elect its officers for a term of two years.
3. The secretariat of the Committee shall be provided by the Secretary General of the United Nations.
4. The meetings of the Committee shall normally be held at United Nations Headquarters.

Para. 1. Provisional rules of procedure were adopted by the Committee at its First and Second Sessions (in 1970), and amended in 1971, 1972 and 1973.

Article 11

1. If a State Party considers that another State Party is not giving effect to the provisions of this Convention, it may bring the matter to the attention of the Committee. The Committee shall then transmit the communication to the State Party concerned. Within three months, the receiving State shall submit to the Committee written explanations or statements clarifying the matter and the remedy, if any, that may have been taken by that State.
2. If the matter is not adjusted to the satisfaction of both parties, either by bilateral negotiations or by any other procedure open to them, within six months after the receipt by the receiving State of the initial communication, either State shall have the right to refer the matter again to the Committee by notifying the Committee and also the other State.
3. The Committee shall deal with a matter referred to it in accordance with paragraph 2 of this article after it has ascertained that all available domestic remedies have been invoked and exhausted in the case, in conformity with the generally recognized principles of international law. This shall not be the rule where the application of the remedies is unreasonably prolonged.
4. In any matter referred to it, the Committee may call upon the States Parties concerned to supply any other relevant information.
5. When any matter arising out of this article is being considered by the Committee, the States Parties concerned shall be entitled to send a representative to take part in the proceedings of the Committee, without voting rights, while the matter is under consideration.

Article 12

1. (a) After the Committee has obtained and collated all the information it deems necessary, the Chairman shall appoint an *ad hoc* Conciliation Commission (hereinafter referred to as the Commission) comprising five persons who may or may not be members of the Committee. The members of the Commission shall be appointed with the unanimous consent of the parties to the dispute, and its good offices shall be made available to the States concerned with a view to an amicable solution of the matter on the basis of respect for this Convention;
(b) If the States parties to the dispute fail to reach agreement within three months on all or part of the composition of the Commission, the members of the Commission not agreed upon by the States parties to the dispute shall be elected by secret ballot by a two-thirds majority vote of the Committee from among its own members.
2. The members of the Commission shall serve in their personal capacity. They shall not be nationals of the States parties to the dispute or of a State not Party to this Convention.
3. The Commission shall elect its own Chairman and adopt its own rules of procedure.
4. The meetings of the Commission shall normally be held at United Nations Headquarters or at any other convenient place as determined by the Commission.

5. The secretariat provided in accordance with article 10, paragraph 3, of this Convention shall also service the Commission whenever a dispute among States Parties brings the Commission into being.

6. The States parties to the dispute shall share equally all the expenses of the members of the Commission in accordance with estimates to be provided by the Secretary-General of the United Nations.

7. The Secretary-General shall be empowered to pay the expenses of the members of the Commission, if necessary, before reimbursement by the States Parties to the dispute in accordance with paragraph 6 of this article.

8. The information obtained and collated by the Committee shall be made available to the Commission, and the Commission may call upon the States concerned to supply any other relevant information.

Article 13

1. When the Commission has fully considered the matter, it shall prepare and submit to the Chairman of the Committee a report embodying its findings on all questions of fact relevant to the issue between the parties and containing such recommendations as it may think proper for the amicable solution of the dispute.

2. The Chairman of the Committee shall communicate the report of the Commission to each of the States Parties to the dispute. These States shall, within three months, inform the Chairman of the Committee whether or not they accept the recommendations contained in the report of the Commission.

3. After the period provided for in paragraph 2 of this article, the Chairman of the Committee shall communicate the report of the Commission and the declarations of the States Parties concerned to the other States Parties to this Convention.

Article 14

1. A State Party may at any time declare that it recognizes the competence of the Committee to receive and consider communications from individuals or groups of individuals within its jurisdiction claiming to be victims of a violation by that State Party of any of the rights set forth in this Convention. No communication shall be received by the Committee if it concerns a State Party which has not made such a declaration.

2. Any State Party which makes a declaration as provided for in paragraph 1 of this article may establish or indicate a body within its national legal order which shall be competent to receive and consider petitions from individuals and groups of individuals within its jurisdiction who claim to be victims of a violation of any of the rights set forth in this Convention and who have exhausted other available local remedies.

3. A declaration made in accordance with paragraph 1 of this article and the name of any body established or indicated in accordance with paragraph 2 of this article shall be deposited by the State Party concerned with the Secretary-General of the United Nations, who shall transmit copies thereof to the other States Parties. A declaration may be withdrawn at any time by notification to the Secretary-General, but such a withdrawal shall not affect communications pending before the Committee.

4. A register of petitions shall be kept by the body established or indicated in accordance with paragraph 2 of this article, and certified copies of the register shall be filed annually through appropriate channels with the Secretary-General on the understanding that the contents shall not be publicly disclosed.

5. In the event of failure to obtain satisfaction from the body established or indicated in accordance with paragraph 2 of this article, the petitioner shall have the right to communicate the matter to the Committee within six months.

6. (a) The Committee shall confidentially bring any communication referred to it to the attention of the State Party alleged to be violating any provision of this Convention, but the identity of the individual or groups of individuals concerned shall not be revealed without his or their express consent. The Committee shall not receive anonymous communications;

(b) Within three months, the receiving State shall submit to the Committee written explanations or statements clarifying the matter and the remedy, if any, that may have been taken by that State.

7. (a) The Committee shall consider communications in the light of all information made available to it by the State Party concerned and by the petitioner. The Committee shall not consider any communication from a petitioner unless it has ascertained that the petitioner has exhausted all available domestic remedies. However, this shall not be the rule where the application of the remedies is unreasonably prolonged;

(b) The Committee shall forward its suggestions and recommendations, if any, to the State Party concerned and to the petitioner.

8. The Committee shall include in its annual report a summary of such communications and, where appropriate, a summary of the explanations and statements of the States Parties concerned and of its own suggestions and recommendations.

9. The Committee shall be competent to exercise the functions provided for in this article only when at least ten States Parties to this Convention are bound by declarations in accordance with paragraph 1 of this article.

Article 15

1. Pending the achievement of the objectives of the Declaration on the Granting of Independence to Colonial Countries and Peoples, contained in General Assembly resolution 1514 (XV) of 14 December 1960, the provisions of this Convention shall in no way limit the right of petition granted to these peoples by other international instruments or by the United Nations and its specialized agencies.

2. (a) The Committee established under article 8, paragraph 1, of this Convention shall receive copies of the petitions from, and submit expressions of opinion and recommendations on these petitions to, the bodies of the United Nations which deal with matters directly related to the principles and objectives of this Convention in their consideration of petitions from the inhabitants of Trust and Non-Self-Governing Territories and all other territories to which General Assembly resolution 1514 (XV) applies, relating to matters covered by this Convention which are before these bodies;

(b) The Committee shall receive from the competent bodies of the United Nations copies of the reports concerning the legislative, judicial, administrative or other measures directly related to the principles and objectives of this Convention applied by the administering Powers within the Territories mentioned in subparagraph (a) of this paragraph, and shall express opinions and make recommendations to these bodies.

3. The Committee shall include in its report to the General Assembly a summary of the petitions and reports it has received from United Nations bodies, and the expressions of opinion and recommendations of the Committee relating to the said petitions and reports.

4. The Committee shall request from the Secretary-General of the United Nations all information relevant to the objectives of this Convention and available to him regarding the Territories mentioned in paragraph 2 (a) of this article.

Article 16

The provisions of this Convention concerning the settlement of disputes or complaints shall be applied without prejudice to other procedures for settling disputes or complaints in the field of discrimination laid down in the constituent instruments of, or conventions adopted by, the United Nations and its specialized agencies, and shall not prevent the States Parties from having recourse to other procedures for settling a dispute in accordance with general or special international agreements in force between them.

PART III

Article 17

1. This Convention is open for signature by any State Member of the United Nations or member of any of its specialized agencies, by any State Party to the Statute of the

International Court of Justice, and by any other State which has been invited by the General Assembly of the United Nations to become a Party to this Convention.

2. This Convention is subject to ratification. Instruments of ratification shall be deposited with the Secretary-General of the United Nations.

Article 18

1. This Convention shall be open to accession by any State referred to in article 17, paragraph 1, of the Convention. 2. Accession shall be effected by the deposit of an instrument of accession with the Secretary-General of the United Nations.

Article 19

1. This Convention shall enter into force on the thirtieth day after the date of the deposit with the Secretary-General of the United Nations of the twenty-seventh instrument of ratification or instrument of accession.

2. For each State ratifying this Convention or acceding to it after the deposit of the twenty-seventh instrument of ratification or instrument of accession, the Convention shall enter into force on the thirtieth day after the date of the deposit of its own instrument of ratification or instrument of accession.

Article 20

1. The Secretary-General of the United Nations shall receive and circulate to all States which are or may become Parties to this Convention reservations made by States at the time of ratification or accession. Any State which objects to the reservation shall, within a period of ninety days from the date of the said communication, notify the Secretary-General that it does not accept it.

2. A reservation incompatible with the object and purpose of this Convention shall not be permitted, nor shall a reservation the effect of which would inhibit the operation of any of the bodies established by this Convention be allowed. A reservation shall be considered incompatible or inhibitive if at least two-thirds of the States Parties to this Convention object to it.

3. Reservations may be withdrawn at any time by notification to this effect addressed to the Secretary-General. Such notification shall take effect on the date on which it is received.

Article 21

A State Party may denounce this Convention by written notification to the Secretary-General of the United Nations. Denunciation shall take effect one year after the date of receipt of the notification by the Secretary General.

Article 22

Any dispute between two or more States Parties with respect to the interpretation or application of this Convention, which is not settled by negotiation or by the procedures expressly provided for in this Convention, shall, at the request of any of the parties to the dispute, be referred to the International Court of Justice for decision, unless the disputants agree to another mode of settlement.

Article 23

1. A request for the revision of this Convention may be made at any time by any State Party by means of a notification in writing addressed to the Secretary-General of the United Nations.

2. The General Assembly of the United Nations shall decide upon the steps, if any, to be taken in respect of such a request.

Article 24

The Secretary-General of the United Nations shall inform all States referred to in article 17, paragraph 1, of this Convention of the following particulars:
(a) Signatures, ratifications and accessions under articles 17 and 18;
(b) The date of entry into force of this Convention under article 19;
(c) Communications and declarations received under articles 14, 20 and 23;
(d) Denunciations under article 21.

Article 25

1. This Convention, of which the Chinese, English, French, Russian and Spanish texts are equally authentic, shall be deposited in the archives of the United Nations.
2. The Secretary-General of the United Nations shall transmit certified copies of this Convention to all States belonging to any of the categories mentioned in article 17, paragraph 1, of the Convention.

2.6: Convention on the Elimination of All Forms of Discrimination against Women

Annex to GA Res. 34/180 of 18 December 1979, 34 *G.A.O.R.*, Suppl. No. 46 (A/34/46) pp. 193 *et seq.* Entered into force on 3 September 1981.

The States Parties to the present Convention,

Noting that the Charter of the United Nations reaffirms faith in fundamental human rights, in the dignity and worth of the human person and in the equal rights of men and women,

Noting that the Universal Declaration of Human Rights affirms the principle of the inadmissibility of discrimination and proclaims that all human beings are born free and equal in dignity and rights and that everyone is entitled to all the rights and freedoms set forth therein, without distinction of any kind, including distinction based on sex,

Noting that the States Parties to the International Covenants on Human Rights have the obligation to ensure the equal rights of men and women to enjoy all economic, social, cultural, civil and political rights,

Considering the international conventions concluded under the auspices of the United Nations and the specialized agencies promoting equality of rights of men and women,

Noting also the resolutions, declarations and recommendations adopted by the United Nations and the specialized agencies promoting equality of rights of men and women,

Concerned, however, that despite these various instruments extensive discrimination against women continues to exist,

Recalling that discrimination against women violates the principles of equality of rights and respect for human dignity, is an obstacle to the participation of women, on equal terms with men, in the political, social, economic and cultural life of their countries, hampers the growth of the prosperity of society and the family and makes more difficult the full development of the potentialities of women in the service of their countries and of humanity,

Concerned that in situations of poverty women have the least access to food, health, education, training and opportunities for employment and other needs,

Convinced that the establishment of the new international economic order based on equity and justice will contribute significantly towards the promotion of equality between men and women,

Emphasizing that the eradication of *apartheid*, all forms of racism, racial discrimination, colonialism, neo-colonialism, aggression, foreign occupation and domination and interference in the internal affairs of States is essential to the full enjoyment of the rights of men and women,

Affirming that the strengthening of international peace and security, the relaxation of international tension, mutual co-operation among all States irrespective of their social and economic systems, general and complete disarmament, in particular nuclear disarmament under strict and effective international control, the affirmation of the principles of justice, equality and mutual benefit in relations among countries and the realization of the right of peoples under alien and colonial domination and foreign occupation to self-determination and independence, as well as respect for national sovereignty and territorial integrity, will promote social progress and development and as a consequence will contribute to the attainment of full equality between men and women,

Convinced that the full and complete development of a country, the welfare of the world and the cause of peace require the maximum participation of women on equal terms with men in all fields,

Bearing in mind the great contribution of women to the welfare of the family and to the development of society, so far not fully recognized, the social significance of maternity and the role of both parents in the family and in the upbringing of children, and aware that the role of women in procreation should not be a basis for discrimination but that the upbringing of children requires a sharing of responsibility between men and women and society as a whole,

Aware that a change in the traditional role of men as well as the role of women in society and in the family is needed to achieve full equality between men and women,

Determined to implement the principles set forth in the Declaration on the Elimination of Discrimination against Women and, for that purpose, to adopt the measures required for the elimination of such discrimination in all its forms and manifestations,

Have agreed on the following:

PART I

Article 1

For the purposes of the present Convention, the term 'discrimination against women' shall mean any distinction, exclusion or restriction made on the basis of sex which has the effect or purpose of impairing or nullifying the recognition, enjoyment or exercise by women, irrespective of their marital status, on a basis of equality of men and women, of human rights and fundamental freedoms in the political, economic, social, cultural, civil or any other field.

Article 2

States Parties condemn discrimination against women in all its forms, agree to pursue by all appropriate means and without delay a policy of eliminating discrimination against women and, to this end, undertake:

(a) To embody the principle of the equality of men and women in their national constitutions or other appropriate legislation if not yet incorporated therein and to ensure, through law and other appropriate means, the practical realization of this principle;

(b) To adopt appropriate legislative and other measures, including sanctions where appropriate, prohibiting all discrimination against women;

(c) To establish legal protection of the rights of women on an equal basis with men and to ensure through competent national tribunals and other public institutions the effective protection of women against any act of discrimination;

(d) To refrain from engaging in any act or practice of discrimination against women and to ensure that public authorities and institutions shall act in conformity with this obligation;

(e) To take all appropriate measures to eliminate discrimination against women by any person, organization or enterprise;

(f) To take all appropriate measures, including legislation, to modify or abolish existing laws, regulations, customs and practices which constitute discrimination against women;

(g) To repeal all national penal provisions which constitute discrimination against women.

Article 3

States Parties shall take in all fields, in particular in the political, social, economic and cultural fields, all appropriate measures, including legislation, to ensure the full development and advancement of women , for the purpose of guaranteeing them the exercise and enjoyment of human rights and fundamental freedoms on a basis of equality with men.

Article 4

1. Adoption by States Parties of temporary special measures aimed at accelerating *de facto* equality between men and women shall not be considered discrimination as defined in the present Convention, but shall in no way entail as a consequence the maintenance of unequal or separate standards; these measures shall be discontinued when the objectives of equality of opportunity and treatment have been achieved.

2. Adoption by States Parties of special measures including those measures contained in the present Convention, aimed at protecting maternity shall not be considered discriminatory.

Article 5

States Parties shall take all appropriate measures:
(a) To modify the social and cultural patterns of conduct of men and women, with a view to achieving the elimination of prejudices and customary and all other practices which are based on the idea of the inferiority or the superiority of either of the sexes or on stereotyped roles for men and women;
(b) To ensure that family education includes a proper understanding of maternity as a social function and the recognition of the common responsibility of men and women in the upbringing and development of their children, it being understood that the interest of the children is the primordial consideration in all cases.

Article 6

States Parties shall take all appropriate measures, including legislation, to suppress all forms of traffic in women and exploitation of prostitution of women.

PART II
Article 7

States Parties shall take all appropriate measures to eliminate discrimination against women in the political and public life of the country and, in particular, shall ensure to women, on equal terms with men, the right:
(a) To vote in all elections and public referenda and to be eligible for election to all publicly elected bodies;
(b) To participate in the formulation of government policy and the implementation thereof and to hold public office and perform all public functions at all levels of government;
(c) To participate in non-governmental organizations and associations concerned with the public and political life of the country.

Article 8

States Parties shall take all appropriate measures to ensure to women, on equal terms with men and without any discrimination, the opportunity to represent their Governments at the international level and to participate in the work of international organizations.

Article 9

1. States Parties shall grant women equal rights with men to acquire, change or retain their nationality. They shall ensure in particular that neither marriage to an alien nor change of nationality by the husband during marriage shall automatically change the nationality of the wife, render her stateless or force upon her the nationality of the husband.
2. States Parties shall grant women equal rights with men with respect to the nationality of their children.

PART III
Article 10

States Parties shall take all appropriate measures to eliminate discrimination against women in order to ensure to them equal rights with men in the field of education and in particular to ensure, on a basis of equality of men and women:
(a) The same conditions for career and vocational guidance, for access to studies and for the achievement of diplomas in educational establishments of all categories in rural as well as in urban areas; this equality shall be ensured in pre-school, general, technical, professional and higher technical education, as well as in all types of vocational training;

130

(b) Access to the same curricula, the same examinations, teaching staff with qualifications of the same standard and school premises and equipment of the same quality;

(c) The elimination of any stereotyped concept of the roles of men and women at all levels and in all forms of education by encouraging coeducation and other types of education which will help to achieve this aim and, in particular, by the revision of textbooks and school programmes and the adaptation of teaching methods;

(d) The same opportunities to benefit from scholarships and other study grants;

(e) The same opportunities for access to programmes of continuing education, including adult and functional literacy programmes, particulary those aimed at reducing, at the earliest possible time, any gap in education existing between men and women;

(f) The reduction of female student drop-out rates and the organization of programmes for girls and women who have left school prematurely;

(g) The same opportunities to participate actively in sports and physical education;

(h) Access to specific educational information to help to ensure the health and well-being of families, including information and advice on family planning.

Article 11

1. States Parties shall take all appropriate measures to eliminate discrimination against women in the field of employment in order to ensure, on a basis of equality of men and women, the same rights, in particular:

(a) The right to work as an inalienable right of all human beings;

(b) The right to the same employment opportunities, including the application of the same criteria for selection in matters of employment;

(c) The right to free choice of profession and employment, the right to promotion, job security and all benefits and conditions of service and the right to receive vocational training and retraining, including apprenticeships, advanced vocational training and recurrent training;

(d) The right to equal remuneration, including benefits, and to equal treatment in respect of work of equal value, as well as equality of treatment in the evaluation of the quality of work;

(e) The right to social security, particularly in cases of retirement, unemployment, sickness, invalidity and old age and other incapacity to work, as well as the right to paid leave;

(f) The right to protection of health and to safety in working conditions, including the safeguarding of the function of reproduction.

2. In order to prevent discrimination against women on the grounds of marriage or maternity and to ensure their effective right to work, States Parties shall take appropriate measures:

(a) To prohibit, subject to the imposition of sanctions, dismissal on the grounds of pregnancy or of maternity leave and discrimination in dismissals on the basis of marital status;

(b) To introduce maternity leave with pay or with comparable social benefits without loss of former employment, seniority or social allowances;

(c) To encourage the provision of the necessary supporting social services to enable parents to combine family obligations with work responsibilities and participation in public life, in particular through promoting the establishment and development of a network of child-care facilities;

(d) To provide special protection to women during pregnancy in types of work proved to be harmful to them.

3. Protective legislation relating to matters covered in this article shall be reviewed periodically in the light of scientific and technological knowledge and shall be revised, repealed or extended as necessary.

Article 12

1. States Parties shall take all appropriate measures to eliminate discrimination against women in the field of health care in order to ensure, on a basis of equality of men and women, access to health care services, including those related to family planning.

2. Notwithstanding the provisions of paragraph 1 of this article, States Parties shall ensure to women appropriate services in connection with pregnancy, confinement and the post-natal period, granting free services where necessary, as well as adequate nutrition during pregnancy and lactation.

Article 13

States Parties shall take all appropriate measures to eliminate discrimination against women in other areas of economic and social life in order to ensure, on a basis of equality of men and women, the same rights, in particular:
(a) The right to family benefits;
(b) The right to bank loans, mortgages and other forms of financial credit;
(c) The right to participate in recreational activities, sports and all aspects of cultural life.

Article 14

1. States Parties shall take into account the particular problems faced by rural women and the significant roles which rural women play in the economic survival of their families, including their work in the non-monetized sectors of the economy, and shall take all appropriate measures to ensure the application of the provisions of the present Convention to women in rural areas.
2. States Parties shall take all appropriate measures to eliminate discrimination against women in rural areas in order to ensure, on a basis of equality of men and women, that they participate in and benefit from rural development and, in particular, shall ensure to such women the right:
(a) To participate in the elaboration and implementation of development planning at all levels;
(b) To have access to adequate health care facilities, including information, counselling and services in family planning;
(c) To benefit directly from social security programmes;
(d) To obtain all types of training and education, formal and non-formal, including that relating to functional literacy, as well as the benefit of all community and extension services, *inter alia*, in order to increase their technical proficiency;
(e) To organize self-help groups and co-operatives in order to obtain equal access to economic opportunities through employment or self employment;
(f) To participate in all community activities;
(g) To have access to agricultural credit and loans, marketing facilities, appropriate technology and equal treatment in land and agrarian reform as well as in land resettlement schemes;
(h) To enjoy adequate living conditions, particularly in relation to housing, sanitation, electricity and water supply, transport and communications.

PART IV

Article 15

1. States Parties shall accord to women equality with men before the law.
2. States Parties shall accord to women, in civil matters, a legal capacity identical to that of men and the same opportunities to exercise that capacity. In particular, they shall give women equal rights to conclude contracts and to administer property and shall treat them equally in all stages of procedure in courts and tribunals.
3. States Parties agree that all contracts and all other private instruments of any kind with a legal effect which is directed at restricting the legal capacity of women shall be deemed null and void.
4. States Parties shall accord to men and women the same rights with regard to the law relating to the movement of persons and the freedom to choose their residence and domicile.

Article 16

1. States Parties shall take all appropriate measures to eliminate discrimination against women in all matters relating to marriage and family relations and in particular shall ensure, on a basis of equality of men and women:
   (a) The same right to enter into marriage;
   (b) The same right freely to choose a spouse and to enter into marriage only with their free and full consent;
   (c) The same rights and responsibilities during marriage and at its dissolution;
   (d) The same rights and responsibilities as parents, irrespective of their marital status, in matters relating to their children; in all cases the interests of the children shall be paramount;
   (e) The same rights to decide freely and responsibly on the number and spacing of their children and to have access to the information, education and means to enable them to exercise these rights;
   (f) The same rights and responsibilities with regard to guardianship, wardship, trustee-ship and adoption of children, or similar institutions where these concepts exist in national legislation; in all cases the interests of the children shall be paramount;
   (g) The same personal rights as husband and wife, including the right to choose a family name, a profession and an occupation;
   (h) The same rights for both spouses in respect of the ownership, acquisition, manage-ment, administration, enjoyment and disposition of property, whether free of charge or for a valuable consideration.
2. The betrothal and the marriage of a child shall have no legal effect, and all necessary action, including legislation, shall be taken to specify a minimum age for marriage and to make the registration of marriages in an official registry compulsory.

PART V

Article 17

1. For the purpose of considering the progress made in the implementation of the present Convention, there shall be established a Committee on the Elimination of Discrimination against Women (hereinafter referred to as the Committee) consisting, at the time of entry into force of the Convention, of eighteen and, after ratification of or accession to the Convention by the thirty-fifth State Party, of twenty-three experts of high moral standing and competence in the field covered by the Convention. The experts shall be elected by States Parties from among their nationals and shall serve in their personal capacity, consideration being given to equitable geographical distribution and to the representation of the different forms of civilization as well as the principal legal systems.
2. The members of the Committee shall be elected by secret ballot from a list of persons nominated by States Parties. Each State Party may nominate one person from among its own nationals.
3. The initial election shall be held six months after the date of the entry into force of the present Convention. At least three months before the date of each election the Secretary-General of the United Nations shall address a letter to the States Parties inviting them to submit their nominations within two months. The Secretary-General shall prepare a list in alphabetical order of all persons thus nominated, indicating the States Parties which have nominated them, and shall submit it to the States Parties.
4. Elections of the members of the Committee shall be held at a meeting of States Parties convened by the Secretary-General at United Nations Headquarters. At that meeting, for which two thirds of the States Parties shall constitute a quorum, the persons elected to the Committee shall be those nominees who obtain the largest number of votes and an absolute majority of the votes of the representatives of States Parties present and voting.
5. The members of the Committee shall be elected for a term of four years. However, the terms of nine of the members elected at the first election shall expire at the end of two years; immediately after the first election the names of these nine members shall be chosen by lot by the Chairman of the Committee.

6. The election of the five additional members of the Committee shall be held in accordance with the provisions of paragraphs 2, 3 and 4 of this article, following the thirty-fifth ratification or accession. The terms of two of the additional members elected on this occasion shall expire at the end of two years, the names of these two members having been chosen by lot by the Chairman of the Committee.

7. For the filling of casual vacancies, the State Party whose expert has ceased to function as a member of the Committee shall appoint another expert from among its nationals, subject to the approval of the Committee.

8. The members of the Committee shall, with the approval of the General Assembly, receive emoluments from United Nations resources on such terms and conditions as the Assembly may decide, having regard to the importance of the Committee's responsibilities.

9. The Secretary-General of the United Nations shall provide the necessary staff and facilities for the effective performance of the functions of the Committee under the present Convention.

Article 18

1. States Parties undertake to submit to the Secretary-General of the United Nations, for consideration by the Committee, a report on the legislative, judicial, administrative or other measures which they have adopted to give effect to the provisions of the present Convention and on the progress made in this respect:

   (a) Within one year after the entry into force for the State concerned;

   (b) Thereafter at least every four years and further whenever the Committee so requests.

2. Reports may indicate factors and difficulties affecting the degree of fulfilment of obligations under the present Convention.

Article 19

1. The Committee shall adopt its own rules of procedure.

2. The Committee shall elect its officers for a term of two years.

Article 20

1. The Committee shall normally meet for a period of not more than two weeks annually in order to consider the reports submitted in accordance with article 18 of the present Convention.

2. The meetings of the Committee shall normally be held at United Nations Headquarters or at any other convenient place as determined by the Committee.

Article 21

1. The Committee shall, through the Economic and Social Council, report annually to the General Assembly of the United Nations on its activities and may make suggestions and general recommendations based on the examination of reports and information received from the States Parties. Such suggestions and general recommendations shall be included in the report of the Committee together with comments, if any, from States Parties.

2. The Secretary-General of the United Nations shall transmit the reports of the Committee to the Commission on the Status of Women for its information.

Article 22

Specialized agencies shall be entitled to be represented at the consideration of the implementation of such provisions of the present Convention as fall within the scope of their activities. The Committee may invite the specialized agencies to submit reports on the implementation of the Convention in areas falling within the scope of their activities.

PART VI

Article 23

Nothing in the present Convention shall affect any provisions that are more conducive to the achievement of equality between men and women which may be contained:

(a) In the legislation of a State Party; or

(b) In any other international convention, treaty or agreement in force for that State.

Article 24

States Parties undertake to adopt all necessary measures at the national level aimed at achieving the full realization of the rights recognized in the present Convention.

Article 25

1. The present Convention shall be open for signature by all States.

2. The Secretary-General of the United Nations is designated as the depositary of the present Convention.

3. The present Convention is subject to ratification. Instruments of ratification shall be deposited with the Secretary-General of the United Nations.

4. The present Convention shall be open to accession by all States. Accession shall be effected by the deposit of an instrument of accession with the Secretary-General of the United Nations.

Article 26

1. A request for the revision of the present Convention may be made at any time by any State Party by means of a notification in writing addressed to the Secretary-General of the United Nations.

2. The General Assembly of the United Nations shall decide upon the steps, if any, to be taken in respect of such a request.

Article 27

1. The present Convention shall enter into force on the thirtieth day after the date of deposit with the Secretary-General of the United Nations of the twentieth instrument of ratification or accession.

2. For each State ratifying the present Convention or acceding to it after the deposit of the twentieth instrument of ratification or accession, the Convention shall enter into force on the thirtieth day after the date of the deposit of its own instrument of ratification or accession.

Article 28

1. The Secretary-General of the United Nations shall receive and circulate to all States the text of reservations made by States at the time of ratification or accession.

2. A reservation incompatible with the object and purpose of the present Convention shall not be permitted.

3. Reservations may be withdrawn at any time by notification to this effect addressed to the Secretary-General of the United Nations, who shall then inform all States thereof. Such notification shall take effect on the date on which it is received.

Article 29

1. Any dispute between two or more States Parties concerning the interpretation or application of the present Convention which is not settled by negotiation shall, at the request of one of them, be submitted to arbitration. If within six months from the date of the request for arbitration the parties are unable to agree on the organization of the arbitration, any one of those parties may refer the dispute to the International Court of Justice by request in conformity with the Statute of the Court.

2. Each State Party may at the time of signature or ratification of the present Convention or accession thereto declare that it does not consider itself bound by paragraph 1 of this article. The other States Parties shall not be bound by that paragraph with respect to any State Party which has made such a reservation.

3. Any State Party which has made a reservation in accordance with paragraph 2 of this article may at any time withdraw that reservation by notification to the Secretary-General of the United Nations.

Article 30

The present Convention, the Arabic, Chinese, English, French, Russian and Spanish texts of which are equally authentic, shall be deposited with the Secretary-General of the United Nations.

IN WITNESS WHEREOF the undersigned, duly authorized, have signed the present Convention.

2.7: African Charter on Human and Peoples' Rights

Adopted 27 June 1981. Entered into force 21 October 1986.

PREAMBLE

The African States members of the Organization of African Unity, parties to the present convention entitled 'African Charter on Human and Peoples' Rights',

Recalling Decision 115 (XVI) of the Assembly of Heads of State and Government at its Sixteenth Ordinary Session held in Monrovia, Liberia, from 17 to 20 July 1979 on the preparation of a 'preliminary draft on an African Charter on Human and Peoples' Rights providing *inter alia* for the establishment of bodies to promote and protect human and peoples' rights';

Considering the Charter of the Organization of African Unity, which stipulates that 'freedom, equality, justice and dignity are essential objectives for the achievement of the legitimate aspirations of the African peoples';

Reaffirming the pledge they solemnly made in Article 2 of the said Charter to eradicate all forms of colonialism from Africa, to coordinate and intensify their cooperation and efforts to achieve a better life for the peoples of Africa and to promote international cooperation having due regard to the Charter of the United Nations. and the Universal Declaration of Human Rights;

Taking into consideration the virtues of their historical tradition and the values of African civilization which should inspire and characterize their reflection on the concept of human and peoples' rights;

Recognizing on the one hand, that fundamental human rights stem from the attributes of human beings which justifies their national and international protection and on the other hand that the reality and respect of peoples' rights should necessarily guarantee human rights;

Considering that the enjoyment of rights and freedoms also implies the performance of duties on the part of everyone;

Convinced that it is henceforth essential to pay a particular attention to the right to development and that civil and political rights cannot be dissociated from economic, social and cultural rights in their conception as well as universality and that the satisfaction of economic, social and cultural rights is a guarantee for the enjoyment of civil and political rights;

Conscious of their duty to achieve the total liberation of Africa, the peoples of which are still struggling for their dignity and genuine independence, and undertaking to eliminate colonialism, neo-colonialism, *apartheid*, zionism and to dismantle aggressive foreign military bases and all forms of discrimination, particularly those based on race, ethnic group, color, sex, language, religion or political opinions;

Reaffirming their adherence to the principles of human and peoples' rights and freedoms contained in the declarations, conventions and other instruments adopted by the Organization of African Unity, the Movement of Non-Aligned Countries and the United Nations;

Firmly convinced of their duty to promote and protect human and people' rights and freedoms taking into account the importance traditionally attached to these rights and freedoms in Africa;

Have agreed as follows:

Chapter I – Human and Peoples' Rights

Article 1

The Member States of the Organization of African Unity parties to the present Charter shall recognize the rights, duties and freedoms enshrined in this Charter and shall undertake to adopt legislative or other measures to give effect to them.

Article 2

Every individual shall be entitled to the enjoyment of the rights and freedoms recognized and guaranteed in the present Charter without distinction of any kind such as race, ethnic group, color, sex, language, religion, political or any other opinion, national and social origin, fortune, birth or other status.

Article 3

1. Every individual shall be equal before the law.
2. Every individual shall be entitled to equal protection of the law.

Article 4

Human beings are inviolable. Every human being shall be entitled to respect for his life and the integrity of his person. No one may be arbitrarily deprived of this right.

Article 5

Every individual shall have the right to the respect of the dignity inherent in a human being and to the recognition of his legal status. All forms of exploitation and degradation of man particularly slavery, slave trade, torture, cruel, inhuman or degrading punishment and treatment shall be prohibited.

Article 6

Every individual shall have the right to liberty and to the security of his person. No one may be deprived of his freedom except for reasons and conditions previously laid down by law. In particular, no one may be arbitrarily arrested or detained.

Article 7

1. Every individual shall have the right to have his cause heard. This comprises:
    (a) the right to an appeal to competent national organs against acts of violating his fundamental rights as recognized and guaranteed by conventions, laws, regulations and customs in force;
    (b) the right to be presumed innocent until proved guilty by a competent court or tribunal;
    (c) the right to defence, including the right to be defended by counsel of his choice;
    (d) the right to be tried within a reasonable time by an impartial court or tribunal.
2. No one may be condemned for an act or omission which did not constitute a legally punishable offence at the time it was committed. No penalty may be inflicted for an offence for which no provision was made at the time it was committed. Punishment is personal and can be imposed only on the offender.

Article 8

Freedom of conscience, the profession and free practice of religion shall be guaranteed. No one may, subject to law and order, be submitted to measures restricting the exercise of these freedoms.

Article 9

1. Every individual shall have the right to receive information.
2. Every individual shall have the right to express and disseminate his opinions within the law.

Article 10

1. Every individual shall have the right to free association provided that he abides by the law.
2. Subject to the obligation of solidarity provided for in Article 29 no one may be compelled to join an association.

Article 11

Every individual shall have the right to assemble freely with others. The exercise of this right shall be subject only to necessary restrictions provided for by law in particular those enacted in the interest of national security, the safety, health, ethics and rights and freedoms of others.

Article 12

1. Every individual shall have the right to freedom of movement and residence within the borders of a State provided he abides by the law.
2. Every individual shall have the right to leave any country including his own, and to return to his country. This right may only be subject to restrictions provided for by law for the protection of national security, law and order, public health or morality.
3. Every individual shall have the right, when persecuted, to seek and obtain asylum in other countries in accordance with laws of those countries and international conventions.
4. A non-national legally admitted in a territory of a State Party to the present Charter, may only be expelled from it by virtue of a decision taken in accordance with the law.
5. The mass expulsion of non-nationals shall be prohibited. Mass expulsion shall be that which is aimed at national, racial, ethnic or religious groups.

Article 13

1. Every citizen shall have the right to participate freely in the government of his country, either directly or through freely chosen representatives in accordance with the provisions of the law.
2. Every citizen shall have the right of equal access to the public service of his country.
3. Every individual shall have the right of access to public property and services in strict equality of all persons before the law.

Article 14

The right to property shall be guaranteed. It may only be encroached upon in the interest of public need or in the general interest of the community and in accordance with the provisions of appropriate laws.

Article 15

Every individual shall have the right to work under equitable and satisfactory conditions, and shall receive equal pay for equal work.

Article 16

1. Every individual shall have the right to enjoy the best attainable state of physical and mental health.
2. States parties to the present Charter shall take the necessary measures to protect the health of their people and to ensure that they receive medical attention when they are sick.

Article 17

1. Every individual shall have the right to education.
2. Every individual may freely, take part in the cultural life of his community.
3. The promotion and protection of morals and traditional values recognized by the community shall be the duty of the State.

Article 18

1. The family shall be the natural unit and basis of society. It shall be protected by the State which shall take care of its physical and moral health.
2. The State shall have the duty to assist the family which is the custodian of morals and traditional values recognized by the community.
3. The State shall ensure the elimination of every discrimination against women and also ensure the protection of the rights of the woman and the child as stipulated in international declarations and conventions.
4. The aged and the disabled shall also have the right to special measures of protection in keeping with their physical or moral needs.

Article 19

All peoples shall be equal; they shall enjoy the same respect and shall have the same rights. Nothing shall justify the domination of a people by another.

Article 20

1. All peoples shall have the right to existence. They shall have the unquestionable and inalienable right to self-determination. They shall freely determine their political status and shall pursue their economic and social development according to the policy they have freely chosen.
2. Colonized or oppressed peoples shall have the right to free themselves from the bonds of domination by resorting to any means recognized by the international community.
3. All peoples shall have the right to the assistance of the States parties to the present Charter in their liberation struggle against foreign domination, be it political, economic or cultural.

Article 21

1. All peoples shall freely dispose of their wealth and natural resources. This right shall be exercised in the exclusive interest of the people. In no case shall a people be deprived of it.
2. In case of spoliation the dispossessed people shall have the right to the lawful recovery of its property as well as to an adequate compensation.
3. The free disposal of wealth and natural resources shall be exercised without prejudice to the obligation of promoting international economic cooperation based on mutual respect, equitable exchange and the principles of international law.
4. States parties to the present Charter shall individually and collectively exercise the right to free disposal of their wealth and natural resources with a view to strengthening African unity and solidarity.
5. States parties to the present Charter shall undertake to eliminate all forms of foreign economic exploitation particularly that practised by international monopolies so as to enable their peoples to fully benefit from the advantages derived from their national resources.

Article 22

1. All peoples shall have the right to their economic, social and cultural development with due regard to their freedom and identity and in the equal enjoyment of the common heritage of mankind.
2. States shall have the duty, individually or collectively, to ensure the exercise of the right to development.

Article 23

1. All peoples shall have the right to national and international peace and security. The principles of solidarity and friendly relations implicitly affirmed by the Charter of the United Nations and reaffirmed by that of the Organization of African Unity shall govern relations between States.

2. For the purpose of strengthening peace, solidarity and friendly relations, States parties to the present Charter shall ensure that:

(a) any individual enjoying the right of asylum under Article 12 of the present Charter shall not engage in subversive activities against his country of origin or any other State party to the present Charter;

(b) their territories shall not be used as bases for subversive or terrorist activities against the people of any other State party to the present Charter.

Article 24

All peoples shall have the right to a general satisfactory environment favorable to their development.

Article 25

States parties to the present Charter shall have the duty to promote and ensure through teaching, education and publication, the respect of the rights and freedoms contained in the present Charter and to see to it that these freedoms and rights as well as corresponding obligations and duties are understood.

Article 26

States parties to the present Charter shall have the duty to guarantee the independence of the Courts and shall allow the establishment and improvement of appropriate national institutions entrusted with the promotion and protection of the rights and freedoms guaranteed by the present Charter.

Chapter II – Duties

Article 27

1. Every individual shall have duties towards his family and society, the State and other legally recognized communities and the international community.

2. The rights and freedoms of each individual shall be exercised with due regard to the rights of others, collective security, morality and common interest.

Article 28

Every individual shall have the duty to respect and consider his fellow beings without discrimination, and to maintain relations aimed at promoting, safeguarding and reinforcing mutual respect and tolerance.

Article 29

The individual shall also have the duty:

1. To preserve the harmonious development of the family and to work for the cohesion and respect of the family; to respect his parents at all times, to maintain them in case of need;

2. To serve his national community by placing his physical and intellectual abilities at its service;

3. Not to compromise the security of the State whose national or resident he is;

4. To preserve and strengthen social and national solidarity, particularly when the latter is threatened;

5. To preserve and strengthen the national independence and the territorial integrity of his country and to contribute to its defence in accordance with the law;

6. To work to the best of his abilities and competence, and to pay taxes imposed by law in the interest of the society;

7. To preserve and strengthen positive African cultural values in his relations with other members of the society, in the spirit of tolerance, dialogue and consultation and, in general, to contribute to the promotion of the moral well being of society;

8. To contribute to the best of his abilities, at all times and at all levels, to the promotion and achievement of African unity.

PART II: MEASURES OF SAFEGUARD

Chapter I – Establishment and Organization of the African Commission on Human and Peoples' Rights

Article 30

An African Commission on Human and Peoples' Rights, hereinafter called 'the Commission', shall be established within the Organization of African Unity to promote human and peoples' rights and ensure their protection in Africa.

Article 31

1. The Commission shall consist of eleven members chosen from amongst African personalities of the highest reputation, known for their high morality, integrity, impartiality and competence in matters of human and peoples' rights; particular consideration being given to persons having legal experience.

2. The members of the Commission shall serve in their personal capacity . . . .

Article 41

The Secretary General of the Organization of African Unity shall appoint the Secretary of the Commission. He shall also provide the staff and services necessary for the effective discharge of the duties of the Commission. The Organization of African Unity shall bear the costs of the staff and services . . .

Chapter II – Mandate of the Commission

Article 45

The functions of the Commission shall be:

1. To promote Human and Peoples' Rights and in particular:
   (a) to collect documents, undertake studies and researches on African problems in the field of human and peoples' rights, organize seminars, symposia and conferences, disseminate information, encourage national and local institutions concerned with human and peoples' rights, and should the case arise, give its views or make recommendations to Governments.
   (b) to formulate and lay down, principles and rules aimed at solving legal problems relating to human and peoples' rights and fundamental freedoms upon which African Governments may base their legislations.
   (c) co-operate with other African and international institutions concerned with the promotion and protection of human and peoples' rights.

2. Ensure the protection of human and peoples' rights under conditions laid down by the present Charter.

3. Interpret all the provisions of the present Charter at the request of a State party, an institution of the OAU or an African Organization recognized by the OAU.

4. Perform any other tasks which may be entrusted to it by the Assembly of Heads of State and Government.

Chapter III – Procedure of the Commission

Article 46

The Commission may resort to any appropriate method of investigation; it may hear from the Secretary General of the Organization of African Unity or any other person capable of enlightening it.

142

Communication From States

Article 47

If a State party to the present Charter has good reasons to believe that another State party to this Charter has violated the provisions of the Charter, it may draw, by written communication, the attention of that State to the matter. This communication shall also be addressed to the Secretary General of the OAU and to the Chairman of the Commission. Within three months of the receipt of the communication, the State to which the communication is addressed shall give the enquiring State, written explanation or statement elucidating the matter. This should include as much as possible relevant information relating to the laws and rules of procedure applied and applicable, and the redress already given or course of action available.

Article 48

If within three months from the date on which the original communication is received by the State to which it is addressed, the issue is not settled to the satisfaction of the two States involved through bilateral negotiation or by any other peaceful procedure, either State shall have the right to submit the matter to the Commission through the Chairman and shall notify the other States involved.

Article 49

Notwithstanding the provisions of 47, if a State party to the present Charter considers that another State party has violated the provisions of the Charter, it may refer the matter directly to the Commission by addressing a communication to the Chairman, to the Secretary General of the Organization of African Unity and the State concerned.

Article 50

The Commission can only deal with a matter submitted to it after making sure that all local remedies, if they exist, have been exhausted, unless it is obvious to the Commission that the procedure of achieving these remedies would be unduly prolonged.

Article 51

1. The Commission may ask the States concerned to provide it with all relevant information.
2. When the Commission is considering the matter, States concerned may be represented before it and submit written or oral representation.

Article 52

After having obtained from the States concerned and from other sources all the information it deems necessary and after having tried all appropriate means to reach an amicable solution based on the respect of Human and Peoples' Rights, the Commission shall prepare, within a reasonable period of time from the notification referred to in 48, a report stating the facts and its findings. This report shall be sent to the States concerned and communicated to the Assembly of Heads of State and Government.

Article 53

While transmitting its report, the Commission may make to the Assembly of Heads of State and Government such recommendations as it deems useful.

Article 54

The Commission shall submit to each ordinary Session of the Assembly of Heads of State and Government a report on its activities.

Other Communications

Article 55

1. Before each Session, the Secretary of the Commission shall make a list of the communications other than those of States parties to the present Charter and transmit them to the members of the Commission, who shall indicate which communications should be considered by the Commission.

2. A communication shall be considered by the Commission if a simple majority of its members so decide.

Article 56

Communications relating to human and peoples' rights referred to in 55 received by the Commission, shall be considered if they:

1. Indicate their authors even if the latter request anonymity,

2. Are compatible with the Charter of the Organization of African Unity or with the present Charter,

3. Are not written in disparaging or insulting language directed against the State concerned and its institutions or to the Organization of African Unity,

4. Are not based exclusively on news disseminated through the mass media,

5. Are sent after exhausting local remedies, if any, unless it is obvious that this procedure is unduly prolonged,

6. Are submitted within a reasonable period from the time local remedies are exhausted or from the date the Commission is seized of the matter, and

7. Do not deal with cases which have been settled by these States involved in accordance with the principles of the Charter of the United Nations, or the Charter of the Organization of African Unity or the provisions of the present Charter.

Article 57

Prior to any substantive consideration, all communications shall be brought to the knowledge of the State concerned by the Chairman of the Commission.

Article 58

1. When it appears after deliberations of the Commission that one or more communications apparently relate to special cases which reveal the existence of a series of serious or massive violations of human and peoples' rights, the Commission shall draw the attention of the Assembly of Heads of State and Government to these special cases.

2. The Assembly of Heads of State and Government may then request the Commission to undertake an in-depth study of these cases and make a factual report, accompanied by its findings and recommendations.

3. A case of emergency duly noticed by the Commission shall be submitted by the latter to the Chairman of the Assembly of Heads of State and Government who may request an in-depth study.

Article 59

1. All measures taken within the provisions of the present Chapter shall remain confidential until such a time as the Assembly of Heads of State and Government shall otherwise decide.

2. However, the report shall be published by the Chairman of the Commission upon the decision of the Assembly of Heads of State and Government.

3. The report on the activities of the Commission shall be published by its Chairman after it has been considered by the Assembly of Heads of State and Government.

Chapter IV – Applicable Principles

Article 60

The Commission shall draw inspiration from international law on human and peoples' rights, particularly from the provisions of various African instruments on human and peoples' rights, the Charter of the United Nations, the Charter of the Organization of African Unity, the Universal Declaration of Human Rights, other instruments adopted by the United Nations and by African countries in the field of human and peoples' rights as well as from the provisions of various instruments adopted within the Specialized Agencies of the United Nations of which the parties to the present Charter are members.

Article 61

The Commission shall also take into consideration, as subsidiary measures to determine the principles of law, other general or special international conventions, laying down rules expressly recognized by member states of the Organization of African Unity, African practices consistent with international norms on human and people's rights, customs generally accepted as law, general principles of law recognized by African states as well as legal precedents and doctrine.

Article 62

Each state party shall undertake to submit every two years, from the date the present Charter comes into force, a report on the legislative or other measures taken with a view to giving effect to the rights and freedoms recognized and guaranteed by the present Charter. . .

2.8: African Charter on the Rights and Welfare of the Child

Adopted 2 May 1948.

PREAMBLE

The African Member States of the Organization of African Unity, Parties to the present Charter entitled '*African Charter on the Rights and Welfare of the Child*';

Considering that the Charter of the Organization of African Unity recognizes the paramountcy of Human Rights and the African Charter on Human and People's Rights proclaimed and agreed that everyone is entitled to all the rights and freedoms recognized and guaranteed therein, without distinction of any kind such as race, ethnic group, colour. sex, language, religion, political or any other opinion, national and social origin, fortune, birth or other status;

Recalling the Declaration on the Rights and Welfare of the African Child (AHG/ST.4 Rev.l) adopted by the Assembly of Heads of State and Government of the Organization of African Unity, at its Sixteenth Ordinary Session in Monrovia, Liberia from 17 to 20 July 1979, recognized the need to take appropriate measures to promote and protect the rights and welfare of the African Child;

Noting with concern that the situation of most African children, remains critical due to the unique factors of their socio-economic, cultural, traditional and developmental circumstances, natural disasters, armed conflicts, exploitation and hunger, and on account of the child's physical and mental immaturity he/she needs special safeguards and care;

Recognizing that the child occupies a unique and privileged position in the African society and that for the full and harmonious development of his personality, the child should grow up in a family environment in an atmosphere of happiness, love and understanding;

Recognizing that the child, due to the needs of his physical and mental development requires particular care with regard to health, physical, mental, moral and social development. and requires legal protection in conditions of freedom, dignity and security;

Taking into consideration the virtues of their cultural heritage, historical background and the values of the African civilization which should inspire and characterize their reflection on the concept of the rights and welfare of the child;

Considering that the promotion and protection of the rights and welfare of the child also implies the performance of duties on the part of everyone;

Reaffirming adherence to the principles of the rights and welfare of the child contained in the declaration, conventions and other instruments of the Organization of African Unity and in the United Nations and in particular the United Nations Convention on the Rights of the Child; and the OAU Heads of State and Government's Declaration on the Rights and Welfare of the African Child.

PART I: RIGHTS AND DUTIES

Chapter One: Rights and Welfare of the Child

Article 1: Obligation of States Parties

1. Member States of the Organization of African Unity Parties to the present Charter shall recognize the rights, freedoms and duties enshrined in this Charter and shall undertake to take the necessary steps, in accordance with their Constitutional processes and with the provisions of the present Charter, to adopt such legislative or other measures as may be necessary to give effect to the provisions of this Charter.

2. Nothing in this Charter shall affect any provisions that are more conducive to the realization of the rights and welfare of the child contained in the law of a State Party or in any other international Convention or agreement in force in that State.

3. Any custom, tradition, cultural or religious practice that is inconsistent with the rights, duties and obligations contained in the present Charter shall to the extent of such inconsistency be discouraged.

Article 2: Definition of a Child

For the purposes of this Charter, a child means every human being below the age of 18 years.

Article 3: Non-Discrimination

Every child shall be entitled to the enjoyment of the rights and freedoms recognized and guaranteed in this Charter irrespective of the child's or his/her parents' or legal guardians' race, ethnic group, colour, sex, language, religion, political or other opinion, national and social origin, fortune, birth or other status.

Article 4: Best Interests of the Child

1. In all actions concerning the child undertaken by any person or authority the best interests of the child shall be the primary consideration.
2. In all judicial or administrative proceedings affecting a child who is capable of communicating his/her own views, an opportunity shall be provided for the views of the child to be heard either directly or through an impartial representative as a party to the proceedings, and those views shall be taken into consideration by the relevant authority in accordance with the provisions of appropriate law.

Article 5: Survival and Development

1. Every child has an inherent right to life. This right shall be protected by law.
2. States Parties to the present Charter shall ensure, to the maximum extent possible, the survival, protection and development of the child.
3. Death sentence shall not be pronounced for crimes committed by children

Article 6: Name and Nationality

1. Every child shall have the right from his birth to a name.
2. Every child shall be registered immediately after birth.
3. Every child has the right to acquire a nationality.
4. States Parties to the present Charter shall undertake to ensure that their Constitutional legislation recognizes the principles according to which a child shall acquire the nationality of the State in the territory of which he has been born if, at the time of the child's birth, he is not granted nationality by any other State in accordance with its laws.

Article 7: Freedom of Expression

Every child who is capable of communicating his or her own views shall be assured the rights to express his opinions freely in all matters and to disseminate his opinions subject to such restrictions as are prescribed by laws.

Article 8: Freedom of Association

Every child shall have the right to free association and freedom of peaceful assembly in conformity with the law.

Article 9: Freedom of Thought, Conscience and Religion

1. Every child shall have the right to freedom of thought, conscience and religion.
2. Parents. and where applicable, legal guardians shall have a duty to provide guidance and direction in the exercise of these rights having regard to the evolving capacities, and best interests of the child.
3. States Parties shall respect the duty of parents and, where applicable, legal guardians to provide guidance and direction in the enjoyment of these rights subject to the national laws and policies.

147

Article 10: Protection of Privacy

No child shall be subject to arbitrary or unlawful interference with his privacy, family home or correspondence, or to the attacks upon his honour or reputation, provided that parents or legal guardians shall have the right to exercise reasonable supervision over the conduct of their children. The child has the right to the protection of the law against such interference or attacks.

Article 11: Education

1. Every child shall have the right to an education.
2. The education of the child shall be directed to:
   (a) the promotion and development of the child's personality, talents and mental and physical abilities to their fullest potential;
   (b) fostering respect for human rights and fundamental freedoms with particular reference to those set out in the provisions of various African instruments on human and peoples' rights and international human rights declarations and conventions;
   (c) the preservation and strengthening of positive African morals, traditional values and cultures;
   (d) the preparation of the child for responsible life in a free society, in the spirit of understanding tolerance, dialogue, mutual respect and friendship among all peoples' ethnic, tribal and religious groups;
   (e) the preservation of national independence and territorial integrity;
   (f) the promotion and achievements of African Unity and Solidarity;
   (g) the development of respect for the environment and natural resources;
   (h) the promotion of the child's understanding of primary health care.
3. States Parties to the present Charter shall take all appropriate measures with a view to achieving the full realization of this right and shall in particular:
   (a) provide free and compulsory basic education;
   (b) encourage the development of secondary education in its different forms and to progressively make it free and accessible to all;
   (c) make the higher education accessible to all on the basis of capacity and ability by every appropriate means;
   (d) take measures to encourage regular attendance at schools and the reduction of drop-out rates;
   (e) take special measures in respect of female, gifted and disadvantaged children, to ensure equal access to education for all sections of the community.
4. States Parties to the present Charter shall respect the rights and duties of parents, and where applicable, of legal guardians to choose for their children schools, other than those established by public authorities, which conform to such minimum standards as may be approved by the State, to ensure the religious and moral education of the child in a manner consistent with the evolving capacities of the child.
5. States Parties to the present Charter shall take all appropriate measures to ensure that a child who is subjected to schools or parental discipline shall be treated with humanity and with respect for the inherent dignity of the child and in conformity with the present Charter.
6. States Parties to the present Charter shall take all appropriate measures to ensure that children who become pregnant before completing their education shall have an opportunity to continue with their education on the basis of their individual ability.
7. No part of this Article shall be construed as to interfere with the liberty of individuals and bodies to establish and direct educational institutions subject to the observance of the principles set out in paragraph 1 of this Article and the requirement that the education given in such institutions shall conform to such minimum standards as may be laid down by the States.

Article 12: Leisure, Recreation and Cultural Activities

1. States Parties recognize the right of the child to rest and leisure, to engage in play and recreational activities appropriate to the age of the child and to participate freely in cultural life and the arts.

2. States Parties shall respect and promote the right of the child to fully participate in cultural and artistic life and shall encourage the provision of appropriate and equal opportunities for cultural, artistic, recreational and leisure activity.

Article 13: Handicapped Children

1. Every child who is mentally or physically disabled shall have the right to special measures of protection in keeping with his physical and moral needs and under conditions which ensure his dignity, promote his self-reliance and active participation in the community.
2. States Parties to the present Charter shall ensure, subject to available resources, to a disabled child and to those responsible for his care, provision of assistance for which application is made and which is appropriate to the child's condition and in particular shall ensure that the disabled child has effective access to training, preparation for employment and recreation opportunities in a manner conducive to the child achieving the fullest possible social integration, individual development and his cultural and moral development.
3. The States Parties to the present Charter shall use their available resources with a view to achieving progressively the full convenience of the mentally and physically disabled person to movement and access to public highway buildings and other places to which the disabled may legitimately want to have access to.

Article 14: Health and Health Services

1. Every child shall have the right to enjoy the best attainable state of physical, mental and spiritual health.
2. States Parties to the present Charter shall undertake to pursue the full implementation of this right and in particular shall take measures:
    (a) to reduce infant and child morality rate;
    (b) to ensure the provision of necessary medical assistance and health care to all children with emphasis on the development of primary health care;
    (c) to ensure the provision of adequate nutrition and safe drinking water;
    (d) to combat disease and malnutrition within the framework of primary health care through the application of appropriate technology;
    (e) to ensure appropriate health care for expectant and nursing mothers;
    (f) to develop preventive health care and family life education and provision of service;
    (g) to integrate basic health service programmes in national development plans;
    (h) to ensure that all sectors of the society, in particular, parents, children, community leaders and community workers are informed and supported in the use of basic knowledge of child health and nutrition, the advantages of breastfeeding, hygiene and environmental sanitation and the prevention of domestic and other accidents;
    (i) to ensure the meaningful participation of non-governmental organizations, local communities and the beneficiary population in the planning and management of a basic service programme for children;
    (j) to support through technical and financial means, the mobilization of local community resources in the development of primary health care for children.

Article 15: Child Labour

1. Every child shall be protected from all forms of economic exploitation and from performing any work that is likely to be hazardous or to interfere with the child's physical, mental, spiritual, moral, or social development.
2. States Parties to the present Charter take all appropriate legislative and administrative measures to ensure the full implementation of this Article which covers both the formal and informal sectors of employment and having regard to the relevant provisions of the International Labour Organisation's instruments relating to children, States Parties shall in particular:
    (a) provide through legislation, minimum wages for admission to every employment;
    (b) provide for appropriate regulation of hours and conditions of employment;
    (c) provide for appropriate penalties or other sanctions to ensure the effective enforcement of this Article;

(d) promote the dissemination of information on the hazards of child labour to all sectors of the community.

Article 16: Protection Against Child Abuse and Torture

1. States Parties to the present Charter shall take specific legislative, administrative, social and educational measures to protect the child from all forms of torture, inhuman or degrading treatment and especially physical or mental injury or abuse, neglect or mal-treatment including sexual abuse, while in the care of a parent, legal guardian or school authority or any other person who has the care of the child.

2. Protective measures under this Article shall include effective procedures for the establishment of special monitoring units to provide necessary support for the child and for those who have the care of the child, as well as other forms of prevention and for identification, reporting, referral, investigation, treatment, and follow-up of instances of child abuse and neglect.

Article 17: Administration of Juvenile Justice

1. Every child accused or found guilty of having infringed penal law shall have the right to special treatment in a manner consistent with the child's sense of dignity and worth and which reinforces the child's respect for human rights and fundamental freedoms of others.

2. States Parties to the present Charter shall in particular:
   (a) ensure that no child who is detained or imprisoned or otherwise deprived of his/her liberty is subjected to torture, inhuman or degrading treatment or punishment;
   (b) ensure that children are separated from adults in their place of detention or imprisonment;
   (c) ensure that every child accused of infringing the penal law:
       (i) shall be presumed innocent until duly recognized guilty;
       (ii) shall be informed promptly in a language that he understands and in detail of the charge against him, and shall be entitled to the assistance of an interpreter if he or she cannot understand the language used;
       (iii) shall be afforded legal and other appropriate assistance in the preparation and presentation of his defence;
       (iv) shall have the matter determined as speedily as possible by an impartial tribunal and if found guilty, be entitled to an appeal by a higher tribunal;
       (v) shall not be compelled to give testimony or confess guilt.
   (d) prohibit the press and the public from trial.

3. The essential aim of treatment of every child during the trial and also if found guilty of infringing the penal law shall be his or her reformation, re-integration into his or her family and social rehabilitation.

4. There shall be a minimum age below which children shall be presumed not to have the capacity to infringe the penal law.

Article 18: Protection of the Family

1. The family shall be the natural unit and basis of society. It shall enjoy the protection and support of the State for its establishment and development.

2. States Parties to the present Charter shall take appropriate steps to ensure equality of rights and responsibilities of spouses with regard to children during marriage and in the event of its dissolution. In case of the dissolution, provision shall be made for the necessary protection of the child.

3. No child shall be deprived of maintenance by reference to the parents' marital status.

Article 19: Parental Care and Protection

1. Every child shall be entitled to the enjoyment of parental care and protection and shall, whenever possible, have the right to reside with his or her parents. No child shall be separated from his parents against his will, except when a judicial authority determines in accordance with the appropriate law, that such separation is in the best interest of the child.

2. Every child who is separated from one or both parents shall have the right to maintain personal relations and direct contact with both parents on a regular basis.
3. Where separation results from the action of a State Party, the State Party shall provide the child, or if appropriate, another member of the family with essential information concerning the whereabouts of the absent member or members of the family. States Parties shall also ensure that the submission of such a request shall not entail any adverse consequences for the person or persons in whose respect it is made.
4. Where a child is apprehended by a State Party, his parents or guardians shall, as soon as possible, be notified of such apprehension by that State Party.

Article 20: Parental Reponsibilities

1. Parents or other persons responsible for the child shall have the primary responsibility of the upbringing and development the child and shall have the duty:
    (a) to ensure that the best interests of the child are their basic concern at all times;
    (b) to secure, within their abilities and financial capacities, conditions of living nece-ssary to the child's development; and
    (c) to ensure that domestic discipline is administered winh humanity and in a manner consistent with the inherent dignity of the child.
2. States Parties to the present Charter shall in accordance with their means and national conditions take all appropriate measures;
    (a) to assist parents and other persons responsible for the child and in case of need provide material assistance and support programmes particularly with regard to nutri-tion, health, education, clothing and housing;
    (b) to assist parents and others responsible for the child in the performance of child-rearing and ensure the development of institutions responsible for providing care of children; and
    (c) to ensure that the children of working parents are provided with care services and facilities.

Article 21: Protection against Harmful Social and Cultural Practices

1. States Parties to the present Charter shall take all appropriate measures to eliminate harmful social and cultural practices affecting the welfare, dignity, normal growth and development of the child and in particular:
    (a) those customs and practices prejudicial to the health or life of the child; and
    (b) those customs and practices discriminatory to the child on the grounds of sex or other status.
2. Child marriage and the betrothal of girls and boys shall be prohibited and effective action, including legislation, shall be taken to specify the minimum age of marriage to be 18 years and make registration of all marriages in an official registry compulsory.

Article 22: Armed Conflicts

1. States Parties to this Charter shall undertake to respect and ensure respect for rules of international humanitarian law applicable in armed conflicts which affect the child.
2. States Parties to the present Charter shall take all necessary measures to ensure that no child shall take a direct part in hostilities and refrain in particular, from recruiting any child.
3. States Parties to the present Charter shall, in accordance with their obligations under international humanitarian law, protect the civilian population in armed conflicts and shall take all feasible measures to ensure the protection and care of children who are affected by armed conflicts. Such rules shall also apply to children in situations of internal armed conflicts, tension and strife.

Article 23: Refugee Children

1. States Parties to the present Charter shall take all appropriate measures to ensure that a child who is seeking refugee status or who is considered a refugee in accordance with

applicable international or domestic law shall, whether unaccompanied or accompanied by parents, legal guardians or close relatives, receive appropriate protection and humanitarian assistance in the enjoyment of the rights set out in this Charter and other international human rights and humanitarian instruments to which the States are Parties.

2. States Parties shall undertake to co-operate with existing international organizations which protect and assist refugees in their efforts to protect and assist such a child and to trace the parents or other close relatives or an unaccompanied refugee child in order to obtain information necessary for reunification with the family.

3. Where no parents, legal guardians or close relatives can be found the child shall be accorded the same protection as any other child permanently or temporarily deprived of his family environment for any reason.

4. The provisions of this Article apply *Mutatis Mutandis* to internally displaced children whether through natural disaster, internal armed conflicts, civil strife, breakdown of economic and social order or howsoever caused.

Article 24: Adoption

States Parties which recognize the system of adoption shall ensure that the best interest of the child shall be the paramount consideration and they shall:

(a) establish competent authorities to determine matters of adoption and ensure that the adoption is carried out in conformity with applicable laws and procedures and on the basis of all relevant and reliable information that the adoption is permissible in view of the child's status concerning parents, relatives and guardians and that, if necessary, the appropriate persons concerned have given their informed consent to the adoption on the basis of appropriate counselling;

(b) recognize that inter-country adoption in those States who have ratified or adhered to the International Convention on the Rights of the Child or this Charter, may, as the last resort, be considered as an alternative means of a child's care, if the child cannot be placed in a foster or an adoptive family or cannot in any suitable manner be cared for in the child's country of origin;

(c) ensure that the child affected by inter-country adoption enjoys safeguards and standards equivalent to those existing in the case of national adoption;

(d) take all appropriate measures to ensure that in inter-country adoption, the placement does not result in trafficking or improper financial gain for those who try to adopt a child;

(e) promote, where appropriate, the objectives of this Article by concluding bilateral or multilateral arrangements or agreements, and endeavour, within this framework to ensure that the placement of the child in another country is carried out by competent authorities or organs;

(f) establish a machinery to monitor the well-being of the adopted child.

Article 25: Separation from Parents

1. Any child who is permanently or temporarily deprived of his family environment for any reason shall be entitled to special protection and assistance;

2. States Parties to the present Charter:

(a) shall ensure that a child who is parentless, or who is temporarily or permanently deprived of his or her family environment, or who in his or her best interest cannot be brought up or allowed to remain in that environment shall be provided with alternative family care, which could include, among others, foster placement, or placement in suitable institutions for the care of children

(b) shall take all necessary measures to trace and re-unite children with parents or relatives where separation is caused by internal and external displacement arising from armed conflicts or natural disasters.

3. When considering alternative family care of the child and the best interests of the child, due regard shall be paid to the desirability of continuity in a child's up-bringing and to the child's ethnic, religious or linguistic background.

Article 26: Protection Against Apartheid and Discrimination

1. States Parties to the present Charter shall individually and collectively undertake to accord the highest priority to the special needs of children living under *apartheid* and in States subject to military destabilization by the *Apartheid* regime.

2. States Parties to the present Charter shall individually and collectively undertake to accord the highest priority to the special needs of children living under regimes practising racial, ethnic, religious or other forms of discrimination as well as in States subject to military destabilization.

3. States Parties shall undertake to provide whenever possible, material assistance to such children and to direct their efforts towards the elimination of all forms of discrimination and *apartheid* on the African Continent.

Article 27: Sexual Exploitation

1. States Parties to the present Charter shall undertake to protect the child from all forms of sexual exploitation and sexual abuse and shall in particular take measures to prevent:

    (a) the inducement, coercion or encouragement of a child to engage in any sexual activity;

    (b) the use of children in prostitution or other sexual practices;

    (c) the use of children in pornographic activities, performances and materials.

Article 28: Drug Abuse

States Parties to the present Charter shall take all appropriate measures to protect the child from the use of narcotics and illicit use of psychotropic substances as defined in the relevant international treaties, and to prevent the use of children in the production and trafficking of such substances

Article 29: Sale, Trafficking and Abduction

States Parties to the present Charter shall take appropriate measures to prevent:

    (a) the abduction, the sale of, or traffic in children for any purpose or in any form, by any person including parents or legal guardians of the child;

    (b) the use of children in all forms of begging.

Article 30: Children of Imprisoned Mothers

States Parties to the present Charter shall undertake to provide special treatment to expectant mothers and to mothers of infants and young children who have been accused or found guilty of infringing the penal law and shall in particular:

    (a) ensure that a non-custodial sentence will always be first considered when sentencing such mothers;

    (b) establish and promote measures alternative to institutional confinement for the treatment of such mothers;

    (c) establish special alternative institutions for holding such mothers;

    (d) ensure that a mother shall not be imprisoned with her child;

    (e) ensure that a death sentence shall not be imposed on such mothers;

    (f) the essential aim of the penitentiary system will be the reformation, the integration of the mother to the family and social rehabilitation.

Article 31: Responsibility of the Child

Every child shall have responsibilities towards his family and society, the State and other legally recognized communities and the international community. The child, subject to his age and ability, and such limitations as may be contained in the present Charter, shall have the duty:

    (a) to work for the cohesion of the family, to respect his parents, superiors and elders at all times and to assist them in case of need;

(b) to serve his national community by placing his physical and intellectual abilities at its service;

(c) to preserve and strengthen social and national solidarity;

(d) to preserve and strengthen African cultural values in his relations with other members of the society, in the spirit of tolerance, dialogue and consultation and to contribute to the moral well-being of society;

(e) to preserve and strengthen the independence and the integrity of his country;

(f) to contribute to the best of his abilities, at all times and at all levels, to the promotion and achievement of African Unity.

PART II

Chapter Two: Establishment and Organization of the Committee on the Rights and Welfare of the Child

Article 32: The Committee

An African Committee of Experts on the Rights and Welfare of the Child hereinafter called 'the Committee' shall be established within the Organization of African Unity to promote and protect the rights and welfare of the child.

Article 33: Composition

1. The Committee shall consist of 11 members of high moral standing, integrity, impartiality and competence in matters of the rights and welfare of the child.
2. The members of the Committee shall serve in their personal capacity.
3. The Committee shall not include more than one national of the same State.

Article 34: Election

As soon as this Charter shall enter into force the members of the Committee shall be elected by secret ballot by the Assembly of Heads of State and Government from a list of persons nominated by the States Parties to the present Charter.

Article 35: Candidates

Each State Party to the present Charter may nominate not more than two candidates. The candidates must have one of the nationalities of the States Parties to the present Charter. When two candidates are nominated by a State, one of them shall not be a national of that State.

Article 36

1. The Secretary-General of the Organization of African Unity shall invite States Parties to the present Charter to nominate candidates at least six months before the elections.
2. The Secretary-General of the Organization of African Unity shall draw up in alphabetical order, a list of persons nominated and communicate it to the Heads of State and Government at least two months before the elections.

Article 37: Term of Office

1. The members of the Committee shall be elected for a term of five years and may not be re-elected, however, the term of four of the members elected at the first election shall expire after two years and the term of six others, after four years.
2. Immediately after the first election, the Chairman of the Assembly of Heads of State and Government of the Organization of African Unity shall draw lots to determine the names of those members referred to in sub-paragraph 1 of this Article.
3. The Secretary-General of the Organization of African Unity shall convene the first meeting of Committee at the Headquarters of the Organization within six months of the election of the members of the Committee, and thereafter the Committee shall be convened by its Chairman whenever necessary, at least once a year.

Article 38: Bureau

1. The Committee shall establish its own Rules of Procedure.
2. The Committee shall elect its officers for a period of two years.
3. Seven Committee members shall form the quorum.
4. In case of an equality of votes, the Chairman shall have a casting vote.
5. The working languages of the Committee shall be the official languages of the OAU.

Article 39: Vacancy

If a member of the Committee vacates his office for any reason other than the normal expiration of a term, the State which nominated that member shall appoint another member from among its nationals to serve for the remainder of the term – subject to the approval of the Assembly.

Article 40: Secretariat

The Secretary-General of the Organization of African Unity shall appoint a Secretary for the Committee.

Article 41: Privileges and Immunities

In discharging their duties, members of the Committee shall enjoy the privileges and immunities provided for in the General Convention on the Privileges and Immunities of the Organization of African Unity.

Chapter Three: Mandate and Procedure of the Committee

Article 42: Mandate

The functions of the Committee shall be:
   (a) To promote and protect the rights enshrined in this Charter and in particular to:
      (i) collect and document information, commission inter-disciplinary assessment of situations on African problems in the fields of the rights and welfare of the child, organize meetings, encourage national and local institutions concerned with the rights and welfare of the child, and where necessary give its views and make recommendations to Governments;
      (ii) formulate and lay down principles and rules aimed at protecting the rights and welfare of children in Africa;
      (iii) co-operate with other African, international and regional Institutions and organizations concerned with the promotion and protection of the rights and welfare of the child.
   (b) To monitor the implementation and ensure protection of the rights enshrined in this Charter.
   (c) To interpret the provisions of the present Charter at the request of a State Party, an Institution of the Organization of African Unity or any other person or Institution recognized by the Organization of African Unity, or any State Party.
   (d) Perform such other task as may be entrusted to it by the Assembly of Heads of State and Government, Secretary-General of the OAU and any other organs of the OAU or the United Nations.

Article 43: Reporting Procedure

1. Every State Party to the present Charter shall undertake to submit to the Committee through the Secretary-General of the Organization of African Unity, reports on the measures they have adopted which give effect to the provisions of this Charter and on the progress made in the enjoyment of these rights:
   (a) within two years of the entry into force of the Charter for the State Party concerned: and
   (b) and thereafter, every three years.

2. Every report made under this Article shall:

(a) contain sufficient information on the implementation of the present Charter to provide the Committee with comprehensive understanding of the implementation of the Charter in the relevant country; and

(b) shall indicate factors and difficulties, if any, affecting the fulfilment of the obligations contained in the Charter.

3. A State Party which has submitted a comprehensive first report to the Committee need not, in its subsequent reports submitted in accordance with paragraph 1 (a) of this Article, repeat the basic information previously provided.

Article 44: Communications

1. The Committee may receive communication, from any person, group or non-governmental organization recognized by the Organization of African Unity, by a Member State, or the United Nations relating to any matter covered by this Charter.

2. Every communication to the Committee shall contain the name and address of the author and shall be treated in confidence.

Article 45: Investigations by the Committee

1. The Committee may resort to any appropriate method of investigating any matter falling within the ambit of the present Charter, request from the States Parties any information relevant to the implementation of the Charter and may also resort to any appropriate method of investigating the measures the State Party has adopted to implement the Charter.

2. The Committee shall submit to each Ordinary Session of the Assembly of Heads of State and Government every two years, a report on its activities and on any communication made under Article [44] of this Charter.

3. The Committee shall publish its report after it has been considered by the Assembly of Heads of State and Government.

4. States Parties shall make the Committee's reports widely available to the public in their own countries.

Chapter Four: Miscellaneous Provisions

Article 46: Sources of Inspiration

The Committee shall draw inspiration from International Law on Human Rights, particularly from the provisions of the African Charter on Human and Peoples' Rights, the Charter of the Organization of African Unity, the Universal Declaration on Human Rights, the International Convention on the Rights of the Child, and other instruments adopted by the United Nations and by African countries in the field of human rights. and from African values and traditions

Article 47: Signature, Ratification or Adherence

1. The present Charter shall be open to signature by all the Member States of the Organization of African Unity.

2. The present Charter shall be subject to ratification or adherence by Member States of the Organization of African Unity. The instruments of ratification or adherence to the present Charter shall be deposited with the Secretary-General of the Organization of African Unity.

3. The present Charter shall come into force 30 days after the reception by the Secretary-General of the Organization of African Unity of the instruments of ratification or adherence of 15 Member States of the Organization of African Unity.

Article 48: Amendment and Revision of the Charter

1. The present Charter may be amended or revised if any State Party makes a written request to that effect to the Secretary-General of the Organization of African Unity,

provided that the proposed amendment is not submitted to the Assembly of Heads of State and Government for consideration until all the States Parties have been duly notified of it and the Committee has given its opinion on the amendment.

2. An amendment shall be approved by a simple majority of the States Parties.

2.9: American Declaration of the Rights and Duties of Man

Adopted 2 May 1948.

PREAMBLE

All men are born free and equal, in dignity and in rights, and, being endowed by nature with reason and conscience, they should conduct themselves as brothers one to another.

The fulfilment of duty by each individual is a prerequisite to the rights of all. Rights and duties are interrelated in every social and political activity of man. While rights exalt individual liberty, duties express the dignity of that liberty.

Duties of a juridical nature presuppose others of a moral nature which support them in principle and constitute their basis.

Inasmuch as spiritual development is the supreme end of human existence and the highest expression thereof, it is the duty of man to serve that end with all his strength and resources.

Since culture is the highest social and historical expression of that spiritual development, it is the duty of man to preserve, practice and foster culture by every means within his power.

And, since moral conduct constitutes the noblest flowering of culture, it is the duty of every man always to hold it in high respect.

CHAPTER ONE: RIGHTS

Article I

Every human being has the right to life, liberty and the security of his person.

Article II

All persons are equal before the law and have the rights and duties established in this Declaration, without distinction as to race, sex, language, creed or any other factor.

Article III

Every person has the right freely to profess a religious faith, and to manifest and practice it both in public and in private.

Article IV

Every person has the right to freedom of investigation, of opinion, and of the expression and dissemination of ideas, by any medium whatsoever.

Article V

Every person has the right to the protection of the law against abusive attacks upon his honor, his reputation, and his private and family life.

Article VI

Every person has the right to establish a family, the basic element of society, and to receive protection therefor.

Article VII

All women, during pregnancy and the nursing period, and all children have the right to special protection, care and aid.

Article VIII

Every person has the right to fix his residence within the territory of the state of which he is a national, to move about freely within such territory, and not to leave it except by his own will.

Article IX

Every person has the right to the inviolability of his home.

Article X

Every person has the right to the inviolability and transmission of his correspondence.

Article XI

Every person has the right to the preservation of his health through sanitary and social measures relating to food, clothing, housing and medical care, to the extent permitted by public and community resources.

Article XII

Every person has the right to an education, which should be based on the principles of liberty, morality and human solidarity.

Likewise every person has the right to an education that will prepare him to attain a decent life, to raise his standard of living, and to be a useful member of society.

The right to an education includes the right to equality of opportunity in every case, in accordance with natural talents, merit and the desire to utilize the resources that the state or the community is in a position to provide.

Every person has the right to receive, free, at least a primary education.

Article XIII

Every person has the right to take part in the cultural life of the community, to enjoy the arts, and to participate in the benefits that result from intellectual progress, especially scientific discoveries.

He likewise has the right to the protection of his moral and material interests as regards his inventions or any literary, scientific or artistic works of which he is the author.

Article XIV

Every person has the right to work, under proper conditions, and to follow his vocation freely, insofar as existing conditions of employment permit.

Every person who works has the right to receive such remuneration as will, in proportion to his capacity and skill, assure him a standard of living suitable for himself and for his family.

Article XV

Every person has the right to leisure time, to wholesome recreation, and to the opportunity for advantageous use of his free time to his spiritual, cultural and physical benefit.

Article XVI

Every person has the right to social security which will protect him from the consequences of unemployment, old age, and any disabilities arising from causes beyond his control that make it physically or mentally impossible for him to earn a living.

Article XVII

Every person has the right to be recognized everywhere as a person having rights and obligations, and to enjoy the basic civil rights.

Article XVIII

Every person may resort to the courts to ensure respect for his legal rights. There should likewise be available to him a simple, brief procedure whereby the courts will protect him from acts of authority that, to his prejudice, violate any fundamental constitutional rights.

Article XIX

Every person has the right to the nationality to which he is entitled by law and to change it, if he so wishes, for the nationality of any other country that is willing to grant it to him.

Article XX

Every person having legal capacity is entitled to participate in the government of his country, directly or through his representatives, and to take part in popular elections, which shall be by secret ballot, and shall be honest, periodic and free.

Article XXI

Every person has the right to assemble peaceably with others in a formal public meeting or an informal gathering, in connection with matters of common interest of any nature.

Article XXII

Every person has the right to associate with others to promote, exercise and protect his legitimate interests of a political, economic, religious, social, cultural, professional, labor union or other nature.

Article XXIII

Every person has a right to own such private property as meets the essential needs of decent living and helps to maintain the dignity of the individual and of the home.

Article XXIV

Every person has the right to submit respectful petitions to any competent authority, for reasons of either general or private interest, and the right to obtain a prompt decision thereon.

Article XXV

No person may be deprived of his liberty except in the cases and according to the procedures established by pre-existing law.

No person may be deprived of liberty for nonfulfilment of obligations of a purely civil character.

Every individual who has been deprived of his liberty has the right to have the legality of his detention ascertained without delay by a court, and the right to be tried without undue delay or, otherwise, to be released. He also has the right to humane treatment during the time he is in custody.

Article XXVI

Every accused person is presumed to be innocent until proved guilty.

Every person accused of an offense has the right to be given an impartial and public hearing, and to be tried by courts previously established in accordance with pre-existing laws, and not to receive cruel, infamous or unusual punishment.

Article XXVII

Every person has the right, in case of pursuit not resulting from ordinary crimes, to seek and receive asylum in foreign territory, in accordance with the laws of each country and with international agreements.

Article XXVIII

The rights of man are limited by the rights of others, by the security of all, and by the just demands of the general welfare and the advancement of democracy.

CHAPTER TWO: DUTIES

Article XXIX

It is the duty of the individual so to conduct himself in relation to others that each and every one may fully form and develop his personality.

Article XXX

It is the duty of every person to aid, support, educate and protect his minor children, and it is the duty of children to honor their parents always and to aid, support and protect them when they need it.

Article XXXI

It is the duty of every person to acquire at least an elementary education.

Article XXXII

It is the duty of every person to vote in the popular elections of the country of which he is a national, when he is legally capable of doing so.

Article XXXIII

It is the duty of every person to obey the law and other legitimate commands of the authorities of his country and those of the country in which he may be.

Article XXXIV

It is the duty of every able-bodied person to render whatever civil and military service his country may require for its defense and preservation, and, in case of public disaster, to render such services as may be in his power.

It is likewise his duty to hold any public office to which he may be elected by popular vote in the state of which he is a national.

Article XXXV

It is the duty of every person to cooperate with the state and the community with respect to social security and welfare, in accordance with his ability and with existing circumstances.

Article XXXVI

It is the duty of every person to pay the taxes established by law for the support of public services.

Article XXXVII

It is the duty of every person to work, as far as his capacity and possibilities permit, in order to obtain the means of livelihood or to benefit his community.

Article XXXVIII

It is the duty of every person to refrain from taking part in political activities that, according to law, are reserved exclusively to the citizens of the state in which he is an alien.

2.10: American Convention on Human Rights

Adopted 22 November 1969. Entered into force 18 July 1978.

PREAMBLE

The American states signatory to the present Convention,

Reaffirming their intention to consolidate in this hemisphere, within the framework of democratic institutions, a system of personal liberty and social justice based on respect for the essential rights of man;

Recognizing that the essential rights of man are not derived from one's being a national of a certain state, but are based upon attributes of the human personality, and that they therefore justify international protection in the form of a convention reinforcing or complementing the protection provided by the domestic law of the American states;

Considering that these principles have been set forth in the Charter of the Organization of American States, in the American Declaration of the Rights and Duties of Man, and in the Universal Declaration of Human Rights, and that they have been reaffirmed and refined in other international instruments, worldwide as well as regional in scope;

Reiterating that, in accordance with the Universal Declaration of Human Rights, the ideal of free men enjoying freedom from fear and want can be achieved only if conditions are created whereby everyone may enjoy his economic, social, and cultural rights, as well as his civil and political rights; and

Considering that the Third Special Inter-American Conference (Buenos Aires, 1967) approved the incorporation into the Charter of the Organization itself of broad standards with respect to economic, social, and educational rights and resolved that an inter-American convention on human rights should determine the structure, competence, and procedure of the organs responsible for these matters,

Have agreed upon the following:

PART I – STATE OBLIGATIONS AND RIGHTS PROTECTED

Chapter I – General Obligations

Article 1. Obligation to Respect Rights

1. The States Parties to this Convention undertake to respect the rights and freedoms recognized herein and to ensure to all persons subject to their jurisdiction the free and full exercise of those rights and freedoms, without any discrimination for reasons of race, color, sex, language, religion, political or other opinion, national or social origin, economic status, birth, or any other social condition.
2. For the purposes of this Convention, 'person' means every human being.

Article 2. Domestic Legal Effects

Where the exercise of any of the rights or freedoms referred to in Article 1 is not already ensured by legislative or other provisions, the States Parties undertake to adopt, in accordance with their constitutional processes and the provisions of this Convention, such legislative or other measures as may be necessary to give effect to those rights or freedoms.

Chapter II – Civil and Political Rights

Article 3. Right to Juridical Personality

Every person has the right to recognition as a person before the law.

Article 4. Right to Life

1. Every person has the right to have his life respected. This right shall be protected by law and, in general, from the moment of conception. No one shall be arbitrarily deprived of his life.

2. In countries that have not abolished the death penalty, it may be imposed only for the most serious crimes and pursuant to a final judgment rendered by a competent court and in accordance with a law establishing such punishment, enacted prior to the commission of the crime. The application of such punishment shall not be extended to crimes to which it does not presently apply.

3. The death penalty shall not be re-established in states that have abolished it.

4. In no case shall capital punishment be inflicted for political offenses or related common crimes.

5. Capital punishment shall not be imposed upon persons who, at the time the crime was committed, were under 18 years of age or over 70 years of age; nor shall it be applied to pregnant women.

6. Every person condemned to death shall have the right to apply for amnesty, pardon, or commutation of sentence, which may be granted in all cases. Capital punishment shall not be imposed while such a petition is pending decision by the competent authority.

Article 5. Right to Humane Treatment

1. Every person has the right to have his physical, mental, and moral integrity respected.

2. No one shall be subjected to torture or to cruel, inhuman, or degrading punishment or treatment. All persons deprived of their liberty shall be treated with respect for the inherent dignity of the human person.

3. Punishment shall not be extended to any person other than the criminal.

4. Accused persons shall, save in exceptional circumstances, be segregated from convicted persons, and shall be subject to separate treatment appropriate to their status as unconvicted persons.

5. Minors while subject to criminal proceedings shall be separated from adults and brought before specialized tribunals, as speedily as possible, so that they may be treated in accordance with their status as minors.

6. Punishments consisting of deprivation of liberty shall have as an essential aim the reform and social readaptation of the prisoners.

Article 6. Freedom from Slavery

1. No one shall be subject to slavery or to involuntary servitude, which are prohibited in all their forms, as are the slave trade and traffic in women.

2. No one shall be required to perform forced or compulsory labor. This provision shall not be interpreted to mean that, in those countries in which the penalty established for certain crimes is deprivation of liberty at forced labor, the carrying out of such a sentence imposed by a competent court is prohibited. Forced labor shall not adversely affect the dignity or the physical or intellectual capacity of the prisoner.

3. For the purposes of this article, the following do not constitute forced or compulsory labor:

(a) work or service normally required of a person imprisoned in execution of sentence or formal decision passed by the competent judicial authority. Such work or service shall be carried out under the supervision and control of public authorities, and any persons performing such work or service shall not be placed at the disposal of any private party, company, or juridical person;

(b) military service and, in countries in which conscientious objectors are recognized, national service that the law may provide for in lieu of military service;

(c) service exacted in time of danger or calamity that threatens the existence or the well-being of the community; or

(d) work or service that forms part of normal civic obligations.

Article 7. Right to Personal Liberty

1. Every person has the right to personal liberty and security.

2. No one shall be deprived of his physical liberty except for the reasons and under the conditions established beforehand by the constitution of the State Party concerned or by a law established pursuant thereto.

3. No one shall be subject to arbitrary arrest or imprisonment.

4. Anyone who is detained shall be informed of the reasons for his detention and shall be promptly notified of the charge or charges against him.

5. Any person detained shall be brought promptly before a judge or other officer authorized by law to exercise judicial power and shall be entitled to trial within a reasonable time or to be released without prejudice to the continuation of the proceedings. His release may be subject to guarantees to assure his appearance for trial.

6. Anyone who is deprived of his liberty shall be entitled to recourse to a competent court, in order that the court may decide without delay on the lawfulness of his arrest or detention and order his release if the arrest or detention is unlawful. In States Parties whose laws provide that anyone who believes himself to be threatened with deprivation of his liberty is entitled to recourse to a competent court in order that it may decide on the lawfulness of such threat, this remedy may not be restricted or abolished. The interested party or another person in his behalf is entitled to seek these remedies.

7. No one shall be detained for debt. This principle shall not limit the orders of a competent judicial authority issued for nonfulfilment of duties of support.

Article 8. *Right to a Fair Trial*

1. Every person has the right to a hearing, with due guarantees and within a reasonable time, by a competent, independent, and impartial tribunal, previously established by law, in the substantiation of any accusation of a criminal nature made against him or for the determination of his rights and obligations of a civil, labor, fiscal, or any other nature.

2. Every person accused of a criminal offense has the right to be presumed innocent so long as his guilt has not been proven according to law. During the proceedings, every person is entitled, with full equality, to the following minimum guarantees:

(a) the right of the accused to be assisted without charge by a translator or interpreter, if he does not understand or does not speak the language of the tribunal or court;

(b) prior notification in detail to the accused of the charges against him;

(c) adequate time and means for the preparation of his defense;

(d) the right of the accused to defend himself personally or to be assisted by legal counsel of his own choosing, and to communicate freely and privately with his counsel;

(e) the inalienable right to be assisted by counsel provided by the state, paid or not as the domestic law provides, if the accused does not defend himself personally or engage his own counsel within the time period established by law;

(f) the right of the defense to examine witnesses present in the court and to obtain the appearance, as witnesses, of experts or other persons who may throw light on the facts;

(g) the right not to be compelled to be a witness against himself or to plead guilty; and

(h) the right to appeal the judgment to a higher court.

3. A confession of guilt by the accused shall be valid only if it is made without coercion of any kind.

4. An accused person acquitted by a nonappealable judgment shall not be subjected to a new trial for the same cause.

5. Criminal proceedings shall be public, except insofar as may be necessary to protect the interests of justice.

Article 9. *Freedom from* Ex Post Facto *Laws*

No one shall be convicted of any act or omission that did not constitute a criminal offense, under the applicable law, at the time it was committed. A heavier penalty shall not be imposed than the one that was applicable at the time the criminal offense was committed. If subsequent to the commission of the offense the law provides for the imposition of a lighter punishment, the guilty person shall benefit therefrom.

Article 10. *Right to Compensation*

Every person has the right to be compensated in accordance with the law in the event he has been sentenced by a final judgment through a miscarriage of justice.

Article 11. Right to Privacy

1. Everyone has the right to have his honor respected and his dignity recognized.
2. No one may be the object of arbitrary or abusive interference with his private life, his family, his home, or his correspondence, or of unlawful attacks on his honor or reputation.
3. Everyone has the right to the protection of the law against such interference or attacks.

Article 12. Freedom of Conscience and Religion

1. Everyone has the right to freedom of conscience and of religion. This right includes freedom to maintain or to change one's religion or beliefs, and freedom to profess or disseminate one's religion or beliefs, either individually or together with others, in public or in private.
2. No one shall be subject to restrictions that might impair his freedom to maintain or to change his religion or beliefs.
3. Freedom to manifest one's religion and beliefs may be subject only to the limitations prescribed by law that are necessary to protect public safety, order, health, or morals, or the rights or freedoms of others.
4. Parents or guardians, as the case may be, have the right to provide for the religious and moral education of their children or wards that is in accord with their own convictions.

Article 13. Freedom of Thought and Expression

1. Everyone has the right to freedom of thought and expression. This right includes freedom to seek, receive, and impart information and ideas of all kinds, regardless of frontiers, either orally, in writing, in print, in the form of art, or through any other medium of one's choice.
2. The exercise of the right provided for in the foregoing paragraph shall not be subject to prior censorship but shall be subject to subsequent imposition of liability, which shall be expressly established by law to the extent necessary to ensure:
    (a) respect for the rights or reputations of others; or
    (b) the protection of national security, public order, or public health or morals.
3. The right of expression may not be restricted by indirect methods or means, such as the abuse of government or private controls over newsprint, radio broadcasting frequencies, or equipment used in the dissemination of information, or by any other means tending to impede the communication and circulation of ideas and opinions.
4. Notwithstanding the provisions of paragraph 2 above, public entertainments may be subject by law to prior censorship for the sole purpose of regulating access to them for the moral protection of childhood and adolescence.
5. Any propaganda for war and any advocacy of national, racial, or religious hatred that constitute incitements to lawless violence or to any other similar action against any person or group of persons on any grounds including those of race, color, religion, language, or national origin shall be considered as offenses punishable by law.

Article 14. Right of Reply

1. Anyone injured by inaccurate or offensive statements or ideas disseminated to the public in general by a legally regulated medium of communication has the right to reply or to make a correction using the same communications outlet, under such conditions as the law may establish.
2. The correction or reply shall not in any case remit other legal liabilities that may have been incurred.
3. For the effective protection of honor and reputation, every publisher, and every newspaper, motion picture, radio, and television company, shall have a person responsible who is not protected by immunities or special privileges.

Article 15. Right of Assembly

The right of peaceful assembly, without arms, is recognized. No restrictions may be placed on the exercise of this right other than those imposed in conformity with the law and necessary in a democratic society in the interest of national security, public safety or public order, or to protect public health or morals or the rights or freedom of others.

Article 16. Freedom of Association

1. Everyone has the right to associate freely for ideological, religious, political, economic, labor, social, cultural, sports, or other purposes.
2. The exercise of this right shall be subject only to such restrictions established by law as may be necessary in a democratic society, in the interest of national security, public safety or public order, or to protect public health or morals or the rights and freedoms of others.
3. The provisions of this article do not bar the imposition of legal restrictions, including even deprivation of the exercise of the right of association, on members of the armed forces and the police.

Article 17. Rights of the Family

1. The family is the natural and fundamental group unit of society and is entitled to protection by society and the state.
2. The right of men and women of marriageable age to marry and to raise a family shall be recognized, if they meet the conditions required by domestic laws, insofar as such conditions do not affect the principle of nondiscrimination established in this Convention.
3. No marriage shall be entered into without the free and full consent of the intending spouses.
4. The States Parties shall take appropriate steps to ensure the equality of rights and the adequate balancing of responsibilities of the spouses as to marriage, during marriage, and in the event of its dissolution. In case of dissolution, provision shall be made for the necessary protection of any children solely on the basis of their own best interests.
5. The law shall recognize equal rights for children born out of wedlock and those born in wedlock.

Article 18. Right to a Name

Every person has the right to a given name and to the surnames of his parents or that of one of them. The law shall regulate the manner in which this right shall be ensured for all, by the use of assumed names if necessary.

Article 19. Rights of the Child

Every minor child has the right to the measures of protection required by his condition as a minor on the part of his family, society, and the state.

Article 20. Right to Nationality

1. Every person has the right to a nationality.
2. Every person has the right to the nationality of the state in whose territory he was born if he does not have the right to any other nationality.
3. No one shall be arbitrarily deprived of his nationality or of the right to change it.

Article 21. Right to Property

1. Everyone has the right to the use and enjoyment of his property. The law may subordinate such use and enjoyment to the interest of society.
2. No one shall be deprived of his property except upon payment of just compensation, for reasons of public utility or social interest, and in the cases and according to the forms established by law.
3. Usury and any other form of exploitation of man by man shall be prohibited by law.

Article 22. Freedom of Movement and Residence

1. Every person lawfully in the territory of a State Party has the right to move about in it, and to reside in it subject to the provisions of the law.

2. Every person has the right to leave any country freely, including his own.

3. The exercise of the foregoing rights may be restricted only pursuant to a law to the extent necessary in a democratic society to prevent crime or to protect national security, public safety, public order, public morals, public health, or the rights or freedoms of others.

4. The exercise of the rights recognized in paragraph 1 may also be restricted by law in designated zones for reasons of public interest.

5. No one can be expelled from the territory of the state of which he is a national or be deprived of the right to enter it.

6. An alien lawfully in the territory of a State Party to this Convention may be expelled from it only pursuant to a decision reached in accordance with law.

7. Every person has the right to seek and be granted asylum in a foreign territory, in accordance with the legislation of the state and international conventions, in the event he is being pursued for political offenses or related common crimes.

8. In no case may an alien be deported or returned to a country, regardless of whether or not it is his country of origin, if in that country his right to life or personal freedom is in danger of being violated because of his race, nationality, religion, social status, or political opinions.

9. The collective expulsion of aliens is prohibited.

Article 23. Right to Participate in Government

1. Every citizen shall enjoy the following rights and opportunities:
    (a) to take part in the conduct of public affairs, directly or through freely chosen representatives;
    (b) to vote and to be elected in genuine periodic elections, which shall be by universal and equal suffrage and by secret ballot that guarantees the free expression of the will of the voters; and
    (c) to have access, under general conditions of equality, to the public service of his country.

2. The law may regulate the exercise of the rights and opportunities referred to in the preceding paragraph only on the basis of age, nationality, residence, language, education, civil and mental capacity, or sentencing by a competent court in criminal proceedings.

Article 24. Right to Equal Protection

All persons are equal before the law. Consequently, they are entitled, without discrimination, to equal protection of the law.

Article 25. Right to Judicial Protection

1. Everyone has the right to simple and prompt recourse, or any other effective recourse, to a competent court or tribunal for protection against acts that violate his fundamental rights recognized by the constitution or laws of the state concerned or by this Convention, even though such violation may have been committed by persons acting in the course of their official duties.

2. The States Parties undertake:
    (a) to ensure that any person claiming such remedy shall have his rights determined by the competent authority provided for by the legal system of the state;
    (b) to develop the possibilities of judicial remedy; and
    (c) to ensure that the competent authorities shall enforce such remedies when granted.

Chapter III – Economic, Social, and Cultural Rights

Article 26. Progressive Development

The States Parties undertake to adopt measures, both internally and through international co-operation, especially those of an economic and technical nature, with a view to achieving progressively, by legislation or other appropriate means, the full realization of the rights implicit in the economic, social, educational, scientific, and cultural standards set forth in the Charter of the Organization of American States as amended by the Protocol of Buenos Aires.

Chapter IV – Suspension of Guarantees, Interpretation, and Application

Article 27. Suspension of Guarantees

1. In time of war, public danger, or other emergency that threatens the independence or security of a State Party, it may take measures derogating from its obligations under the present Convention to the extent and for the period of time strictly required by the exigencies of the situation, provided that such measures are not inconsistent with its other obligations under international law and do not involve discrimination on the ground of race, color, sex, language, religion, or social origin.
2. The foregoing provision does not authorize any suspension of the following articles: Article 3 (Right to Juridical Personality), Article 4 (Right to Life), Article 5 (Right to Humane Treatment), Article 6 (Freedom from Slavery), Article 9 (Freedom from *Ex Post Facto* Laws), Article 12 (Freedom of Conscience and Religion), Article 17 (Rights of the Family), Article 18 (Right to a Name), Article 19 (Rights of the Child), Article 20 (Right to Nationality), and Article 23 (Right to Participate in Government), or of the judicial guarantees essential for the protection of such rights.
3. Any State Party availing itself of the right of suspension shall immediately inform the other States Parties, through the Secretary General of the Organization of American States, of the provisions the application of which it has suspended, the reasons that gave rise to the suspension, and the date set for the termination of such suspension.

Article 28. Federal Clause

1. Where a State Party is constituted as a federal state, the national government of such State Party shall implement all the provisions of the Convention over whose subject matter it exercises legislative and judicial jurisdiction.
2. With respect to the provisions over whose subject matter the constituent units of the federal state have jurisdiction, the national government shall immediately take suitable measures, in accordance with its constitution and its laws, to the end that the competent authorities of the constituent units may adopt appropriate provisions for the fulfilment of this Convention.
3. Whenever two or more States Parties agree to form a federation or other type of association, they shall take care that the resulting federal or other compact contains the provisions necessary for continuing and rendering effective the standards of this Convention in the new state that is organized.

Article 29. Restrictions Regarding Interpretation

No provision of this Convention shall be interpreted as:
(a) permitting any State Party, group, or person to suppress the enjoyment or exercise of the rights and freedoms recognized in this Convention or to restrict them to a greater extent than is provided for herein;
(b) restricting the enjoyment or exercise of any right or freedom recognized by virtue of the laws of any State Party or by virtue of another convention to which one of the said states is a party;
(c) precluding other rights or guarantees that are inherent in the human personality or derived from representative democracy as a form of government; or
(d) excluding or limiting the effect that the American Declaration of the Rights and Duties of Man and other international acts of the same nature may have.

Article 30. Scope of Restrictions

The restrictions that, pursuant to this Convention, may be placed on the enjoyment or exercise of the rights or freedoms recognized herein may not be applied except in accordance with laws enacted for reasons of general interest and in accordance with the purpose for which such restrictions have been established.

Article 31. Recognition of Other Rights

Other rights and freedoms recognized in accordance with the procedures established in Articles 76 and 77 may be included in the system of protection of this Convention.

Chapter V – Personal Responsibilities

Article 32. Relationship between Duties and Rights

1. Every person has reponsibilities to his family, his community, and mankind.
2. The rights of each person are limited by the rights of others, by the security of all, and by the just demands of the general welfare, in a democratic society.

PART II – MEANS OF PROTECTION

Chapter VI – Competent Organs

Article 33

The following organs shall have competence with respect to matters relating to the fulfilment of the commitments made by the States Parties to this Convention:
(a) the Inter-American Commission on Human Rights, referred to as 'The Commission'; and
(b) the Inter-American Court of Human Rights, referred to as 'The Court'.

Chapter VII – Inter-American Commission on Human Rights

Section 1. Organization

Article 34

The Inter-American Commission on Human Rights shall be composed of seven members, who shall be persons of high moral character and recognized competence in the field of human rights.

Article 35

The Commission shall represent all the member countries of the Organization of American States.

Article 36

1. The members of the Commission shall be elected in a personal capacity by the General Assembly of the Organization from a list of candidates proposed by the governments of the member states.
2. Each of those governments may propose up to three candidates, who may be nationals of the states proposing them or of any other member state of the Organization of American States. When a slate of three is proposed, at least one of the candidates shall be a national of a state other than the one proposing the slate.

Article 37

1. The members of the Commission shall be elected for a term of four years and may be re-elected only once, but the terms of three of the members chosen in the first election shall expire at the end of two years. Immediately following that election the General Assembly shall determine the names of those three members by lot.
2. No two nationals of the same state may be members of the Commission.

Article 38

Vacancies that may occur on the Commission for reasons other than the normal expiration of a term shall be filled by the Permanent Council of the Organization in accordance with the provisions of the Statute of the Commission.

Article 39

The Commission shall prepare its Statute, which it shall submit to the General Assembly for approval. It shall establish its own Regulations.

Article 40

Secretariat services for the Commission shall be furnished by the appropriate specialized unit of the General Secretariat of the Organization. This unit shall be provided with the resources required to accomplish the tasks assigned to it by the Commission.

Section 2. Functions

Article 41

The main function of the Commission shall be to promote respect for and defense of human rights. In the exercise of its mandate, it shall have the following functions and powers:

(a) to develop an awareness of human rights among the peoples of America;

(b) to make recommendations to the governments of the member states, when it considers such action advisable, for the adoption of progressive measures in favor of human rights within the framework of their domestic law and constitutional provisions as well as appropriate measures to further the observance of those rights;

(c) to prepare such studies or reports as it considers advisable in the performance of its duties;

(d) to request the governments of the member states to supply it with information on the measures adopted by them in matters of human rights;

(e) to respond, through the General Secretariat of the Organization of American States, to inquiries made by the member states on matters related to human rights and, within the limits of its possibilities, to provide those states with the advisory services they request;

(f) to take action on petitions and other communications pursuant to its authority under the provisions of Articles 44 through 51 of this Convention; and

(g) to submit an annual report to the General Assembly of the Organization of American States.

Article 42

The States Parties shall transmit to the Commission a copy of each of the reports and studies that they submit annually to the Executive Committees of the Inter-American Economic and Social Council and the Inter-American Council for Education, Science, and Culture, in their respective fields, so that the Commission may watch over the promotion of the rights implicit in the economic, social, educational, scientific, and cultural standards set forth in the Charter of the Organization of American States as amended by the Protocol of Buenos Aires.

Article 43

The States Parties undertake to provide the Commission with such information as it may request of them as to the manner in which their domestic law ensures the effective application of any provisions of this Convention.

Section 3. Competence

Article 44

Any person or group of persons, or any nongovernmental entity legally recognized in one or more member states of the Organization, may lodge petitions with the Commission containing denunciations or complaints of violation of this Convention by a State Party.

Article 45

1. Any State Party may, when it deposits its instrument of ratification of or adherence to this Convention, or at any later time, declare that it recognizes the competence of the Commission to receive and examine communications in which a State Party alleges that another State Party has committed a violation of a human right set forth in this Convention.
2. Communications presented by virtue of this article may be admitted and examined only if they are presented by a State Party that has made a declaration recognizing the aforementioned competence of the Commission. The Commission shall not admit any communication against a State Party that has not made such a declaration.
3. A declaration concerning recognition of competence may be made to be valid for an indefinite time, for a specified period, or for a specific case.
4. Declarations shall be deposited with the General Secretariat of the Organization of American States, which shall transmit copies thereof to the member states of that Organization.

Article 46

1. Admission by the Commission of a petition or communication lodged in accordance with Articles 44 or 45 shall be subject to the following requirements:
   (a) that the remedies under domestic law have been pursued and exhausted in accordance with generally recognized principles of international law;
   (b) that the petition or communication is lodged within a period of six months from the date on which the party alleging violation of his rights was notified of the final judgment;
   (c) that the subject of the petition or communication is not pending in another international proceeding for settlement; and
   (d) that, in the case of Article 44, the petition contains the name, nationality, profession, domicile, and signature of the person or persons or of the legal representative of the entity lodging the petition.
2. The provisions of paragraphs 1.a and 1.b of this article shall not be applicable when:
   (a) the domestic legislation of the state concerned does not afford due process of law for the protection of the right or rights that have allegedly been violated;
   (b) the party alleging violation of his rights has been denied access to the remedies under domestic law or has been prevented from exhausting them or
   (c) there has been unwarranted delay in rendering a final judgment under the aforementioned remedies.

Article 47

The Commission shall consider inadmissible any petition or communication submitted under Articles 44 or 45 if:
   (a) any of the requirements indicated in Article 46 has not been met;
   (b) the petition or communication does not state facts that tend to establish a violation of the rights guaranteed by this Convention;
   (c) the statements of the petitioner or of the state indicate that the petition or communication is manifestly groundless or obviously out of order; or
   (d) the petition or communication is substantially the same as one previously studied by the Commission or by another international organization.

Section 4. Procedure

Article 48

1. When the Commission receives a petition or communication alleging violation of any of the rights protected by this Convention, it shall proceed as follows:

(a) If it considers the petition or communication admissible, it shall request information from the government of the state indicated as being responsible for the alleged violations and shall furnish that government a transcript of the pertinent portions of the petition or communication. This information shall be submitted within a reasonable period to be determined by the Commission in accordance with the circumstances of each case.

(b) After the information has been received, or after the period established has elapsed and the information has not been received, the Commission shall ascertain whether the grounds for the petition or communication still exist. If they do not, the Commission shall order the record to be closed.

(c) The Commision may also declare the petition or communication inadmissible or out of order on the basis of information or evidence subsequently received.

(d) If the record has not been closed, the Commission shall, with the knowledge of the parties, examine the matter set forth in the petition or communication in order to verify the facts. If necessary and advisable, the Commission shall carry out an investigation, for the effective conduct of which it shall request, and the states concerned shall furnish to it, all necessary facilities.

(e) The Commission may request the states concerned to furnish any pertinent information and, if so requested, shall hear oral statements or receive written statements from the parties concerned.

(f) The Commission shall place itself at the disposal of the parties concerned with a view to reaching a friendly settlement of the matter on the basis of respect for the human rights recognized in this Convention.

2. However, in serious and urgent cases, only the presentation of a petition or communication that fulfils all the formal requirements of admissibility shall be necessary in order for the Commission to conduct an investigation with the prior consent of the state in whose territory a violation has allegedly been committed.

Article 49

If a friendly settlement has been reached in accordance with paragraph 1.f of Article 48, the Commission shall draw up a report, which shall be transmitted to the petitioner and to the States Parties to this Convention, and shall then be communicated to the Secretary General of the Organization of American States for publication. This report shall contain a brief statement of the facts and of the solution reached. If any party in the case so requests, the fullest possible information shall be provided to it.

Article 50

1. If a settlement is not reached, the Commission shall, within the time limit established by its Statute, draw up a report setting forth the facts and stating its conclusions. If the report, in whole or in part, does not represent the unanimous agreement of the members of the Commission, any member may attach to it a separate opinion. The written and oral statements made by the parties in accordance with paragraph 1.e of Article 48 shall also be attached to the report.

2. The report shall be transmitted to the states concerned, which shall not be at liberty to publish it.

3. In transmitting the report, the Commission may make such proposals and recommendations as it sees fit.

Article 51

1. If, within a period of three months from the date of the transmittal of the report of the Commission to the states concerned, the matter has not either been settled or submitted

172

by the Commission or by the state concerned to the Court and its jurisdiction accepted, the Commission may, by the vote of an absolute majority of its members, set forth its opinion and conclusions concerning the question submitted for its consideration.

2. Where appropriate, the Commission shall make pertinent recommendations and shall prescribe a period within which the state is to take the measures that are incumbent upon it to remedy the situation examined.

3. When the prescribed period has expired, the Commission shall decide by the vote of an absolute majority of its members whether the state has taken adequate measures and whether to publish its report.

Chapter VIII – Inter-American Court of Human Rights

Section 1. Organization

Article 52

1. The Court shall consist of seven judges, nationals of the member states of the Organization, elected in an individual capacity from among jurists of the highest moral authority and of recognized competence in the field of human rights, who possess the qualifications required for the exercise of the highest judicial functions in conformity with the law of the state of which they are nationals or of the state that proposes them as candidates.

2. No two judges may be nationals of the same state.

Article 53

1. The judges of the Court shall be elected by secret ballot by an absolute majority vote of the States Parties to the Convention, in the General Assembly of the Organization, from a panel of candidates proposed by those states.

2. Each of the States Parties may propose up to three candidates, nationals of the state that proposes them or of any other member state of the Organization of American States. When a slate of three is proposed, at least one of the candidates shall be a national of a state other than the one proposing the slate.

Article 54

1. The judges of the Court shall be elected for a term of six years and may be re-elected only once. The term of three of the judges chosen in the first election shall expire at the end of three years. Immediately after the election, the names of the three judges shall be determined by lot in the General Assembly.

2. A judge elected to replace a judge whose term has not expired shall complete the term of the latter.

3. The judges shall continue in office until the expiration of their term. However, they shall continue to serve with regard to cases that they have begun to hear and that are still pending, for which purposes they shall not be replaced by the newly elected judges.

Article 55

1. If a judge is a national of any of the States Parties to a case submitted to the Court, he shall retain his right to hear that case.

2. If one of the judges called upon to hear a case should be a national of one of the States Parties to the case, any other State Party in the case may appoint a person of its choice to serve on the Court as an *ad hoc* judge.

3. If among the judges called upon to hear a case none is a national of any of the States Parties to the case, each of the latter may appoint an *ad hoc* judge.

4. An *ad hoc* judge shall possess the qualifications indicated in Article 52.

5. If several States Parties to the Convention should have the same interest in a case, they shall be considered as a single party for purposes of the above provisions. In case of doubt, the Court shall decide.

Article 56

Five judges shall constitute a quorum for the transaction of business by the Court.

Article 57

The Commission shall appear in all cases before the Court.

Article 58

1. The Court shall have its seat at the place determined by the States Parties to the Convention in the General Assembly of the Organization; however, it may convene in the territory of any member state of the Organization of American States when a majority of the Court considers it desirable, and with the prior consent of the state concerned. The seat of the Court may be changed by the States Parties to the Convention in the General Assembly by a two-thirds vote.
2. The Court shall appoint its own Secretary.
3. The Secretary shall have his office at the place where the Court has its seat and shall attend the meetings that the Court may hold away from its seat.

Article 59

The Court shall establish its Secretariat, which shall function under the direction of the Secretary of the Court, in accordance with the administrative standards of the General Secretariat of the Organization in all respects not incompatible with the independence of the Court. The staff of the Court's Secretariat shall be appointed by the Secretary General of the Organization, in consultation with the Secretary of the Court.

Article 60

The Court shall draw up its Statute which it shall submit to the General Assembly for approval. It shall adopt its own Rules of Procedure.

Section 2. Jurisdiction and Functions

Article 61

1. Only the States Parties and the Commission shall have the right to submit a case to the Court.
2. In order for the Court to hear a case, it is necessary that the procedures set forth in Articles 48 and 50 shall have been completed.

Article 62

1. A State Party may, upon depositing its instrument of ratification or adherence to this Convention, or at any subsequent time, declare that it recognizes as binding, *ipso facto*, and not requiring special agreement, the jurisdiction of the Court on all matters relating to the interpretation or application of this Convention.
2. Such declaration may be made unconditionally, on the condition of reciprocity, for a specified period, or for specific cases. It shall be presented to the Secretary General of the Organization, who shall transmit copies thereof to the other member states of the Organization and to the Secretary of the Court.
3. The jurisdiction of the Court shall comprise all cases concerning the interpretation and application of the provisions of this Convention that are submitted to it, provided that the States Parties to the case recognize or have recognized such jurisdiction, whether by special declaration pursuant to the preceding paragraphs, or by a special agreement.

Article 63

1. If the Court finds that there has been a violation of a right or freedom protected by this Convention, the Court shall rule that the injured party be ensured the enjoyment of his

right or freedom that was violated. It shall also rule, if appropriate, that the consequences of the measure or situation that constituted the breach of such right or freedom be remedied and that fair compensation be paid to the injured party.

2. In cases of extreme gravity and urgency, and when necessary to avoid irreparable damage to persons, the Court shall adopt such provisional measures as it deems pertinent in matters it has under consideration. With respect to a case not yet submitted to the Court, it may act at the request of the Commission.

Article 64

1. The member states of the Organization may consult the Court regarding the interpretation of this Convention or of other treaties concerning the protection of human rights in the American states. Within their spheres of competence, the organs listed in Chapter X of the Charter of the Organization of American States, as amended by the Protocol of Buenos Aires, may in like manner consult the Court.

2. The Court, at the request of a member state of the Organization, may provide that state with opinions regarding the compatibility of any of its domestic laws with the aforesaid international instruments.

Article 65

To each regular session of the General Assembly of the Organization of American States the Court shall submit, for the Assembly's consideration, a report on its work during the previous year. It shall specify, in particular, the cases in which a state has not complied with its judgments, making any pertinent recommendations.

Section 3. Procedure

Article 66

1. Reasons shall be given for the judgment of the Court.

2. If the judgment does not represent in whole or in part the unanimous opinion of the judges, any judge shall be entitled to have his dissenting or separate opinion attached to the judgment.

Article 67

The judgment of the Court shall be final and not subject to appeal. In case of disagreement as to the meaning or scope of the judgment, the Court shall interpret it at the request of any of the parties, provided the request is made within ninety days from the date of notification of the judgment.

Article 68

1. The States Parties to the Convention undertake to comply with the judgment of the Court in any case to which they are parties.

2. That part of a judgment that stipulates compensatory damages may be executed in the country concerned in accordance with domestic procedure governing the execution of judgments against the state.

Article 69

The parties to the case shall be notified of the judgment of the Court and it shall be transmitted to the States Parties to the Convention.

Chapter IX – Common Provisions

Article 70

1. The judges of the Court and the members of the Commission shall enjoy, from the moment of their election and throughout their term of office, the immunities extended to

diplomatic agents in accordance with international law. During the exercise of their official function they shall, in addition, enjoy the diplomatic privileges necessary for the performance of their duties.

2. At no time shall the judges of the Court or the members of the Commission be held liable for any decisions or opinions issued in the exercise of their functions.

Article 71

The position of judge of the Court or member of the Commission is incompatible with any other activity that might affect the independence or impartiality of such judge or member, as determined in the respective statutes.

Article 72

The judges of the Court and the members of the Commission shall receive emoluments and travel allowances in the form and under the conditions set forth in their statutes, with due regard for the importance and independence of their office. Such emoluments and travel allowances shall be determined in the budget of the Organization of American States, which shall also include the expenses of the Court and its Secretariat. To this end, the Court shall draw up its own budget and submit it for approval to the General Assembly through the General Secretariat. The latter may not introduce any changes in it.

Article 73

The General Assembly may, only at the request of the Commission or the Court, as the case may be, determine sanctions to be applied against members of the Commission or judges of the Court when there are justifiable grounds for such action as set forth in the respective statutes. A vote of a two-thirds majority of the member states of the Organization shall be required for a decision in the case of members of the Commission and, in the case of judges of the Court, a two-thirds majority vote of the States Parties to the Convention shall also be required.

PART III – GENERAL AND TRANSITORY PROVISIONS
Chapter X – Signature, Ratification, Reservations, Amendments, Protocols, and Denunciation

Article 74

1. This Convention shall be open for signature and ratification by or adherence of any member state of the Organization of American States.

2. Ratification of or adherence to this Convention shall be made by the deposit of an instrument of ratification or adherence with the General Secretariat of the Organization of American States. As soon as eleven states have deposited their instruments of ratification or adherence, the Convention shall enter into force. With respect to any state that ratifies or adheres thereafter, the Convention shall enter into force on the date of the deposit of its instrument of ratification or adherence.

3. The Secretary General shall inform all member states of the Organization of the entry into force of the Convention.

Article 75

This Convention shall be subject to reservations only in conformity with the provisions of the Vienna Convention on the Law of Treaties signed on May 23, 1969.

Article 76

1. Proposals to amend this Convention may be submitted to the General Assembly for the action it deems appropriate by any State Party directly, and by the Commission or the Court through the Secretary General.

2. Amendments shall enter into force for the States ratifying them on the date when two-thirds of the States Parties to this Convention have deposited their respective instruments of ratification. With respect to the other States Parties, the amendments shall enter into force on the dates on which they deposit their respective instruments of ratification.

Article 77

1. In accordance with Article 31, any State Party and the Commission may submit proposed protocols to this Convention for consideration by the States Parties at the General Assembly with a view to gradually including other rights and freedoms within its system of protection.
2. Each protocol shall determine the manner of its entry into force and shall be applied only among the States Parties to it.

Article 78

1. The States Parties may denounce this Convention at the expiration of a five-year period from the date of its entry into force and by means of notice given one year in advance. Notice of the denunciation shall be addressed to the Secretary General of the Organization, who shall inform the other States Parties.
2. Such a denunciation shall not have the effect of releasing the State Party concerned from the obligations contained in this Convention with respect to any act that may constitute a violation of those obligations and that has been taken by that state prior to the effective date of denunciation.

Chapter XI – Transitory Provisions

Section 1. Inter-American Commission on Human Rights

Article 79

Upon the entry into force of this Convention, the Secretary General shall, in writing, request each member state of the Organization to present, within ninety days, its candidates for membership on the Inter-American Commission on Human Rights. The Secretary General shall prepare a list in alphabetical order of the candidates presented, and transmit it to the member states of the Organization at least thirty days prior to the next session of the General Assembly.

Article 80

The members of the Commission shall be elected by secret ballot of the General Assembly from the list of candidates referred to in Article 79. The candidates who obtain the largest number of votes and an absolute majority of the votes of the representatives of the member states shall be declared elected. Should it become necessary to have several ballots in order to elect all the members of the Commission, the candidates who receive the smallest number of votes shall be eliminated successively, in the manner determined by the General Assembly.

Section 2. Inter-American Court of Human Rights

Article 81

Upon the entry into force of this Convention, the Secretary General shall, in writing, request each State Party to present, within ninety days, its candidates for membership on the Inter-American Court of Human Rights. The Secretary General shall prepare a list in alphabetical order of the candidates presented and transmit it to the States Parties at least thirty days prior to the next session of the General Assembly.

Article 82

The judges of the Court shall be elected from the list of candidates referred to in Article 81, by secret ballot of the States Parties to the Convention in the General Assembly. The candidates who obtain the largest number of votes and an absolute majority of the votes of the representatives of the States Parties shall be declared elected. Should it become necessary to have several ballots in order to elect all the judges of the Court, the candidates who receive the smallest number of votes shall be eliminated successively, in the manner determined by the States Parties.

2.11: Additional Protocol to the American Convention on Human Rights in the Area of Economic, Social and Cultural Rights

'Protocol of San Salvador', O.A.S. Treaty Series No. 69 (1988), signed November 17, 1988.

PREAMBLE

The States Parties to the American Convention on Human Rights 'Pact San Jos, Costa Rica,',

Reaffirming their intention to consolidate in this hemisphere, within the framework of democratic institutions, a system of personal liberty and social justice based on respect for the essential rights of man;

Recognizing that the essential rights of man are not derived from one's being a national of a certain State, but are based upon attributes of the human person, for which reason they merit international protection in the form of a convention reinforcing or complementing the protection provided by the domestic law of the American States;

Considering the close relationship that exists between economic, social and cultural rights, and civil and political rights, in that the different categories of rights constitute an indivisible whole based on the recognition of the dignity of the human person, for which reason both require permanent protection and promotion if they are to be fully realized, and the violation of some rights in favor of the realization of others can never be justified;

Recognizing the benefits that stem from the promotion and development of cooperation among States and international relations;

Recalling that, in accordance with the Universal Declaration of Human Rights and the American Convention on Human Rights, the ideal of free human beings enjoying freedom from fear and want can only be achieved if conditions are created whereby everyone may enjoy his economic, social and cultural rights as well as his civil and political rights;

Bearing in mind that, although fundamental economic, social and cultural rights have been recognized in earlier international instruments of both world and regional scope, it is essential that those rights be reaffirmed, developed, perfected and protected in order to consolidate in America, on the basis of full respect for the rights of the individual, the democratic representative form of government as well as the right of its peoples to development, self-determination, and the free disposal of their wealth and natural resources; and

Considering that the American Convention on Human Rights provides that draft additional protocols to that Convention may be submitted for consideration to the States Parties, meeting together on the occasion of the General Assembly of the Organization of American States, for the purpose of gradually incorporating other rights and freedoms into the protective system thereof,

Have agreed upon the following Additional Protocol to the American Convention on Human Rights 'Protocol of San Salvador:'

Article 1 Obligation to Adopt Measures

The States Parties to this Additional Protocol to the American Convention on Human Rights undertake to adopt the necessary measures, both domestically and through international cooperation, especially economic and technical, to the extent allowed by their available resources, and taking into account their degree of development, for the purpose of achieving progressively and pursuant to their internal legislations, the full observance of the rights recognized in this Protocol.

Article 2 Obligation to Enact Domestic Legislation

If the exercise of the rights set forth in this Protocol is not already guaranteed by legislative or other provisions, the States Parties undertake to adopt, in accordance with their constitutional processes and the provisions of this Protocol, such legislative or other measures as may be necessary for making those rights a reality.

Article 3 Obligation of Nondiscrimination

The State Parties to this Protocol undertake to guarantee the exercise of the rights set forth herein without discrimination of any kind for reasons related to race, color, sex, language, religion, political or other opinions, national or social origin, economic status, birth or any other social condition.

Article 4 Inadmissibility of Restrictions

A right which is recognized or in effect in a State by virtue of its internal legislation or international conventions may not be restricted or curtailed on the pretext that this Protocol does not recognize the right or recognizes it to a lesser degree.

Article 5 Scope of Restrictions and Limitations

The State Parties may establish restrictions and limitations on the enjoyment and exercise of the rights established herein by means of laws promulgated for the purpose of preserving the general welfare in a democratic society only to the extent that they are not incompatible with the purpose and reason underlying those rights.

Article 6 Right to Work

1. Everyone has the right to work, which includes the opportunity to secure the means for living a dignified and decent existence by performing a freely elected or accepted lawful activity.
2. The State Parties undertake to adopt measures that will make the right to work fully effective, especially with regard to the achievement of full employment, vocational guidance, and the development of technical and vocational training projects, in particular those directed to the disabled. The States Parties also undertake to implement and strengthen programs that help to ensure suitable family care, so that women may enjoy a real opportunity to exercise the right to work.

Article 7 Just, Equitable, and Satisfactory Conditions of Work

The States Parties to this Protocol recognize that the right to work to which the foregoing article refers presupposes that everyone shall enjoy that right under just, equitable, and satisfactory conditions, which the States Parties undertake to guarantee in their internal legislation, particularly with respect to:

(a) Remuneration which guarantees, as a minimum, to all workers dignified and decent living conditions for them and their families and fair and equal wages for equal work, without distinction;

(b) The right of every worker to follow his vocation and to devote himself to the activity that best fulfils his expectations and to change employment in accordance with the pertinent national regulations;

(c) The right of every worker to promotion or upward mobility in his employment, for which purpose account shall be taken of his qualifications, competence, integrity and seniority;

(d) Stability of employment, subject to the nature of each industry and occupation and the causes for just separation. In cases of unjustified dismissal, the worker shall have the right to indemnity or to reinstatement on the job or any other benefits provided by domestic legislation;

(e) Safety and hygiene at work;

(f) The prohibition of night work or unhealthy or dangerous working conditions and, in general, of all work which jeopardizes health, safety, or morals, for persons under 18 years of age. As regards minors under the age of 16, the work day shall be subordinated to the provisions regarding compulsory education and in no case shall work constitute an impediment to school attendance or a limitation on benefiting from education received;

(g) A reasonable limitation of working hours, both daily and weekly. The days shall be shorter in the case of dangerous or unhealthy work or of night work;

(h) Rest, leisure and paid vacations as well as remuneration for national holidays.

Article 8 Trade Union Rights

1. The States Parties shall ensure:

(a) The right of workers to organize trade unions and to join the union of their choice for the purpose of protecting and promoting their interests. As an extension of that right, the States Parties shall permit trade unions to establish national federations or confederations, or to affiliate with those that already exist, as well as to form international trade union organizations and to affiliate with that of their choice. The States Parties shall also permit trade unions, federations and confederations to function freely;

(b) The right to strike.

2. The exercise of the rights set forth above may be subject only to restrictions established by law, provided that such restrictions are characteristic of a democratic society and necessary for safeguarding public order or for protecting public health or morals or the rights and freedoms of others. Members of the armed forces and the police and of other essential public services shall be subject to limitations and restrictions established by law.

3. No one may be compelled to belong to a trade union.

Article 9 Right to Social Security

1. Everyone shall have the right to social security protecting him from the consequences of old age and of disability which prevents him, physically or mentally, from securing the means for a dignified and decent existence. In the event of the death of a beneficiary, social security benefits shall be applied to his dependents.

2. In the case of persons who are employed, the right to social security shall cover at least medical care and an allowance or retirement benefit in the case of work accidents or occupational disease and, in the case of women, paid maternity leave before and after childbirth.

Article 10 Right to Health

1. Everyone shall have the right to health, understood to mean the enjoyment of the highest level of physical, mental and social well-being.

2. In order to ensure the exercise of the right to health, the States Parties agree to recognize health as a public good and, particularly, to adopt the following measures to ensure that right:

(a) Primary health care, that is, essential health care made available to all individuals and families in the community;

(b) Extension of the benefits of health services to all individuals subject to the State's jurisdiction;

(c) Universal immunization against the principal infectious diseases;

(d) Prevention and treatment of endemic, occupational and other diseases;

(e) Education of the population on the prevention and treatment of health problems, and

(f) Satisfaction of the health needs of the highest risk groups and of those whose poverty makes them the most vulnerable.

Article 11 Right to a Healthy Environment

1. Everyone shall have the right to live in a healthy environment and to have access to basic public services.

2. The States Parties shall promote the protection, preservation, and improvement of the environment.

Article 12 Right to Food

1. Everyone has the right to adequate nutrition which guarantees the possibility of enjoying the highest level of physical, emotional and intellectual development.
2. In order to promote the exercise of this right and eradicate malnutrition, the States Parties undertake to improve methods of production, supply and distribution of food, and to this end, agree to promote greater international cooperation in support of the relevant national policies.

Article 13 Right to Education

1. Everyone has the right to education.
2. The States Parties to this Protocol agree that education should be directed towards the full development of the human personality and human dignity and should strengthen respect for human rights, ideological pluralism, fundamental freedoms, justice and peace. They further agree that education ought to enable everyone to participate effectively in a democratic and pluralistic society and achieve a decent existence and should foster understanding, tolerance and friendship among all nations and all racial, ethnic or religious groups and promote activities for the maintenance of peace.
3. The States Parties to this Protocol recognize that in order to achieve the full exercise of the right to education:
(a) Primary education should be compulsory and accessible to all without cost;
(b) Secondary education in its different forms, including technical and vocational secondary education, should be made generally available and accessible to all by every appropriate means, and in particular, by the progressive introduction of free education;
(c) Higher education should be made equally accessible to all, on the basis of individual capacity, by every appropriate means, and in particular, by the progressive introduction of free education;
(d) Basic education should be encouraged or intensified as far as possible for those persons who have not received or completed the whole cycle of primary instruction;
(e) Programs of special education should be established for the handicapped, so as to provide special instruction and training to persons with physical disabilities or mental deficiencies.
4. In conformity with the domestic legislation of the States Parties, parents should have the right to select the type of education to be given to their children, provided that it conforms to the principles set forth above.
5. Nothing in this Protocol shall be interpreted as a restriction of the freedom of individuals and entities to establish and direct educational institutions in accordance with the domestic legislation of the States Parties.

Article 14 Right to the Benefits of Culture

1. The States Parties to this Protocol recognize the right of everyone:
(a) To take part in the cultural and artistic life of the community;
(b) To enjoy the benefits of scientific and technological progress;
(c) To benefit from the protection of moral and material interests deriving from any scientific, literary or artistic production of which he is the author.
2. The steps to be taken by the States Parties to this Protocol to ensure the full exercise of this right shall include those necessary for the conservation, development and dissemination of science, culture and art.
3. The States Parties to this Protocol undertake to respect the freedom indispensable for scientific research and creative activity.
4. The States Parties to this Protocol recognize the benefits to be derived from the encouragement and development of international cooperation and relations in the fields of science, arts and culture, and accordingly agree to foster greater international cooperation in these fields.

Article 15 Right to the Formation and the Protection of Families

1. The family is the natural and fundamental element of society and ought to be protected by the State, which should see to the improvement of its spiritual and material conditions.
2. Everyone has the right to form a family, which shall be exercised in accordance with the provisions of the pertinent domestic legislation.
3. The States Parties hereby undertake to accord adequate protection to the family unit and in particular:

(a) To provide special care and assistance to mothers during a reasonable period before and after childbirth;

(b) To guarantee adequate nutrition for children at the nursing stage and during school attendance years;

(c) To adopt special measures for the protection of adolescents in order to ensure the full development of their physical, intellectual and moral capacities;

(d) To undertake special programs of family training so as to help create a stable and positive environment in which children will receive and develop the values of understanding, solidarity, respect and responsibility.

Article 16 Rights of Children

Every child, whatever his parentage, has the right to the protection that his status as a minor requires from his family, society and the State. Every child has the right to grow under the protection and responsibility of his parents; save in exceptional, judicially-recognized circumstances, a child of young age ought not to be separated from his mother. Every child has the right to free and compulsory education, at least in the elementary phase, and to continue his training at higher levels of the educational system.

Article 17 Protection of the Elderly

Everyone has the right to special protection in old age. With this in view the States Parties agree to take progressively the necessary steps to make this right a reality and, particularly, to:

(a) Provide suitable facilities, as well as food and specialized medical care, for elderly individuals who lack them and are unable to provide them for themselves;

(b) Undertake work programs specifically designed to give the elderly the opportunity to engage in a productive activity suited to their abilities and consistent with their vocations or desires;

(c) Foster the establishment of social organizations aimed at improving the quality of life for the elderly.

Article 18 Protection of the Handicapped

Everyone affected by a diminution of his physical or mental capacities is entitled to receive special attention designed to help him achieve the greatest possible development of his personality. The States Parties agree to adopt such measures as may be necessary for this purpose and, especially, to:

(a) Undertake programs specifically aimed at providing the handicapped with the resources and environment needed for attaining this goal, including work programs consistent with their possibilities and freely accepted by them or their legal representatives, as the case may be;

(b) Provide special training to the families of the handicapped in order to help them solve the problems of coexistence and convert them into active agents in the physical, mental and emotional development of the latter;

(c) Include the consideration of solutions to specific requirements arising from needs of this group as a priority component of their urban development plans;

(d) Encourage the establishment of social groups in which the handicapped can be helped to enjoy a fuller life.

Article 19 Means of Protection

1. Pursuant to the provisions of this article and the corresponding rules to be formulated for this purpose by the General Assembly of the Organization of American States, the States Parties to this Protocol undertake to submit periodic reports on the progressive measures they have taken to ensure due respect for the rights set forth in this Protocol.

2. All reports shall be submitted to the Secretary General of the OAS, who shall transmit them to the Inter-American Economic and Social Council and the Inter-American Council for Education, Science and Culture so that they may examine them in accordance with the provisions of this article. The Secretary General shall send a copy of such reports to the Inter-American Commission on Human Rights.

3. The Secretary General of the Organization of American States shall also transmit to the specialized organizations of the inter-American system of which the States Parties to the present Protocol are members, copies or pertinent portions of the reports submitted, insofar as they relate to matters within the purview of those organizations, as established by their constituent instruments.

4. The specialized organizations of the inter-American system may submit reports to the Inter-American Economic and Social Council and the Inter-American Council for Education, Science and Culture relative to compliance with the provisions of the present Protocol in their fields of activity.

5. The annual reports submitted to the General Assembly by the Inter-American Economic and Social Council and the Inter-American Council for Education, Science and Culture shall contain a summary of the information received from the States Parties to the present Protocol and the specialized organizations concerning the progressive measures adopted in order to ensure respect for the rights acknowledged in the Protocol itself and the general recommendations they consider to be appropriate in this respect.

6. Any instance in which the rights established in paragraph a) of Article 8 and in Article 13 are violated by action directly attributable to a State Party to this Protocol may give rise, through participation of the Inter-American Commission on Human Rights and, when applicable, of the Inter-American Court of Human Rights, to application of the system of individual petitions governed by Article 44 through 51 and 61 through 69 of the American Convention on Human Rights.

7. Without prejudice to the provisions of the preceding paragraph, the Inter-American Commission on Human Rights may formulate such observations and recommendations as it deems pertinent concerning the status of the economic, social and cultural rights established in the present Protocol in all or some of the States Parties, which it may include in its Annual Report to the General Assembly or in a special report, whichever it considers more appropriate.

8. The Councils and the Inter-American Commission on Human Rights, in discharging the functions conferred upon them in this article, shall take into account the progressive nature of the observance of the rights subject to protection by this Protocol.

Article 20 Reservations

The States Parties may, at the time of approval, signature, ratification or accession, make reservations to one or more specific provisions of this Protocol, provided that such reservations are not incompatible with the object and purpose of the Protocol.

Article 21 Signature, Ratification or Accession

Entry into Effect

1. This Protocol shall remain open to signature and ratification or accession by any State Party to the American Convention on Human Rights.

2. Ratification of or accession to this Protocol shall be effected by depositing an instrument of ratification or accession with the General Secretariat of the Organization of American States.

3. The Protocol shall enter into effect when eleven States have deposited their respective instruments of ratification or accession.

4. The Secretary General shall notify all the member states of the Organization of American States of the entry of the Protocol into effect.

Article 22 Inclusion of other Rights and Expansion of those Recognized

1. Any State Party and the Inter-American Commission on Human Rights may submit for the consideration of the States Parties meeting on the occasion of the General Assembly proposed amendments to include the recognition of other rights or freedoms or to extend or expand rights or freedoms recognized in this Protocol.

2. Such amendments shall enter into effect for the States that ratify them on the date of deposit of the instrument of ratification corresponding to the number representing two-thirds of the States Parties to this Protocol. For all other States Parties they shall enter into effect on the date on which they deposit their respective instrument of ratification.

2.12: European Convention for the Protection of Human Rights and Fundamental Freedoms

Adopted 4 November 1950. Entered into force 3 September 1958.

The Governments signatory hereto, being Members of the Council of Europe,

Considering the Universal Declaration of Human Rights proclaimed by the General Assembly of the United Nations on 10th December 1948;

Considering that this Declaration aims at securing the universal and effective recognition and observance of the Rights therein declared;

Considering that the aim of the Council of Europe is the achievement of greater unity between its Members and that one of the methods by which that aim is to be pursued is the maintenance and further realization of Human Rights and Fundamental Freedoms;

Reaffirming their profound belief in those Fundamental Freedoms which are the foundation of justice and peace in the world and are best maintained on the one hand by an effective political democracy and on the other by a common understanding and observance of the Human Rights upon which they depend;

Being resolved, as the Governments of European countries which are like-minded and have a common heritage of political traditions, ideals, freedom and the rule of law, to take the first steps for the collective enforcement of certain of the Rights stated in the Universal Declaration;

Have agreed as follows

Article 1

The High Contracting Parties shall secure to everyone within their jurisdiction the rights and freedoms defined in Section I of this Convention.

Section I

Article 2

1. Everyone's right to life shall be protected by law. No one shall be deprived of his life intentionally save in the execution of a sentence of a court following his conviction of a crime for which this penalty is provided by law.
2. Deprivation of life shall not be regarded as inflicted in contravention of this Article when it results from the use of force which is no more than absolutely necessary:
    (a) in defence of any person from unlawful violence;
    (b) in order to effect a lawful arrest or to prevent the escape of a person lawfully detained;
    (c) in action lawfully taken for the purpose of quelling a riot or insurrection.

Article 3

No one shall be subjected to torture or to inhuman or degrading treatment or punishment.

Article 4

1. No one shall be held in slavery or servitude.
2. No one shall be required to perform forced or compulsory labour.
3. For the purpose of this Article the term 'forced or compulsory labour' shall not include
    (a) any work required to be done in the ordinary course of detention imposed according to the provisions of Article 5 of this Convention or during conditional release from such detention;
    (b) any service of a military character or, in case of conscientious objectors in countries where they are recognised, service exacted instead of compulsory military service;

(c) any service exacted in case of an emergency or calamity threatening the life or well-being of the community;
(d) any work or service which forms part of normal civil obligations.

Article 5

1. Everyone has the right to liberty and security of person. No one shall be deprived of his liberty save in the following cases and in accordance with the procedure prescribed by law:
    (a) the lawful detention of a person after conviction by a competent court;
    (b) the lawful arrest or detention of a person for non-compliance with the lawful order of a court or in order to secure the fulfilment of any obligation prescribed by law;
    (c) the lawful arrest or detention of a person effected for the purpose of bringing him before the competent legal authority on reasonable suspicion of having committed an offence or when it is reasonably considered necessary to prevent his committing an offence or fleeing after having done so;
    (d) the detention of a minor by lawful order for the purpose of educational supervision or his lawful detention for the purpose of bringing him before the competent legal authority;
    (e) the lawful detention of persons for the prevention of the spreading of infectious diseases, of persons of unsound mind, alcoholics or drug addicts or vagrants;
    (f) the lawful arrest or detention of a person to prevent his effecting an unauthorised entry into the country or of a person against whom action is being taken with a view to deportation or extradition.
2. Everyone who is arrested shall be informed promptly, in a language which he understands, of the reasons for his arrest and of any charge against him.
3. Everyone arrested or detained in accordance with the provisions of paragraph 1(c) of this Article shall be brought promptly before a judge or other officer authorised by law to exercise judicial power and shall be entitled to trial within a reasonable time or to release pending trial. Release may be conditioned by guarantees to appear for trial.
4. Everyone who is deprived of his liberty by arrest or detention shall be entitled to take proceedings by which the lawfulness of his detention shall be decided speedily by a court and his release ordered if the detention is not lawful.
5. Everyone who has been the victim of arrest or detention in contravention of the provisions of this Article shall have an enforceable right to compensation.

Article 6

1. In the determination of his civil rights and obligations or of any criminal charge against him, everyone is entitled to a fair and public hearing within a reasonable time by an independent and impartial tribunal established by law. Judgment shall be pronounced publicly but the press and public may be excluded from all or part of the trial in the interests of morals, public order or national security in a democratic society, where the interests of juveniles or the protection of the private life of the parties so require, or to the extent strictly necessary in the opinion of the court in special circumstances where publicity would prejudice the interests of justice.
2. Everyone charged with a criminal offence shall be presumed innocent until proved guilty according to law.
3. Everyone charged with a criminal offence has the following minimum rights:
    (a) to be informed promptly, in a language which he understands and in detail, of the nature and cause of the accusation against him;
    (b) to have adequate time and facilities for the preparation of his defence;
    (c) to defend himself in person or through legal assistance of his own choosing or, if he has not sufficient means to pay for legal assistance, to be given it free when the interests of justice so require;
    (d) to examine or have examined witnesses against him and to obtain the attendance and examination of witnesses on his behalf under the same conditions as witnesses against him;

(e) to have the free assistance of an interpreter if he cannot understand or speak the language used in court.

Article 7

1. No one shall be held guilty of any criminal offence on account of any act or omission which did not constitute a criminal offence under national or international law at the time when it was committed. Nor shall a heavier penalty be imposed than the one that was applicable at the time the criminal offence was committed.
2. This Article shall not prejudice the trial and punishment of any person for any act or omission which, at the time when it was committed, was criminal according to the general principles of law recognised by civilised nations.

Article 8

1. Everyone has the right to respect for his private and family life, his home and his correspondence.
2. There shall be no interference by a public authority with the exercise of this right except such as is in accordance with the law and is necessary in a democratic society in the interests of national security, public safety or the economic well-being of the country, for the prevention of disorder or crime, for the protection of health or morals, or for the protection of the rights and freedoms of others.

Article 9

1. Everyone has the right to freedom of thought, conscience and religion; this right includes freedom to change his religion or belief and freedom, either alone or in community with others and in public or private, to manifest his religion or belief, in worship, teaching, practice and observance.
2. Freedom to manifest one's religion or beliefs shall be subject only to such limitations as are prescribed by law and are necessary in a democratic society in the interests of public safety, for the protection of public order, health or morals, or for the protection of the rights and freedoms of others.

Article 10

1. Everyone has the right to freedom of expression. This right shall include freedom to hold opinions and to receive and impart information and ideas without interference by public authority and regardless of frontiers. This Article shall not prevent States from requiring the licensing of broadcasting, television or cinema enterprises.
2. The exercise of these freedoms, since it carries with it duties and responsibilities, may be subject to such formalities, conditions, restrictions or penalties as are prescribed by law and are necessary in a democratic society, in the interests of national security, territorial integrity or public safety, for the prevention of disorder or crime, for the protection of health or morals, for the protection of the reputation or rights of others, for preventing the disclosure of information received in confidence, or for maintaining the authority and impartiality of the judiciary.

Article 11

1. Everyone has the right to freedom of peaceful assembly and to freedom of association with others, including the right to form and to join trade unions for the protection of his interests.
2. No restrictions shall be placed on the exercise of these rights other than such as are prescribed by law and are necessary in a democratic society in the interests of national security or public safety, for the prevention of disorder or crime, for the protection of health or morals or for the protection of the rights and freedoms of others. This Article shall not prevent the imposition of lawful restrictions on the exercise of these rights by members of the armed forces, of the police or of the administration of the State.

Article 12

Men and women of marriageable age have the right to marry and to found a family, according to the national laws governing the exercise of this right.

Article 13

Everyone whose rights and freedoms as set forth in this Convention are violated shall have an effective remedy before a national authority notwithstanding that the violation has been committed by persons acting in an official capacity.

Article 14

The enjoyment of the rights and freedoms set forth in this Convention shall be secured without discrimination on any ground such as sex, race, colour, language, religion, political or other opinion, national or social origin, association with a national minority, property, birth or other status.

Article 15

1. In time of war or other public emergency threatening the life of the nation any High Contracting Party may take measures derogating from its obligations under this Convention to the extent strictly required by the exigencies of the situation, provided that such measures are not inconsistent with its other obligations under international law.
2. No derogation from Article 2, except in respect of deaths resulting from lawful acts of war, or from Articles 3, 4 (paragraph 1) and 7 shall be made under this provision.
3. Any High Contracting Party availing itself of this right of derogation shall keep the Secretary-General of the Council of Europe fully informed of the measures which it has taken and the reasons therefor. It shall also inform the Secretary-General of the Council of Europe when such measures have ceased to operate and the provisions of the Convention are again being fully executed.

Article 16

Nothing in Articles 10, 11 and 14 shall be regarded as preventing the High Contracting Parties from imposing restrictions on the political activity of aliens.

Article 17

Nothing in this Convention may be interpreted as implying for any State, group or person any right to engage in any activity or perform any act aimed at the destruction of any of the rights and freedoms set forth herein or at their limitation to a greater extent than is provided for in the Convention.

Article 18

The restrictions permitted under this Convention to the said rights and freedoms shall not be applied for any purpose other than those for which they have been prescribed.

Section II

Article 19

To ensure the observance of the engagements undertaken by the High Contracting Parties in the present Convention, there shall be set up:
1. A European Commission of Human Rights hereinafter referred to as the Commission.
2. A European Court of Human Rights, hereinafter referred to as the Court.

Section III

Article 20

The Commission shall consist of a number of members equal to that of the High Contracting Parties. No two members of the Commission may be nationals of the same State.

Article 21

1. The members of the Commission shall be elected by the Committee of Ministers by an absolute majority of votes, from a list of names drawn up by the Bureau of the Consultative Assembly; each group of the Representatives of the High Contracting Parties in the Consultative Assembly shall put forward three candidates, of whom two at least shall be its nationals.

2. As far as applicable, the same procedure shall be followed to complete the Commission in the event of other States subsequently becoming Parties to this Convention, and in filling casual vacancies.

Article 22

1. The members of the Commission shall be elected for a period of six years. They may be re-elected. However, of the members elected at the first election, the terms of seven members shall expire at the end of three years.

2. The members whose terms are to expire at the end of the initial period of three years shall be chosen by lot by the Secretary-General of the Council of Europe immediately after the first election has been completed.

3. A member of the Commission elected to replace a member whose term of office has not expired shall hold office for the remainder of his predecessor's term.

4. The members of the Commission shall hold office until replaced. After having been replaced, they shall continue to deal with such cases as they already have under consideration.

Article 23

The members of the Commission shall sit on the Commission in their individual capacity.

Article 24

Any High Contracting Party may refer to the Commission, through the Secretary-General of the Council of Europe, any alleged breach of the provisions of the Convention by another High Contracting Party.

Article 25

1. The Commission may receive petitions addressed to the Secretary-General of the Council of Europe from any person, non-governmental organisation or group of individuals claiming to be the victim of a violation by one of the High Contracting Parties of the rights set forth in this Convention, provided that the High Contracting Party against which the complaint has been lodged has declared that it recognises the competence of the Commission to receive such petitions. Those of the High Contracting Parties who have made such a declaration undertake not to hinder in any way the effective exercise of this right.

2. Such declarations may be made for a specific period.

3. The declarations shall be deposited with the Secretary-General of the Council of Europe who shall transmit copies thereof to the High Contracting Parties and publish them.

4. The Commission shall only exercise the powers provided for in this Article when at least six High Contracting Parties are bound by declarations made in accordance with the preceding paragraphs.

Article 26

The Commission may only deal with the matter after all domestic remedies have been exhausted, according to the generally recognised rules of international law, and within a period of six months from the date on which the final decision was taken.

Article 27

1. The Commission shall not deal with any petition submitted under Article 25 which

(a) is anonymous, or

(b) is substantially the same as a matter which has already been examined by the Commission or has already been submitted to another procedure of international investigation or settlement and if it contains no relevant new information.

2. The Commission shall consider inadmissible any petition submitted under Article 25 which it considers incompatible with the provisions of the present Convention, manifestly ill-founded, or an abuse of the right of petition.

3. The Commission shall reject any petition referred to it which it considers inadmissible under Article 26.

Article 28

In the event of the Commission accepting a petition referred to it:

(a) it shall, with a view to ascertaining the facts, undertake together with the representatives of the parties an examination of the petition and, if need be, an investigation, for the effective conduct of which the States concerned shall furnish all necessary facilities, after an exchange of views with the Commission;

(b) it shall place itself at the disposal of the parties concerned with a view to securing a friendly settlement of the matter on the basis of respect for Human Rights as defined in this Convention.

Article 29

After it has accepted a petition submitted under Article 25, the Commission may nevertheless decide unanimously to reject the petition if, in the course of its examination, it finds that the existence of one of the grounds for non-acceptance provided for in Article 27 has been established. In such a case, the decision shall be communicated to the parties.

Article 30

If the Commission succeeds in effecting a friendly settlement in accordance with Article 28, it shall draw up a Report which shall be sent to the States concerned, to the Committee of Ministers and to the Secretary-General of the Council of Europe for publication. This Report shall be confined to a brief statement of the facts and of the solution reached.

Article 31

1. If a solution is not reached, the Commission shall draw up a Report on the facts and state its opinion as to whether the facts found disclose a breach by the State concerned of its obligations under the Convention. The opinions of all the members of the Commission on this point may be stated in the Report.

2. The Report shall be transmitted to the Committee of Ministers. It shall also be transmitted to the States concerned, who shall not be at liberty to publish it.

3. In transmitting the Report to the Committee of Ministers the Commission may make such proposals as it thinks fit.

Article 32

1. If the question is not referred to the Court in accordance with Article 48 of this Convention within a period of three months from the date of the transmission of the Report to the Committee of Ministers, the Committee of Ministers shall decide by a majority of two-thirds of the members entitled to sit on the Committee whether there has been a violation of the Convention.

2. In the affirmative case the Committee of Ministers shall prescribe a period during which the High Contracting Party concerned must take the measures required by the decision of the Committee of Ministers.

3. If the High Contracting Party concerned has not taken satisfactory measures within the prescribed period, the Committee of Ministers shall decide by the majority provided for in paragraph (1) above what effect shall be given to its original decision and shall publish the Report.

4. The High Contracting Parties undertake to regard as binding on them any decision which the Committee of Ministers may take in application of the preceding paragraphs.

Article 33

The Commission shall meet in camera.

Article 34

Subject to the provisions of Article 29, the Commission shall take its decisions by a majority of the Members present and voting.

Article 35

The Commission shall meet as the circumstances require. The meetings shall be convened by the Secretary-General of the Council of Europe.

Article 36

The Commission shall draw up its own rules of procedure.

Article 37

The secretariat of the Commission shall be provided by the Secretary-General of the Council of Europe.

Section IV

Article 38

The European Court of Human Rights shall consist of a number of judges equal to that of the Members of the Council of Europe. No two judges may be nationals of the same State.

Article 39

1. The members of the Court shall be elected by the Consultative Assembly by a majority of the votes cast from a list of persons nominated by the Members of the Council of Europe; each Member shall nominate three candidates, of whom two at least shall be its nationals.
2. As far as applicable, the same procedure shall be followed to complete the Court in the event of the admission of new Members of the Council of Europe, and in filling casual vacancies.
3. The candidates shall be of high moral character and must either possess the qualifications required for appointment to high judicial office or be jurisconsults of recognised competence.

Article 40

1. The members of the Court shall be elected for a period of nine years. They may be re-elected. However, of the members elected at the first election the terms of four members shall expire at the end of three years, and the terms of four more members shall expire at the end of six years.
2. The members whose terms are to expire at the end of the initial periods of three and six years shall be chosen by lot by the Secretary-General immediately after the first election has been completed.
3. A member of the Court elected to replace a member whose term of office has not expired shall hold office for the remainder of his predecessor's term.
4. The members of the Court shall hold office until replaced. After having been replaced, they shall continue to deal with such cases as they already have under consideration.

Article 41

The Court shall elect its President and Vice-President for a period of three years. They may be re-elected.

Article 42

The members of the Court shall receive for each day of duty a compensation to be determined by the Committee of Ministers.

Article 43

For the consideration of each case brought before it the Court shall consist of a Chamber composed of seven judges. There shall sit as an *ex officio* member of the Chamber the judge who is a national of any State Party concerned, or, if there is none, a person of its choice who shall sit in the capacity of judge; the names of the other judges shall be chosen by lot by the President before the opening of the case.

Article 44

Only the High Contracting Parties and the Commission shall have the right to bring a case before the Court.

Article 45

The jurisdiction of the Court shall extend to all cases concerning the interpretation and application of the present Convention which the High Contracting Parties or the Commission shall refer to it in accordance with Article 48.

Article 46

1. Any of the High Contracting Parties may at any time declare that it recognises as compulsory *ipso facto* and without special agreement the jurisdiction of the Court in all matters concerning the interpretation and application of the present Convention.
2. The declarations referred to above may be made unconditionally or on condition of reciprocity on the part of several or certain other High Contracting Parties or for a specified period.
3. These declarations shall be deposited with the Secretary-General of the Council of Europe who shall transmit copies thereof to the High Contracting Parties.

Article 47

The Court may only deal with a case after the Commission has acknowledged the failure of efforts for a friendly settlement and within the period of three months provided for in Article 32.

Article 48

The following may bring a case before the Court, provided that the High Contracting Party concerned, if there is only one, or the High Contracting Parties concerned, if there is more than one, are subject to the compulsory jurisdiction of the Court or, failing that, with the consent of the High Contracting Party concerned, if there is only one, or of the High Contracting Parties concerned if there is more than one:
  (a) the Commission;
  (b) a High Contracting Party whose national is alleged to be a victim;
  (c) a High Contracting Party which referred the case to the Commission;
  (d) a High Contracting Party against which the complaint has been lodged.

Article 49

In the event of dispute as to whether the Court has jurisdiction, the matter shall be settled by the decision of the Court.

Article 50

If the Court finds that a decision or a measure taken by a legal authority or any other authority of a High Contracting Party is completely or partially in conflict with the obligations arising from the present Convention, and if the internal law of the said Party allows only partial reparation to be made for the consequences of this decision or measure, the decision of the Court shall, if necessary, afford just satisfaction to the injured party.

Article 51

1. Reasons shall be given for the judgment of the Court.
2. If the judgment does not represent in whole or in part the unanimous opinion of the judges, any judge shall be entitled to deliver a separate opinion.

Article 52

The judgment of the Court shall be final.

Article 53

The High Contracting Parties undertake to abide by the decision of the Court in any case to which they are parties.

Article 54

The judgment of the Court shall be transmitted to the Committee of Ministers which shall supervise its execution.

Article 55

The Court shall draw up its own rules and shall determine its own procedure.

Article 56

1. The first election of the members of the Court shall take place after the declarations by the High Contracting Parties mentioned in Article 46 have reached a total of eight.
2. No case can be brought before the Court before this election.

Section V

Article 57

On receipt of a request from the Secretary-General of the Council of Europe any High Contracting Party shall furnish an explanation of the manner in which its internal law ensures the effective implementation of any of the provisions of this Convention.

Article 58

The expenses of the Commission and the Court shall be borne by the Council of Europe.

Article 59

The members of the Commission and of the Court shall be entitled, during the discharge of their functions, to the privileges and immunities provided for in Article 40 of the Statute of the Council of Europe and in the agreements made thereunder.

Article 60

Nothing in this Convention shall be construed as limiting or derogating from any of the human rights and fundamental freedoms which may be ensured under the laws of any High Contracting Party or under any other agreement to which it is a Party.

Nothing in this Convention shall prejudice the powers conferred on the Committee of Ministers by the Statute of the Council of Europe.

Article 62

The High Contracting Parties agree that, except by special agreement, they will not avail themselves of treaties, conventions or declarations in force between them for the purpose of submitting, by way of petition, a dispute arising out of the interpretation or application of this Convention to a means of settlement other than those provided for in this Convention.

Article 63

1. Any State may at the time of its ratification or at any time thereafter declare by notification addressed to the Secretary-General of the Council of Europe that the present Convention shall extend to all or any of the territories for whose international relations it is responsible.
2. The Convention shall extend to the territory or territories named in the notification as from the thirtieth day after the receipt of this notification by the Secretary-General of the Council of Europe.
3. The provisions of this Convention shall be applied in such territories with due regard, however, to local requirements.
4. Any State which has made a declaration in accordance with paragraph 1 of this Article may at any time thereafter declare on behalf of one or more of the territories to which the declaration relates that it accepts the competence of the Commission to receive petitions from individuals, non-governmental organisations or groups of individuals in accordance with Article 25 of the present Convention.

Article 64

1. Any State may, when signing this Convention or when depositing its instrument of ratification, make a reservation in respect of any particular provision of the Convention to the extent that any law then in force in its territory is not in conformity with the provision. Reservations of a general character shall not be permitted under this Article.
2. Any reservation made under this Article shall contain a brief statement of the law concerned.

Article 65

1. A High Contracting Party may denounce the present Convention only after the expiry of five years from the date on which it became a Party to it and after six months' notice contained in a notification addressed to the Secretary-General of the Council of Europe, who shall inform the other High Contracting Parties.
2. Such a denunciation shall not have the effect of releasing the High Contracting Party concerned from its obligations under this Convention in respect of any act which, being capable of constituting a violation of such obligations, may have been performed by it before the date at which the denunciation became effective.
3. Any High Contracting Party which shall cease to be a Member of the Council of Europe shall cease to be a Party to this Convention under the same conditions.
4. The Convention may be denounced in accordance with the provisions of the preceding paragraphs in respect of any territory to which it has been declared to extend under the terms of Article 63.

Article 66

1. This Convention shall be open to the signature of the Members of the Council of Europe. It shall be ratified. Ratifications shall be deposited with the Secretary-General of the Council of Europe.

2. The present Convention shall come into force after the deposit of ten instruments of ratification.

3. As regards any signatory ratifying subsequently, the Convention shall come into force at the date of the deposit of its instrument of ratification.

4. The Secretary-General of the Council of Europe shall notify all the Members of the Council of Europe of the entry into force of the Convention, the names of the High Contracting Parties who have ratified it, and the deposit of all instruments of ratification which may be effected subsequently.

DONE AT ROME this 4th day of November 1950 in English and French, both texts being equally authentic, in a single copy which shall remain deposited in the archives of the Council of Europe. The Secretary-General shall transmit certified copies to each of the signatories.

2.13: European Convention on the Exercise of Children's Rights

The member States of the Council of Europe and the other States signatory hereto;

Considering that the aim of the Council of Europe is to achieve greater unity between its members;

Having regard to the United Nations Convention on the rights of the child and in particular Article 4 which requires States Parties to undertake all appropriate legislative, administrative and other measures for the implementation of the rights recognised in the said Convention;

Noting the contents of Recommendation 1121 (1990) of the Parliamentary Assembly on the rights of the child;

Convinced that the rights and best interests of children should be promoted and to that end children should have the opportunity to exercise their rights, in particular in family proceedings affecting them;

Recognising that children should be provided with relevant information to enable such rights and best interests to be promoted and that due weight should be given to the views of children;

Recognising the importance of the parental role in protecting and promoting the rights and best interests of children and considering that, where necessary, States should also engage in such protection and promotion;

Considering, however, that in the event of conflict it is desirable for families to try to reach agreement before bringing the matter before a judicial authority,

Have agreed as follows:

CHAPTER I – SCOPE AND OBJECT OF THE CONVENTION AND DEFINITIONS

Article 1 – Scope and object of the Convention

1. This Convention shall apply to children who have not reached the age of 18 years.
2. The object of the present Convention is, in the best interests of children, to promote their rights, to grant them procedural rights and to facilitate the exercise of these rights by ensuring that children are, themselves or through other persons or bodies, informed and allowed to participate in proceedings affecting them before a judicial authority.
3. For the purposes of this Convention proceedings before a judicial authority affecting children are family proceedings, in particular those involving the exercise of parental responsibilities such as residence and access to children.
4. Every State shall, at the time of signature or when depositing its instrument of ratification, acceptance, approval or accession, by a declaration addressed to the Secretary-General of the Council of Europe, specify at least three categories of family cases before a judicial authority to which this Convention is to apply.
5. Any Party may, by further declaration, specify additional categories of family cases to which this Convention is to apply or provide information concerning the application of Article 5, paragraph 2 of Article 9, paragraph 2 of Article 10 and Article 11.
6. Nothing in this Convention shall prevent Parties from applying rules more favourable to the promotion and the exercise of children's rights.

Article 2 – Definitions

For the purposes of this Convention:

(a) the term 'judicial authority' means a court or an administrative authority having equivalent powers:

(b) the term 'holders of parental responsibilities' means parents and other persons or bodies entitled to exercise some or all parental responsibilities;

(c) the term 'representative' means a person, such as a lawyer, or a body appointed to act before a judicial authority on behalf of a child;

(d) the term 'relevant information' means information which is appropriate to the age and understanding of the child, and which will be given to enable the child to exercise his or her rights fully unless the provision of such information were contrary to the welfare of the child.

CHAPTER II – PROCEDURAL MEASURES TO PROMOTE THE EXERCISE OF CHILDREN'S RIGHTS

A. Procedural Rights of a Child

Article 3 – Right to be Informed and to Express his or her Views in Proceedings

A child considered by internal law as having sufficient understanding, in the case of proceedings before a judicial authority affecting him or her, shall be granted, and shall be entitled to request, the following rights:

(a) to receive all relevant information;

(b) to be consulted and express his or her views;

(c) to be informed of the possible consequences of compliance with these views and the possible consequences of any decision.

Article 4 – Right to apply for the Appointment of a Special Representative

1. Subject to Article 9, the child shall have the right to apply, in person or through other persons or bodies, for a special representative in proceedings before a judicial authority affecting the child where the internal law precludes the holders of parental responsibilities from representing the child as a result of a conflict of interest with the latter.

2. States are free to limit the right in paragraph 1 to children who are considered by internal law to have sufficient understanding.

Article 5 – Other Possible Procedural Rights

Parties shall consider granting children additional procedural rights in relation to proceedings before a judicial authority affecting them, in particular:

(a) the right to apply to be assisted by an appropriate person of their choice in order to help them express their views;

(b) the right to apply themselves or through other persons or bodies for the appointment of a separate representative, in appropriate cases a lawyer;

(c) the right to appoint their own representative;

(d) the right to exercise some or all of the rights of parties to such proceedings.

B. Role of Judicial Authorities

Article 6 – Decision-making Process

In proceedings affecting a child, the judicial authority, before taking a decision, shall:

(a) consider whether it has sufficient information at its disposal in order to take a decision in the best interests of the child and, where necessary, it shall obtain further information, in particular from the holders of parental responsibilities;

(b) in a case where the child is considered by internal law as having sufficient understanding:

– ensure that the child has received all relevant information;

– consult the child in person in appropriate cases, if necessary privately, itself or through other persons or bodies, in a manner appropriate to his or her understanding, unless this would be manifestly contrary to the best interests of the child;

– allow the child to express his or her views;

(c) give due weight to the views expressed by the child.

Article 7 – Duty to Act Speedily

In proceedings affecting a child the judicial authority shall act speedily to avoid any unnecessary delay and procedures shall be available to ensure that its decisions are rapidly enforced. In urgent cases, the judicial authority shall have the power, where appropriate, to take decisions which are immediately enforceable.

Article 8 – Acting on Own Motion

In proceedings affecting a child the judicial authority shall have the power to act on its own motion in cases determined by internal law where the welfare of a child is in serious danger.

Article 9 – Appointment of a Representative

1. In proceedings affecting a child where, by internal law, the holders of parental responsibilities are precluded from representing the child as a result of a conflict of interest between them and the child, the judicial authority shall have the power to appoint a special representative for the child in those proceedings.
2. Parties shall consider providing that, in proceedings affecting a child, the judicial authority shall have the power to appoint a separate representative, in appropriate cases a lawyer, to represent the child.

C. Role of Representatives

Article 10

1. In the case of proceedings before a judicial authority affecting a child the representative shall, unless this would be manifestly contrary to the best interests of the child:
   (a) provide all relevant information to the child, if the child is considered by internal law as having sufficient understanding;
   (b) provide explanations to the child if the child is considered by internal law as having sufficient understanding, concerning the possible consequences of compliance with his or her views and the possible consequences of any action by the representative;
   (c) determine the views of the child and present these views to the judicial authority.
2. Parties shall consider extending the provisions of paragraph 1 to the holders of parental responsibilities.

D. Extension of Certain Provisions

Article 11

Parties shall consider extending the provisions of Articles 3, 4 and 9 to proceedings affecting children before other bodies and to matters affecting children which are not the subject of proceedings.

E. National Bodies

Article 12

1. Parties shall encourage, through bodies which perform, *inter alia*, the functions set out in paragraph 2, the promotion and the exercise of children's rights.
2. The functions are as follows:
   (a) to make proposals to strengthen the law relating to the exercise of children's rights;
   (b) to give opinions concerning draft legislation relating to the exercise of children's rights;
   (c) to provide general information concerning the exercise of children's rights to the media, the public and persons and bodies dealing with questions relating to children;
   (d) to seek the views of children and provide them with relevant information.

199

F. Other Matters

Article 13 – Mediation or other Processes to Resolve Disputes

In order to prevent or resolve disputes or to avoid proceedings before a judicial authority affecting children, Parties shall encourage the provision of mediation or other processes to resolve disputes and their use to reach agreement in appropriate cases to be determined by Parties.

Article 14 – Legal Aid and Advice

Where internal law provides for legal aid or advice for the representation of children in proceedings before a judicial authority affecting children, such provisions shall apply in relation to the matters covered by Articles 4 and 9.

Article 15 – Relations with Other International Instruments

This Convention shall not restrict the application of any other international instrument which deals with specific issues arising in the context of the protection of children and families, and to which a Party to this Convention is, or becomes, a Party.

CHAPTER III – STANDING COMMITTEE

Article 16 – Establishment and Functions of the Standing Committee

1. A Standing Committee is set up for the purposes of this Convention.
2. The Standing Committee shall keep under review problems relating to this Convention. It may, in particular:
   (a) consider any relevant questions concerning the interpretation or implementation of the Convention. The Standing Committee's conclusions concerning the implementation of the Convention may take the form of a recommendation; recommendations shall be adopted by a three-quarters majority of the votes cast;
   (b) propose amendments to the Convention and examine those proposed in accordance with Article 20;
   (c) provide advice and assistance to the national bodies having the functions under paragraph 2 of Article 12 and promote international co-operation between them.

Article 17 – Composition

1. Each Party may be represented on the Standing Committee by one or more delegates. Each Party shall have one vote.
2. Any State referred to in Article 21, which is not a Party to this Convention, may be represented in the Standing Committee by an observer. The same applies to any other State or to the European Community after having been invited to accede to the Convention in accordance with the provisions of Article 22.
3. Unless a Party has informed the Secretary-General of its objection, at least one month before the meeting, the Standing Committee may invite the following to attend as observers at all its meetings or at one meeting or part of a meeting:
   – any State not referred to in paragraph 2 above;
   – the United Nations Committee on the Rights of the Child;
   – the European Community;
   – any international governmental body;
   – any international non-governmental body with one or more functions mentioned under paragraph 2 of Article 12;
   – any national governmental or non-governmental body with one or more functions mentioned under paragraph 2 of Article 12.
4. The Standing Committee may exchange information with relevant organisations dealing with the exercise of children's rights.

Article 18 – Meetings

1. At the end of the third year following the date of the entry into force of this Convention and, on his or her own initiative, at any time after this date, the Secretary-General of the Council of Europe shall invite the Standing Committee to meet.
2. Decisions may only be taken in the Standing Committee if at least one-half of the Parties are present.
3. Subject to Articles 16 and 20 the decisions of the Standing Committee shall be taken by a majority of the members present.
4. Subject to the provisions of this Convention the Standing Committee shall draw up its own rules of procedure and the rules of procedure of any working party it may set up to carry out all appropriate tasks under the convention.

Article 19 – Reports of the Standing Committee

After each meeting, the Standing Committee shall forward to the Parties and the Committee of Ministers of the Council of Europe a report on its discussions and any decisions taken.

CHAPTER IV – AMENDMENTS TO THE CONVENTION
Article 20

1. Any amendment to the articles of this Convention proposed by a Party or the Standing Committee shall be communicated to the Secretary-General of the Council of Europe and forwarded by him or her, at least two months before the next meeting of the Standing Committee, to the member States of the Council of Europe, any signatory, any Party, any State invited to sign this Convention in accordance with the provisions of Article 21 and any State or the European Community invited to accede to it in accordance with the provisions of Article 22.
2. Any amendment proposed in accordance with the provisions of the preceding paragraph shall be examined by the Standing Committee which shall submit the text adopted by a three-quarters majority of the votes cast to the Committee of Ministers for approval. After its approval, this text shall be forwarded to the Parties for acceptance.
3. Any amendment shall enter into force on the first day of the month following the expiration of a period of one month after the date on which all Parties have informed the Secretary-General that they have accepted it.

CHAPTER V – FINAL CLAUSES
Article 21 – Signature, Ratification and Entry into Force

1. This Convention shall be open for signature by the member states of the Council of Europe and the non-member States which have participated in its elaboration.
2. This Convention is subject to ratification, acceptance or approval. Instruments of ratification, acceptance or approval shall be deposited with the Secretary-General of the Council of Europe.
3. This Convention shall enter into force on the first day of the month following the expiration of a period of three months after the date on which three States, including at least two member States of the Council of Europe, have expressed their consent to be bound by the Convention in accordance with the provisions of the preceding paragraph.
4. In respect of any signatory which subsequently expresses its consent to be bound by it, the Convention shall enter into force on the first day of the month following the expiration of a period of three months after the date of the deposit of its instrument of ratification, acceptance or approval.

Article 22 – Non-member States and the European Community

1. After the entry into force of this Convention, the Committee of Ministers of the Council of Europe may, on its own initiative or following a proposal from the Standing Committee and after consultation of the Parties, invite any non-member State of the Council of Europe, which has not participated in the elaboration of the Convention, as well as the European Community

to accede to this Convention by a decision taken by the majority provided for in Article 20 sub-paragraph (d) of the Statute of the Council of Europe, and by the unanimous vote of the representatives of the contracting States entitled to sit on the Committee of Ministers.

2. In respect of any acceding State or the European Community, the Convention shall enter into force on the first day of the month following the expiration of a period of three months after the date of deposit of the instrument of accession with the Secretary-General of the Council of Europe.

Article 23 – Territorial Application

1. Any State may, at the time of signature or when depositing its instrument of ratification, acceptance, approval or accession, specify the territory or territories to which this Convention shall apply.

2. Any Party may, at any later date, by a declaration addressed to the Secretary-General of the Council of Europe, extend the application of this Convention to any other territory specified in the declaration and for whose international relations it is responsible or on whose behalf it is authorised to give undertakings. In respect of such territory the Convention shall enter into force on the first day of the month following the expiration of a period of three months after the date of receipt of such declaration by the Secretary-General.

3. Any declaration made under the two preceding paragraphs may, in respect of any territory specified in such declaration, be withdrawn by a notification addressed to the Secretary-General. The withdrawal shall become effective on the first day of the month following the expiration of a period of three months after the date of receipt of such notification by the Secretary-General.

Article 24 – Reservations

No reservation may be made to the Convention.

Article 25 – Denunciation

1. Any Party may at any time denounce this Convention by means of a notification addressed to the Secretary-General of the Council of Europe.

2. Such denunciation shall become effective on the first day of the month following the expiration of a period of three months after the date of receipt of notification by the Secretary-General.

Article 26 – Notifications

The Secretary-General of the Council of Europe shall notify the member States of the Council, any signatory, any Party and any other State or the European Community which has been invited to accede to this Convention of:

(a) any signature;

(b) the deposit of any instrument of ratification, acceptance, approval or accession;

(c) any date of entry into force of this Convention in accordance with Articles 21 or 22;

(d) any amendment adopted in accordance with Article 20 and the date on which such an amendment enters into force;

(e) any declaration made under the provisions of Articles 1 and 23;

(f) any denunciation made in pursuance of the provisions of Article 25;

(g) any other act, notification or communication relating to this Convention.

In witness whereof the undersigned, being duly authorised thereto, have signed this Convention.

Done at Strasbourg, the 25th January 1996, in English and French, both texts being equally authentic, in a single copy which shall be deposited in the archives of the Council of Europe. The Secretary-General of the Council of Europe shall transmit certified copies to each member State of the Council of Europe, to the non-member States which have participated in the elaboration of this Convention, to the European Community and to any State invited to accede to this Convention.

2.14: Slavery Convention

Entered into force 9 March 1927.

Whereas the signatories of the General Act of the Brussels Conference of 1889–90 declared that they were equally animated by the firm intention of putting an end to the traffic in African slaves,

Whereas the signatories of the Convention of Saint-Germain-en-Laye of 1919, to revise the General Act of Berlin of 1885 and the General Act and Declaration of Brussels of 1890, affirmed their intention of securing the complete suppression of slavery in all its forms and of the slave trade by land and sea,

Taking into consideration the report of the Temporary Slavery Commission appointed by the Council of the League of Nations on June 12th, 1924,

Desiring to complete and extend the work accomplished under the Brussels Act and to find a means of giving practical effect throughout the world to such intentions as were expressed in regard to slave trade and slavery by the signatories of the Convention of Saint-Germain-en-Laye, and recognising that it is necessary to conclude to that end more detailed arrangements than are contained in that Convention,

Considering, moreover, that it is necessary to prevent forced labour from developing into conditions analogous to slavery,

Have decided to conclude a Convention and have accordingly appointed as their Plenipotentiaries [names omitted] . . . have agreed as follows:

Article 1

For the purpose of the present Convention, the following definitions are agreed upon:
1. Slavery is the status or condition of a person over whom any or all of the powers attaching to the right of ownership are exercised.
2. The slave trade includes all acts involved in the capture, acquisition or disposal of a person with intent to reduce him to slavery; all acts involved in the acquisition of a slave with a view to selling or exchanging him; all acts of disposal by sale or exchange of a slave acquired with a view to being sold or exchanged, and, in general, every act of trade or transport in slaves.

Article 2

The High Contracting Parties undertake, each in respect of the territories placed under its sovereignty, jurisdiction, protection, suzerainty or tutelage, so far as they have not already taken the necessary steps:
  (a) To prevent and suppress the slave trade;
  (b) To bring about, progressively and as soon as possible, the complete abolition of slavery in all its forms.

Article 3

The High Contracting Parties undertake to adopt all appropriate measures with a view to preventing and suppressing the embarkation, disembarkation and transport of slaves in their territorial waters and upon all vessels flying their respective flags.

The High Contracting Parties undertake to negotiate as soon as possible a general Convention with regard to the slave trade which will give them rights and impose upon them duties of the same nature as those provided for in the Convention of June 17th, of any High Contracting Parties in a position different from that of the other High Contracting Parties.

It is also understood that, before or after the coming into force of this general Convention, the High Contracting Parties are entirely free to conclude between themselves, without, however, derogating from the principles laid down in the preceding paragraph, such special agreements as, by reason of their peculiar situation, might appear to be suitable in order to bring about as soon as possible the complete disappearance of the slave trade.

Article 4

The High Contracting Parties shall give to one another every assistance with the object of securing the abolition of slavery and the slave trade.

Article 5

The High Contracting Parties recognise that recourse to compulsory or forced labour may have grave consequences and undertake, each in respect of the territories placed under its sovereignty, jurisdiction, protection, suzerainty or tutelage, to take all necessary measures to prevent compulsory or forced labour from developing into conditions analogous to slavery.

It is agreed that:

1. Subject to the transitional provisions laid down in paragraph (2) below, compulsory or forced labour may only be exacted for public purposes.

2. In territories in which compulsory or forced labour for other than public purposes still survives, the High Contracting Parties shall endeavour progressively and as soon as possible to put an end to the practice. So long as such forced or compulsory labour exists, this labour shall invariably be of an exceptional character, shall always receive adequate remuneration, and shall not involve the removal of the labourers from their usual place of residence.

3. In all cases, the responsibility for any recourse to compulsory or forced labour shall rest with the competent central authorities of the territory concerned.

Article 6

Those of the High Contracting Parties whose laws do not at present make adequate provision for the punishment of infractions of laws and regulations enacted with a view to giving effect to the purposes of the present Convention undertake to adopt the necessary measures in order that severe penalties may be imposed in respect of such infractions.

Article 7

The High Contracting Parties undertake to communicate to each other and to the Secretary-General of the League of Nations any laws and regulations which they may enact with a view to the application of the provisions of the present Convention.

Article 8

The High Contracting Parties agree that disputes arising between them relating to the interpretation or application of this Convention shall, if they cannot be settled by direct negotiation, be referred for decision to the Permanent Court of International Justice. In case either or both of the States Parties to such a dispute should not be Parties to the Protocol of December 16th, 1920, relating to the Permanent Court of International Justice, the dispute shall be referred, at the choice of the Parties and in accordance with the constitutional procedure of each State, either to the Permanent Court of International Justice or to a court of arbitration constituted in accordance with the Convention of October 18th, 1907, for the Pacific Settlement of International Disputes, or to some other court of arbitration.

Article 9

At the time of signature or of ratification or of accession, any High Contracting Party may declare that its acceptance of the present Convention does not bind some or all of the territories placed under its sovereignty, jurisdiction, protection, suzerainty or tutelage in respect of all or any provisions of the Convention; it may subsequently accede separately on behalf of any one of them or in respect of any provision to which any one of them is not a Party.

Article 10

In the event of a High Contracting Party wishing to denounce the present Convention, the denunciation shall be notified in writing to the Secretary-General of the League of Nations, who will at once communicate a certified true copy of the notification to all the other High Contracting Parties, informing them of the date on which it was received.

The denunciation shall only have effect in regard to the notifying State, and one year after the notification has reached the Secretary-General of the League of Nations.

Denunciation may also be made separately in respect of any territory placed under its sovereignty, jurisdiction, protection, suzerainty or tutelage.

Article 11

The present Convention, which will bear this day's date and of which the French and English texts are both authentic, will remain open for signature by the States Members of the League of Nations until April 1st, 1927.

The Secretary-General of the League of Nations will subsequently bring the present Convention to the notice of States which have not signed it, including States which are not Members of the League of Nations, and invite them to accede thereto.

A State desiring to accede to the Convention shall notify its intention in writing to the Secretary-General of the League of Nations and transmit to him the instrument of accession, which shall be deposited in the archives of the League.

The Secretary-General shall immediately transmit to all the other High Contracting Parties a certified true copy of the notification and of the instrument of accession, informing them of the date on which he received them.

Article 12

The present Convention will be ratified and the instruments of ratification shall be deposited in the office of the Secretary-General of the League of Nations. The Secretary-General will inform all the High Contracting Parties of such deposit.

The Convention will come into operation for each State on the date of the deposit of its ratification or of its accession.

IN FAITH WHEREOF the Plenipotentiaries signed the present Convention.

DONE at Geneva the twenty-fifth day of September, one thousand nine hundred and twenty-six, in one copy, which will be deposited in the archives of the League of Nations. A certified copy shall be forwarded to each signatory State.

2.15: Convention[1] for the Suppression of the Traffic in Persons and of the Exploitation of the Prostitution of Others

Opened for signature at Lake Success, New York, on 21 March 1950. Entered into force 25 July 1951.

PREAMBLE

Whereas prostitution and the accompanying evil of the traffic in persons for the purpose of prostitution are incompatible with the dignity and worth of the human person and endanger the welfare of the individual, the family and the community,

Whereas, with respect to the suppression of the traffic in women and children, the following international instruments are in force:

1. International Agreement of 18 May 1904 for the Suppression of the White Slave Traffic, as amended by the Protocol approved by the General Assembly of the United Nations on 3 December 1948,[2]

2. International Convention of 4 May 1910 for the Suppression of the White Slave Traffic, as amended by the above-mentioned Protocol,[3]

3. International Convention of 30 September 1921 for the Suppression of the Traffic in Women and Children, as amended by the Protocol approved by the General Assembly of the United Nations on 20 October 1947,[4]

4. International Convention of 11 October 1933 for the Suppression of the Traffic in Women of Full Age, as amended by the aforesaid Protocol,[5]

Whereas the League of Nations in 1937 prepared a draft Convention[6] extending the scope of the above-mentioned instruments, and

Whereas developments since 1937 make feasible the conclusion of a convention consolidating the above-mentioned instruments and embodying the substance of the 1937 draft Convention as well as desirable alterations therein;

Now therefore
The Contracting Parties
Hereby agree as hereinafter provided:

Article 1

The Parties to the present Convention agree to punish any person who, to gratify the passions of another:

1. Procures, entices or leads away, for purposes of prostitution, another person, even with the consent of that person;

2. Exploits the prostitution of another person, even with the consent of that person.

Article 2

The Parties to the present Convention further agree to punish any person who:

1. Keeps or manages, or knowingly finances or takes part in the financing of a brothel;

---

[1] Came into force on 25 July 1951, the ninetieth day following the date of deposit of the second instrument of ratification or accession, in accordance with article 24.

The following States deposited with the Secretary-General of the United Nations their instruments of ratification or accession on the dates indicated:

        Accession.—Israel .... 28 December 1950

        Ratification.—Yugoslavia .... 26 April 1951

[2] United Nations, *Treaty Series*, Vol. 92, p. 19.

[3] United Nations, *Treaty Series*, Vol. 98, p. 109.

[4] United Nations, *Treaty Series*, Vol. 53, p. 39, Vol. 65, p. 333; Vol. 76, p. 281, and Vol. 77, p. 364.

[5] United Nations, *Treaty Series*, Vol. 53, p. 49; Vol. 65, p. 334; Vol. 76, p. 281, and Vol. 77, p. 365.

[6] League of Nations, document C.331.M.223.1937.IV.

2. Knowingly lets or rents a building or other place or any part thereof for the purpose of the prostitution of others.

Article 3

To the extent permitted by domestic law, attempts to commit any of the offences referred to in articles 1 and 2, and acts preparatory to the commission thereof, shall also be punished.

Article 4

To the extent permitted by domestic law, intentional participation in the acts referred to in articles 1 and 2 above shall also be punishable.

To the extent permitted by domestic law, acts of participation shall be treated as separate offences whenever this is necessary to prevent impunity.

Article 5

In cases where injured persons are entitled under domestic law to be parties to proceedings in respect of any of the offences referred to in the present Convention, aliens shall be so entitled upon the same terms as nationals.

Article 6

Each Party to the present Convention agrees to take all the necessary measures to repeal or abolish any existing law, regulation or administrative provision by virtue of which persons who engage in or are suspected of engaging in prostitution are subject either to special registration or to the possession of a special document or to any exceptional requirements for supervision or notification.

Article 7

Previous convictions pronounced in foreign States for offences referred to in the present Convention shall, to the extent permitted by domestic law, be taken into account for the purpose of:
1. Establishing recidivism;
2. Disqualifying the offender from the exercise of civil rights.

Article 8

The offences referred to in articles 1 and 2 of the present Convention shall be regarded as extraditable offences in any extradition treaty which has been or may hereafter be concluded between any of the Parties to this Convention.

The Parties to the present Convention which do not make extradition conditional on the existence of a treaty shall henceforward recognize the offences referred to in articles 1 and 2 of the present Convention as cases for extradition between themselves.

Extradition shall be granted in accordance with the law of the State to which the request is made.

Article 9

In States where the extradition of nationals is not permitted by law, nationals who have returned to their own State after the commission abroad of any of the offences referred to in articles 1 and 2 of the present Convention shall be prosecuted in and punished by the courts of their own State.

This provision shall not apply if, in a similar case between the Parties to the present Convention, the extradition of an alien cannot be granted.

Article 10

The provisions of article 9 shall not apply when the person charged with the offence has been tried in a foreign State and, if convicted, has served his sentence or had it remitted or reduced in conformity with the laws of that foreign State.

Article 11

Nothing in the present Convention shall be interpreted as determining the attitude of a Party towards the general question of the limits of criminal jurisdiction under international law.

Article 12

The present Convention does not affect the principle that the offences to which it refers shall in each State be defined, prosecuted and punished in conformity with its domestic law.

Article 13

The Parties to the present Convention shall be bound to execute letters of request relating to offences referred to in the Convention in accordance with their domestic law and practice.

The transmission of letters of request shall be effected:

1. By direct communication between the judicial authorities; or
2. By direct communication between the Ministers of Justice of the two States, or by direct communication from another competent authority of the State making the request to the Minister of Justice of the State to which the request is made; or
3. Through the diplomatic or consular representative of the State making the request in the State to which the request is made; this representative shall send the letters of request direct to the competent judicial authority or to the authority indicated by the Government of the State to which the request is made, and shall receive direct from such authority the papers constituting the execution of the letters of request.

In cases 1 and 3 a copy of the letters of request shall always be sent to the superior authority of the State to which application is made.

Unless otherwise agreed, the letters of request shall be drawn up in the language of the authority making the request, provided always that the State to which the request is made may require a translation in its own language, certified correct by the authority making the request.

Each Party to the present Convention shall notify to each of the other Parties to the Convention the method or methods of transmission mentioned above which it will recognize for the letters of request of the latter State.

Until such notification is made by a State, its existing procedure in regard to letters of request shall remain in force.

Execution of letters of request shall not give rise to a claim for reimbursement of charges or expenses of any nature whatever other than expenses of experts.

Nothing in the present article shall be construed as an undertaking on the part of the Parties to the present Convention to adopt in criminal matters any form or methods of proof contrary to their own domestic laws.

Article 14

Each Party to the present Convention shall establish or maintain a service charged with the co-ordination and centralization of the results of the investigation of offences referred to in the present Convention.

Such services should compile all information calculated to facilitate the prevention and punishment of the offences referred to in the present Convention and should be in close contact with the corresponding services in other States.

Article 15

To the extent permitted by domestic law and to the extent to which the authorities responsible for the services referred to in article 14 may judge desirable, they shall furnish to the authorities responsible for the corresponding services in other States the following information:

1. Particulars of any offence referred to in the present Convention or any attempt to commit such offence;

2. Particulars of any search for and any prosecution, arrest, conviction, refusal of admission or expulsion of persons guilty of any of the offences referred to in the present Convention, the movements of such persons and any other useful information with regard to them.

The information so furnished shall include descriptions of the offenders, their fingerprints, photographs, methods of operation, police records and records of conviction.

Article 16

The Parties to the present Convention agree to take or to encourage, through their public and private educational, health, social, economic and other related services, measures for the prevention of prostitution and for the rehabilitation and social adjustment of the victims of prostitution and of the offences referred to in the present Convention.

Article 17

The Parties to the present Convention undertake, in connexion with immigration and emigration, to adopt or maintain such measures as are required in terms of their obligations under the present Convention, to check the traffic in persons of either sex for the purpose of prostitution.

In particular they undertake:
1. To make such relegations as are necessary for the protection of immigrants or emigrants, and in particular, women and children, both at the place of arrival and departure and while *en route*;
2. To arrange for appropriate publicity warning the public of the dangers of the aforesaid traffic;
3. To take appropriate measures to ensure supervision of railway stations, airports, seaports and *en route*, and of other public places, in order to prevent international traffic in persons for the purpose of prostitution;
4. To take appropriate measures in order that the appropriate authorities be informed of the arrival of persons who appear, *prima facie*, to be the principals and accomplices in or victims of such traffic.

Article 18

The Parties to the present Convention undertake, in accordance with the conditions laid down by domestic law, to have declarations taken from aliens who are prostitutes, in order to establish their identity and civil status and to discover who has caused them to leave their State. The information obtained shall be communicated to the authorities of the State of origin of the said persons with a view to their eventual repatriation.

Article 19

The Parties to the present Convention undertake, in accordance with the conditions laid down by domestic law and without prejudice to prosecution or other action for violations thereunder and so far as possible:
1. Pending the completion of arrangements for the repatriation of destitute victims of international traffic in persons for the purpose of prostitution, to make suitable provisions for their temporary care and maintenance;
2. To repatriate persons referred to in article 18 who desire to be repatriated or who may be claimed by persons exercising authority over them or whose expulsion is ordered in conformity with the law. Repatriation shall take place only after agreement is reached with the State of destination as to identity and nationality as well as to the place and date of arrival at frontiers. Each Party to the present Convention shall facilitate the passage of such persons through its territory.

Where the persons referred to in the preceding paragraph cannot themselves repay the cost of repatriation and have neither spouse, relatives nor guardian to pay for them, the cost of repatriation as far as the nearest frontier or port of embarkation or airport in the direction of the State of origin shall be borne by the State where they are in residence, and the cost of the remainder of the journey shall be borne by the State of origin.

Article 20

The Parties to the present Convention shall, if they have not already done so, take the necessary measures for the supervision of employment agencies in order to prevent persons seeking employment, in particular women and children, from being exposed to the danger of prostitution.

Article 21

The Parties to the present Convention shall communicate to the Secretary-General of the United Nations such laws and regulations as have already been promulgated in their States, and thereafter annually such laws and regulations as may be promulgated, relating to the subjects of the present Convention, as well as all measures taken by them concerning the application of the Convention. The information received shall be published periodically by the Secretary-General and sent to all Members of the United Nations and to non-member States to which the present Convention is officially communicated in accordance with article 23.

Article 22

If any dispute shall arise between the Parties to the present Convention relating to its interpretation or application and if such dispute cannot be settled by other means, the dispute shall, at the request of any one of the Parties to the dispute, be referred to the International Court of Justice.

Article 23

The present Convention shall be open for signature on behalf of any Member of the United Nations and also on behalf of any other State to which an invitation has been addressed by the Economic and Social Council.

The present Convention shall be ratified and the instruments of ratification shall be deposited with the Secretary-General of the United Nations.

The States mentioned in the first paragraph which have not signed the Convention may accede to it.

Accession shall be effected by deposit of an instrument of accession with the Secretary-General of the United Nations.

For the purpose of the present Convention the word 'State' shall include all the colonies and Trust Territories of a State signatory or acceding to the Convention and all territories for which such State is internationally responsible.

Article 24

The present Convention shall come into force on the ninetieth day following the day of deposit of the second instrument of ratification or accession.

For each State ratifying or acceding to the Convention after the deposit of the second instrument of ratification or accession, the Convention shall enter into force ninety days after the deposit by such State of its instrument of ratification or accession.

Article 25

After the expiration of five years from the entry into force of the present Convention, any Party to the Convention may denounce it by a written notification addressed to the Secretary-General of the United Nations.

Such denunciation shall take effect to the Party making it one year from the date upon which it is received by the Secretary-General of the United Nations.

Article 26

The Secretary-General of the United Nations shall inform all Members of the United Nations and non-member States referred to in article 23:

(a) Of signatures, ratifications and accessions received in accordance with article 23;

(b) Of the date on which the present Convention will come into force in accordance with article 24;

(c) Of denunciations received in accordance with article 25.

Article 27

Each Party to the present Convention undertakes to adopt, in accordance with its Constitution, the legislative or other measures necessary to ensure the application of the Convention.

Article 28

The provisions of the present Convention shall supersede in the relations between the Parties thereto the provisions of the international instruments referred to in sub-paragraphs 1, 2, 3 and 4 of the second paragraph of the Preamble, each of which shall be deemed to be terminated when all the Parties thereto shall have become Parties to the present Convention.

IN FAITH WHEREOF the undersigned, being duly authorized thereto by their respective Governments, have signed the present Convention, opened for signature at Lake Success, New York, on the twenty-first day of March, one thousand nine hundred and fifty, a certified true copy of which shall be transmitted by the Secretary-General to all the Members of the United Nations and to the non-member States referred to in article 23.

C3: TABLES OF TREATY RATIFICATIONS, RESERVATIONS, AND STATE REPORTING SCHEDULES

Treaty Index

Abbreviations

a	accession	When a State combines signature and ratification in one act.
d	succession	When a newly independent State agrees to abide by a treaty previously signed and applied to its territory by the formerly responsible State.
r	ratification	When ratification was made subsequent to signature.
s	signature	When a State signs the convention but doesn't ratify it so it is not binding on that State (it however denotes an intention to ratify at a later stage).
Rsv.		Reservations made by countries upon ratification.
NR		Year in which a report must be submitted to the U.N. Committee stating all the measures that have been taken by the State Party to pursue the provisions of the Convention.
NR*		The parties to the present Convention shall communicate to the Secretary-General of the U.N. annually such laws and regulations as may be promulgated in their States as well as the measures taken by them concerning the application of the present Convention. This information will be published periodically by the Secretary-General and sent to all members of the U.N. and non-member States to which the present Convention is officially communicated.
NR**		The State Parties to the present Covenant undertake to submit reports on the measures which they have adopted and the progress made in achieving the observance of the rights recognised therein [no submission periods have been specified].
NR***		Under this Covenant a Committee with representatives from all participant states was created. This Committee shall submit to the General Assembly of the U.N. an annual report on its activities and to this end, all participants states shall submit to the Committee an initial report (due one year after ratification) on measures adopted and thereafter every time the Committee requires them to do so.

Notes

For ease of reference, all Treaty articles mentioned on the following charts have been abridged. For further information please refer to the text of the treaty.

The dates by which reports are required to be submitted to the U.N. Committee (as mentioned under NR heading) may differ if the parties submit the reports later than the date stipulated. For instance, if a report was due in 1996 and it was submitted in 1997, the next due date will count from the date of submission and not from the date it was due.

The reservations mentioned under the Rsv. heading do not include some declarations which State Parties have made upon signature and ratification.

Convention on the Rights of the Child

Participant	Rsv.	Dates	NR
Afghanistan		28-03-1994 r	2001
Albania	14-1, 2; i	27-02-1992 r	1999
Algeria		16-04-1993 r	2000
Andorra		02-01-1996 r	2002
Angola		05-12-1990 r	1997
Antigua & Barbuda		05-10-1993 r	2000
Argentina	21-b,c,d,e	04-12-1990 r	1997
Armenia		23-06-1993 a	2000
Australia	37-c	17-12-1990 r	1997
Austria	ii; 17	06-08-1992 r	1999
Azerbaijan		13-08-1992 a	1999
Bahamas	2	20-02-1991 r	1998
Bahrain		13-02-1992 a	1999
Bangladesh	14-1; 21	03-08-1990 r	1997
Barbados		09-10-1990 r	1997
Belarus		01-10-1990 r	1997
Belgium	2; ii; 40-2bv	16-12-1991 r	1998
Belize		02-05-1990 r	1997
Benin		03-08-1990 r	1997
Bhutan		01-08-1990 r	1997
Bolivia		26-06-1990 r	1997
Bosnia & Herz.	9-1	01-09-1993 s	—
Botswana	1	14-03-1995 a	2002
Brazil		24-09-1995 r	1997
Brunei Dar.	iii	27-12-1995 a	2002
Bulgaria		03-06-1991 r	1998
Burkina Faso		31-08-1990 r	1997
Burundi		19-10-1990 r	1997
Cambodia		15-10-1992 a	1999
Cameroon		11-01-1993 r	2000
Canada	21; 37c	13-12-1991 r	1998
Cape Verde		04-06-1992 a	1999
Central A. Rep.		23-04-1992 r	1999
Chad		02-10-1990 r	1997
Chile		13-08-1990 r	1997
China	6	02-03-1992 r	1999
Colombia		28-01-1991 r	1998
Comoros		22-06-1993 r	2000
Congo		14-10-1993 a	2000
Costa Rica		21-08-1990 r	1997
Côte d'Ivoire		04-02-1991 r	1998
Croatia	9-1	12-10-1992 s	—
Cuba	1	21-08-1991 r	1998
Cyprus		07-02-1991 r	1998
Czech Rep.		22-02-1993 s	—
D.P.R. Korea	40-2bv*	21-09-1990 r	1997
Denmark		19-07-1991 r	1998
Djibouti	iii	06-12-1990 r	1997
Dominica		13-03-1991 r	1998
Dominic. Rep.		11-06-1991 r	1998
Ecuador		23-03-1990 r	1997
Egypt	20; 21	06-07-1990 r	1997
El Salvador		10-07-1990 r	1997
Equat. Guinea		15-06-1992 a	1999
Eritrea		03-08-1994 r	2000
Estonia		21-10-1991 a	1998
Ethiopia		14-05-1991 a	1998
Fiji		13-08-1993 r	2000
Finland		20-06-1991 r	1998
France	6*; 30; 40-2bv**	07-08-1990 r	1997
Gabon		09-02-1994 r	2000
Gambia		08-08-1990 r	1997
Georgia		02-06-1994 a	2001
Germany	18-1; 40-2bii, v**	06-03-1992 r	1999
Ghana		05-02-1990 r	1997
Greece		13-05-1993 r	1998
Grenada		05-11-1990 r	1997
Guatemala		06-06-1990 r	1997
Guinea		13-07-1990 a	1997
Guinea-Bissau		20-08-1990 r	1997
Guyana		14-01-1991 r	1998
Haiti		08-06-1995 r	2002
Holy See	24-2; iv	20-04-1990 r	1997
Honduras		10-08-1990 r	1997
Hungary		07-10-1991 r	1998
Iceland	v	28-10-1992 r	1999
India		11-12-1992 a	1999
Indonesia	vii	05-09-1990 r	1997
Iran (Isl. Rep.)	iii	13-07-1994 r	2001
Iraq	14-1	15-06-1994 a	2001
Ireland		28-09-1992 r	1999
Israel		03-10-1991 r	1998
Italy		05-09-1991 r	1998
Jamaica		14-05-1991 r	1998
Japan	37-c; 9-1*; 10-1	22-04-1994 r	2001
Kazakhstan		12-08-1994 r	1998
Kenya		30-07-1990 r	—
Kiribati	vii	12-12-1995 a	1997
Kuwait	iv; 7; 21*	21-10-1991 r	
Kyrgyztan		07-10-1994 a	
Lao P.D. Rep.		08-05-1991 a	
Latvia		14-04-1992 a	
Lebanon		14-05-1991 r	
Lesotho		10-03-1992 r	
Liberia		04-06-1993 r	
Libyan A.J.		15-04-1993 a	
Liechtenstein	7*; 10	22-12-1995 a	
Lithuania		31-01-1992 a	
Luxembourg	6**; 7**; 15	07-03-1994 r	
Macedonia		02-12-1993 s	
Madagascar		19-03-1991 r	
Malawi		02-01-1991 r	
Malaysia		17-02-1995 a	
Maldives	viii	11-02-1991 r	
Mali	21*; 14	20-09-1990 r	
Malta	26	30-09-1990 r	
Marshall Isl.		04-10-1993 r	
Mauritania	iii	16-05-1991 r	
Mauritius	22	26-07-1990 r	
Mexico		21-09-1990 r	
Micronesia		05-05-1993 a	
Monaco	7*; 40-2bv**	21-06-1993 a	
Mongolia		05-07-1990 r	
Morocco	14	21-06-1993 r	
Mozambique		26-04-1994 r	
Myanmar		15-07-1991 a	
Namibia		30-09-1990 r	
Nauru		27-07-1994 a	
Nepal		14-09-1990 r	
Netherlands	ix	06-02-1995 a	
New Zealand	32-1; 37-c*	06-04-1993 r	
Nicaragua		05-10-1990 r	
Niger		30-09-1990 r	
Nigeria		19-04-1991 r	
Niue		20-12-1995 a	
Norway		08-01-1991 r	
Pakistan	iii	12-11-1990 r	
Palau		04-08-1995 a	

214

Convention on the Rights of the Child (continued)

Participant	Rsv.	Dates	NR	Participant	Rsv.	Dates	NR
Panama		12-12-1990 r	1997	Sudan		03-08-1990 r	1997
Papua New Guinea		02-03-1993 r	2000	Suriname		01-03-1993 r	——
Paraguay		25-09-1990 r	1997	Swaziland		07-09-1995 r	2000
Peru		04-09-1990 r	1997	Sweden		29-06-1990 r	2000
Philippines	7; x 24-2	21-08-1990 r	1997	Switzerland		01-05-1991 s	1999
Poland		07-06-1991 r	1998	Syrian A. Rep.	iii; 14, 21*	15-07-1993 r	1997
Portugal		21-09-1990 r	1997	Tajikistan		26-10-1993 a	2002
Qatar	iii	03-04-1995 r	2002	Thailand	7*; 22; 29	27-03-1992 a	1998
Rep. of Korea	9-3; 21-a; 40-2bv*	20-11-1991 r	1998	Togo		01-08-1990 r	1999
Rep. of Moldova		26-01-1993 a	2001	Tonga		06-11-1995 a	2002
Romania		28-09-1990 r	1997	Trinidad & Tobago		05-12-1991 r	2000
Russian Fed.		16-08-1990 r	1998	Tunisia	iii; 6*; 2; 40-2bv**; 7*	30-01-1992 r	2002
Rwanda		24-01-1991 r	1998	Turkey	17*; 29; 30*	04-04-1995 r	1997
St. Kitts & Nevis		24-07-1990 r	1997	Turkmenistan		20-09-1993 a	1998
St. Vincent & the Grenadines		26-10-1993 r	2000	Tuvalu		22-09-1995 a	1998
St. Lucia		16-06-1993 r	2001	Uganda		17-08-1990 r	——
Samoa	28-1a	29-11-1994 r	2001	Ukraine		16-12-1991 r	1997
San Marino		25-11-1991 a	1998	United Kingdom		10-06-1991 r	2001
São Tomé & Principe		14-05-1991 a	1998	U. Rep. Tanzania		16-02-1995 s	2000
Saudi Arabia		26-01-1996	2003	United St. of America	xiii; 32; 37-c*,d	20-11-1990 r	1997
Senegal		31-07-1991 r	1998	Uruguay		29-06-1994 a	1997
Seychelles		07-09-1990 a	1997	Uzbekistan		07-07-1993 r	1998
Sierra Leone		18-06-1990 r	1997	Vanuatu		13-09-1990 r	1998
Singapore	xi; 32; 28-1a	05-10-1995 a	2002	Venezuela		28-02-1990 r	1997
Slovak Rep.		28-05-1993 s	——	Vietnam		01-05-1991 r	1998
Slovenia	9-1	06-07-1992 s	——	Yemen		03-01-1991 r	1997
Solomon Islands		10-04-1995 a	2002	Yugoslavia	9-1**	27-09-1990 r	1997
South Africa		16-06-1995 r	2002	Zaire		06-12-1991 r	2000
Spain	21-d	06-12-1990 r	1997	Zambia		11-09-1990 r	2002
Sri Lanka		12-07-1991 r	1998				

Optional Protocol to the International Covenant on Civil and Political Rights

Participant	Rsv.	Dates	NR***
Algeria		12-09-1989 a	
Angola		10-01-1992 a	
Argentina		08-08-1986 a	
Armenia		23-06-1993 a	
Australia		25-09-1991 a	
Austria	5–2	10-12-1978 r	
Barbados		05-01-1973 a	
Belarus		30-09-1992 a	
Belgium		17-05-1994 a	
Benin		12-03-1992 a	
Bolivia		12-08-1982 a	
Bosnia & Herzegovina		01-03-1995 r	
Bulgaria		26-03-1992 a	
Cameroon		27-06-1984 a	
Canada		19-05-1976 a	
Central African Rep.		08-05-1981 a	
Chad		09-06-1995 a	
Chile	1	27-05-1992 a	
Colombia		29-10-1969 r	
Congo		05-10-1983 a	
Costa Rica		29-11-1968 r	
Croatia	1, 5–2*	12-10-1995 a	
Cyprus		15-04-1992 r	
Czech Republic		22-02-1993 d	
Denmark	5–2*	06-01-1972 r	
Dominican Republic		04-01-1978 a	
Ecuador		06-03-1969 r	
El Salvador	1, 5–2*	06-06-1995 r	
Equatorial Guinea		25-09-1987 a	
Estonia		21-10-1991 a	
Finland		19-08-1975 r	
France	1, 5–2*	17-02-1984 a	
Gambia		09-06-1988 a	
Georgia		03-05-1994 a	
Germany	5–2**	25-08-1993 a	
Guinea		17-06-1993 r	
Guyana		10-05-1993 a	
Honduras		19-12-1966 s	
Hungary		07-09-1988 a	
Iceland	5–2*	22-08-1979 a	
Ireland	5–2*	08-12-1989 a	
Italy	5–2*	15-09-1978 r	
Jamaica		03-10-1975 r	
Kyrgyzstan		07-10-1994 a	
Latvia		22-06-1994 a	
Libyan Arab Jamahiriya		16-05-1989 a	
Lithuania		20-11-1991 a	
Luxembourg	5–2*	18-08-1983 a	
Madagascar		21-06-1971 r	
Malta	1, 5–2*	13-09-1990 a	
Mauritius		12-12-1973 a	
Mongolia		16-04-1991 a	
Namibia		28-11-1994 a	
Netherlands		11-12-1978 r	
Nepal		14-05-1991 a	
New Zealand		26-05-1989 a	
Nicaragua		12-03-1980 a	
Niger		07-03-1986 a	
Norway	5–2*	13-09-1972 r	
Panama		08-03-1977 r	
Paraguay		10-01-1995 a	
Peru		03-10-1980 r	
Philippines		22-08-1989 r	
Poland	5–2*	07-11-1991 a	
Portugal		03-05-1983 r	
Rep. of Korea		10-04-1990 a	
Romania	5–2*	20-07-1993 a	
Russian Fed.	1, 5–2*	01-10-1991 a	
St. Vincent & Grenadines		09-11-1981 a	
San Marino		18-10-1985 a	
Senegal		13-02-1978 r	
Seychelles		05-05-1992 a	
Slovakia		28-05-1993 d	
Slovenia	1, 5–2*	16-07-1993 a	
Somalia		24-01-1990 a	
Spain	5–2*	25-01-1985 a	
Suriname		28-12-1976 a	
Sweden	5–2*	06-12-1971 r	
the former Yugoslav Rep. of Macedonia		12-12-1994 r	
Togo		30-03-1988 a	
Trinidad & Tobago		14-11-1980 a	
Uganda	5–2*	14-11-1995 a	
Ukraine		25-07-1991 a	
Uruguay		01-04-1970 r	
Uzbekistan		28-09-1995 a	
Venezuela	i	10-05-1978 r	
Yugoslavia		14-03-1990 s	
Zaire		01-11-1976 a	
Zambia		10-04-1984 a	

i

The State Party ratifies the Optional Protocol on the understanding that Article 60-5 of its Constitution shall be respected. This Article establishes that 'No person shall be convicted in a criminal trial unless he has first been personally notified of the charges and heard in the manner prescribed by law. Persons accused of an offence against the *res publica* with the guarantees and in the manner prescribed by law'

Article 1 [recognition of the Committee to consider claims from individuals of violations of rights set out in the Covenant]
The State Party accepts the competence of the Committee in claims which result either from acts, omissions, developments or events occurring after the date on which the Protocol enters into force in the State Party.

Article 5–2 [The Committee shall not consider any communication from an individual unless it has ascertained that the same matter is not being examined under another procedure of international investigation]
The State party ratifies the Protocol on the understanding that the Committee shall not accept any claim unless it has ascertained that the same has not been examined by the European Commission on Human Rights.

Article 5–2* [The Committee shall not consider any communication from an individual unless it has ascertained that the same matter is not being examined under another procedure of international investigation]
The State Party makes a reservation with respect to the competence of the Committee to consider a claim if the matter has already been considered under other procedures of international investigation.

Optional Protocol to the International Covenant on Civil and Political Rights

Article 5–2** [*The Committee shall not consider any communication from an individual unless it has ascertained that the same matter is not being examined under another procedure of international investigation*]
The State Party reserves the right not to recognise the competence of the Committee to claims: (a) which have already been considered under another procedure of international investigation; (b) by means of which a violation of rights is reprimanded having its origin in events occurring prior to the entry into force of the Protocol; (c) by means of which a violation is reprimanded, in so far as the reprimand violation refers to rights other than those guaranteed under the Covenant.

STATE PARTIES

AMERICA

Argentina
Barbados***
Bolivia
Canada
Chad
Chile
Columbia
Costa Rica
Dominican Rep.
Ecuador
El Salvador
Guyana
Honduras
Jamaica***
Nicaragua
Panama
Paraguay
Peru
St. Vincent &
    Grenadines***
Suriname
Trinidad & Tobago***
Uruguay
Venezuela

EUROPE

Austria
Belarus
Belgium
Bosnia & Herz.
Bulgaria
Croatia

Cyprus
Czech Rep.
Denmark
Estonia
Finland
France
Germany
Hungary
Iceland
Ireland
Italy
Latvia
Lithuania
Luxembourg
Malta
Netherlands
Norway
Poland
Portugal
Romania
Russian Fed.*
San Marino
Slovakia
Slovenia
Spain
Sweden
the former Yugoslav
Rep. of Macedonia
Ukraine
Yugoslavia

AFRICA

Algeria
Angola

Benin
Cameroon
Central Af. Rep.
Congo
Equatorial Guinea
Gambia
Guinea
Libyan Arab Jam.
Madagascar
Mauritius**
Namibia
Nigeria
Senegal
Seychelles**
Somalia
Togo
Uganda
Zaire
Zambia

ASIA

Armenia
Georgia
Kyrgyzstan
Mongolia
Nepal
Philippines
Rep. of Korea
Uzbekistan

AUSTRALIA

Australia
New Zealand

*   Eurasia
**   Indian Ocean
*** West Indies

Convention on the Rights of the Child

i

Articles 13 [right to freedom of expression], 16 [right to privacy, family, home and non-unlawful interference with correspondence] and 17 [right to access to information especially that aimed at the promotion of his or her spiritual, social and moral well being] shall be applied while taking account of the interest of the child and the need to safeguard its physical and mental integrity.

ii

The State Party will apply Articles 13 [right to freedom of expression] and 15 [right to freedom of association and to freedom of peaceful assembly] provided that they will not affect legal restrictions in accordance with Article 10 and 11 of the European Convention on the Protection of Human Rights and Fundamental Freedoms.

iii

Reserves the right not to be bound to any provisions which may be contrary to its Constitution and to the beliefs and principles of Islam.

iv

The State Party interprets this Convention in a way which safeguards the primary and inalienable rights of parents, in particular insofar as these rights concern education, religion, association with others and privacy.

v

The State Party declares that Article 9 [to ensure that a child shall not be separated from his parents against their will] and Article 37-c [every child deprived of liberty shall be treated with humanity and respect; in particular should be separated from adults] shall be applicable according to its own law.

vi

The State Party declares that Articles 1 [a child means every human being below the age of eighteen unless the law applicable, majority is attained earlier], 14 [the right to freedom of thought, conscience and religion], 16 [right to privacy, family, home and non-unlawful interference with correspondence], 17 [right to access to information especially that aimed at the promotion of his or her spiritual, social and moral well being], 21 [to permit the system of adoption in the best interests of the child], 22 [to ensure that a child who is seeking refugee status receive appropriate protection] and 29 [the education of the child shall be directed to the development of his personality, talents and mental and physical abilities] shall be applied in conformity with its Constitution.

vii

The State Party reserves the right not to be bound by Article 24-2b,c,d,e,f [to ensure the provision of medical assistance; to combat disease and malnutrition; to ensure appropriate pre- and post-natal health care; to ensure people are informed and have access to health education; to develop preventive health care and family planning]; Article 26 [the right of every child to benefit from social security] and Article 28-b,c,d [to encourage the development of different forms of secondary education; to make higher education accessible; make educational and vocational information and guidance available].

viii

The State Party reserves the right not to be bound to the Articles below and declares that these shall be applicable only if they are in conformity with its Constitution and national laws.

Articles: 1 [a child means every human being below the age of eighteen unless under the law applicable, majority is attained earlier]; 2 [the rights set in this Convention shall be applicable without discrimination of any kind]; 7 [the right to be registered after birth and to be given a name and acquire nationality]; 13 [the right to freedom of expression]; 14 [the child's right to freedom of thought, conscience and religion] 15 [the right to freedom of association and freedom of peaceful assembly]; 22 [to ensure that a child who is seeking refugee status shall receive appropriate protection]; 28 [the right to education]; 37 [to ensure that no child shall be subject to torture or other cruel, inhuman or degrading treatment or punishment]; 40-3,4 [the right of every child alleged as, accused of, or recognised as having infringed the penal law to be treated in a manner consistent with the promotion of the child's sense of dignity and worth]; 44 [to submit the Committee reports on the measures adopted which give effect to the rights recognised under this Convention]; 45 [the specialised agencies of the U.N. shall be entitled to be represented at the consideration of the implementation of the provision of this Convention].

ix

The State Party reserves the right to apply the following Articles and with the following exceptions: Article 26 [the right to benefit from social security] shall not imply an independent entitlement of children to social security; Article 37 [every child deprived of liberty shall be treated with humanity and respect; in particular should it be separated from adults] shall not prevent the application of adult penal law to children of sixteen years and older; Article 40 [the right of every child alleged as, accused of, or recognised as having infringed the law to be treated with dignity; and to this end to be informed promptly and directly of the charges against him through his parents or other appropriate assistance] is accepted with the reservation that cases involving minor offences may be tried without the presence of legal assistance; Article 22 [to ensure that a child who is seeking refugee status shall receive appropriate protection] does not prevent the submission of a request for admission from being made subject to certain conditions, failure to meet such conditions resulting in inadmissibility.

x

Articles 12 [to assure to the child who is capable of forming his own views the right to express those views freely] and 16 [right to privacy, family, home and non-unlawful interference with correspondence] shall be exercised with respect for parents' authority, in accordance with the State Party's customs and traditions.

xi

The State Party declares that Articles 12 [to assure to the child who is capable of forming his own views the right to express those views freely] and 16 [right to privacy, family, home and non-unlawful interference with correspondence] and 17 [right to access to information especially that aimed at the promotion of the child's spiritual, social and moral well being] shall be exercised with respect for the authority of parents, schools and other persons who are entrusted with the care of the child.

The State Party further considers that Articles 19 [to take all appropriate measures to protect the child from all forms of physical or mental violence] and 37 [to ensure that no child shall be subjected to torture or other cruel, inhuman or degrading treatment or punishment] do not prohibit the application of (i) any prevailing measures prescribed by its law for maintaining law and order or (ii) which are necessary in the interests of national security or (iii) the judicious application of corporal punishment in the best interest of the child.

The State Party declares that its accession to this Convention does not imply the acceptance of obligations going beyond the limits prescribed by its law nor the acceptance of any obligation to introduce any right beyond those prescribed under its law.

The State Party reserves the right to apply such legislation and conditions concerning the entry into, stay in and departure of those who do not or who no longer have the right to enter and remain in its territory, and to the acquisition and possession of citizenship, as it may deem necessary from time to time and in accordance with its nationals laws.

In connection with Article 28-1a, the State Party reserves the right to provide primary education free only to children who are citizens of its territory.

xii
The State Party interprets the word 'parents' to mean only those who, as a matter of national law, are treated as parents. The State Party reserves the right to apply such legislation and conditions concerning the entry into, stay in and departure of those who do not or who no longer have the right to enter and remain in its territory, and to the acquisition and possession of citizenship, as it may deem necessary from time to time and in accordance with its national laws.

Article 1 [a child means every human being below the age of eighteen unless under the law applicable, majority is attained earlier]
The State Party reserves the right not to be bound by this Article insofar as it conflicts with its laws.

Article 2 [the rights set in this Convention shall be applicable without discrimination of any kind]
The State Party reserves the right not to apply the provisions of this Article insofar as they relate to the conferment of citizenship upon a child.

Article 2* [the right set in this Convention shall be applicable without discrimination of any kind]
The State Party reserves the right to apply this Article in accordance with its legislation.

Article 6 [the right to life]
The State Party shall fulfil its obligations under this Article provided that these do not conflict with its family planning legislation and its Law of Minor Children.

Article 6* [the right to life]
The State Party declares that this Article cannot be interpreted as constituting any obstacle to the implementation of the provision of its legal system regarding the voluntary interruption of pregnancy.

Article 6** [the right to life]
The State Party declares that this Article cannot be interpreted as constituting any obstacle to the implementation of the provision of its legal system regarding sex information, the prevention of back-street abortion and the regulation of pregnancy termination.

Article 7 [the right to be registered after birth and to be given a name and acquire nationality]
The State Party understands the concepts of this Article to signify the right of the child who was born in Kuwait and whose parents are unknown to be granted the State's nationality.

Article 7* [the right to be registered after birth and to be given a name and acquire nationality]
The State Party reserves the right to apply its legislation regarding nationality.

Article 7** [the right to be registered after birth and to be given a name and acquire nationality]
The State Party declares that this Article shall not present any obstacle to the legal process in respect of anonymous births.

Article 7*** [the right to be registered after birth... and, as far as possible, the right to know and be cared for by his parents]
The State Party stipulates that the right of an adopted child to know its natural parents shall be subject to the limitations imposed by binding legal arrangements that enable adoptive parents to maintain the confidentiality of the child's origin.

Article 9-1 [to ensure that a child shall not be separated from his parents against their will]
The State Party reserves the right not to apply this Article.

Article 9-1* [to ensure that a child shall not be separated from his parents against their will]
The State Party declares that this Article shall not apply to a case where a child is separated from his parents as a result of deportation in accordance with its immigration laws.

Article 9-1** [to ensure that a child shall not be separated from his parents against their will]
The State Party may under this Article make decisions to deprive parents of their right to raise their children without prior judicial determination in accordance with its legislation.

Article 9-3 [to respect the right of the child who is separated from one or both parents to maintain personal relations with them]
The State Party reserves the right not to be bound by this Article.

Article 10 [applications by a child or his parents to enter or leave for the purpose of family reunification shall be dealt with in a positive, humane and expeditious manner]
The State Party reserves the right not to be bound by this Article.

Article 10 [applications by a child or his parents to enter or leave for the purpose of family reunification shall be dealt with in a positive, humane and expeditious manner]
The State Party reserves the right to apply its legislation according to which family reunification for certain categories of foreigners is not guaranteed.

Article 10-1 [applications by a child or his parents to enter or leave for the purpose of family reunification shall be dealt with in a positive, humane and expeditious manner]
The State Party declares that this Article, i.e. the obligation to deal with applications in a 'positive, humane and expeditious manner' shall not affect the outcome of such applications.

Article 14 [the child's right to freedom of thought, conscience and religion]
The State Party reserves the right not to be bound by this Article.

Article 14-1 [the child's right to freedom of thought, conscience and religion] 2 [the rights of parents to provide direction to the child in the exercise of this right]
The State Party interprets this Article in accordance with the basic foundations of its legal system.

Article 15 [the right to freedom of association and freedom of peaceful assembly]
The State Party declares that this Article does not impede the provisions of its legislation concerning the exercise of this right.

Article 17 [right to access to information especially that aimed at the promotion of the child's spiritual, social and moral well-being]
The State Party will apply this Article to the extent that it is compatible with the basic rights of others, in particular with the basic rights of freedom of information and freedom of press.

Article 17* [right to access to information especially that aimed at the promotion of the child's spiritual, social and moral well-being]
The State Party reserves the right to apply this Article in accordance with its legislation.

Article 18-1 [to ensure recognition of the principle that both parents have common responsibilities for the upbringing and development of the child]
The State Party is of the opinion that this Article does not imply that parental custody automatically applies to both parents.

Article 20 [*a child temporarily or permanently deprived of his family environment shall be entitled to special protection*]
The State Party reserves the right not to be bound by this Article.

Article 21 [*to permit the system of adoption in the best interests of the child*]
The State Party shall only apply this Article subject to its existing laws and practices.

Article 21* [*to permit the system of adoption in the best interests of the child*]
The State Party reserves the right not to be bound by this Article.

Article 21-a [*to ensure that the adoption of a child is authorised only by competent authorities*]
The State Party reserves the right not to be bound by this Article.

Article 21-b [*inter-country adoption*], *c* [*safeguards to inter-country adoption*], *d* [*scrutiny to improper financial gain in inter-country adoptions*], *e* [*procuring bilateral or multilateral arrangements concerning inter-country adoption*
The State Party does not consider itself bound by these provisions.

Article 21-d [*to take all appropriate measures to ensure that inter-country adoption does not result in improper financial gain for those involved*]
The State Party understands that this Article may never be construed to permit financial benefits other than those needed to cover strictly necessary expenditure which may have arisen from the adoption of children residing in another country.

Article 22 [*to ensure that a child who is seeking refugee status shall receive appropriate protection*]
The State Party reserves the right not to be bound by this Article.

Article 22* [*to ensure that a child who is seeking refugee status shall receive appropriate protection*]
The State Party reserves the right to apply this Article in accordance with its legislation.

Article 24-2 [*the right to the enjoyment of the highest attainable standard of health; and to this end State Parties shall take appropriate measures to diminish child mortality; to provide medical assistance; to combat disease and malnutrition; to ensure pre-natal and post-natal health care for mothers; to endure parents are informed and have access to health education; to develop preventive health care and family planning education*]
The State Party interprets 'family planning' to mean only those methods which it considers morally acceptable.

Article 26 [*the right to benefit from social security*]
The State Party is bound by the obligations arising out of this Article to the extent of present social security legislation.

Article 28-1a [*the right to education and with a view to achieving this right to make primary education compulsory and available free*]
The State Party reserves the right not to be bound by this Article.

Article 29 [*the education of the child shall be directed to the development of his personality, talents and mental and physical abilities*]
The State Party reserves the right to apply this Article in accordance with its legislation.

Article 30 [*a child belonging to a minority group shall not be denied the right to enjoy his culture*]
The State Party declares that in the light of its Constitution, this Article is not applicable.

Article 30* [*a child belonging to a minority group shall not be denied the right to enjoy his culture*]
The State Party reserves the right to apply this Article in accordance with its legislation.

Article 32 [*the right to be protected from economic exploitation*]
The State Party reserves the right to apply this Article subject to its employment legislation.

Article 32-1 [*the right to be protected from economic exploitation*]
The State Party considers that the rights under this Article are adequately protected by its existing law and therefore reserves the right not to legislate further on the matter.

Article 37-c [*every child deprived of liberty shall be treated with humanity and respect; in particular should it be separated from adults*]
The State Party accepts the general principles of this Article but only accepts it to the extent that the imprisonment is considered by the authorities to be feasible and consistent with the obligation that children be able to maintain contact with their families, i.e. unless it is considered in the child's best interest not to do so.

Article 37-c* [*every child deprived of liberty shall be treated with humanity and respect; in particular should be separated from adults*]
The State Party reserves the right not to be bound by this Article in circumstances where the shortage of suitable facilities makes the mixing of juveniles and adults unavoidable.

Article 37-d [*every child deprived of liberty shall have the right to prompt access to legal assistance*]
The State Party reserves the right to apply this Article in accordance with its legislation.

Article 40-2bv [*the right of every child alleged as, accused of, or recognised as having infringed the law to be treated with dignity; and to this end the guarantee that if considered to have infringed the penal law to have this decision reviewed by a higher authority*]
The State Party considers that the expression 'according to law' means that his provision does not apply to minors who, under the State Party's law: (i) are declared guilty and are sentenced in a higher court following an appeal against their acquittal in a first instance court; (ii) are referred directly to a higher court.

Article 40-2bv* [*the right of every child alleged as, accused of, or recognised as having infringed the law to be treated with dignity; and to this end the guarantee that if considered to have infringed the penal law to have this decision reviewed by a higher authority*]
The State Party reserves the right not to be bound by this Article.

Article 40-2bv** [*the right of every child alleged as, accused of, or recognised as having infringed the law to be treated with dignity; and to this end the guarantee that if considered to have infringed the penal law to have this decision reviewed by a higher authority*]
The State Party construes this Article as establishing a general principle to which limited exceptions may be made under law.

Article 40-2bii [*the right of every child alleged as, accused of, or recognised as having infringed the law to be treated with dignity; and to this end to be informed promptly and directly of the charges against him through his parents or other appropriate assistance*]
The State Party declares that this Article shall be applied in such a way that, in the case of minor infringement of the penal law, there shall not in each and every case exist: (i) a right to 'legal or other appropriate assistance'.

STATE PARTIES BY CONTINENTS

AMERICA

Antigua & Barbuda
Argentina
Bahamas
Barbados***
Belize
Bolivia
Brazil
Canada
Chile
Colombia
Costa Rica
Cuba
Dominica***
Dominican Rep.
El Salvador
Ecuador
Grenada***
Guatemala
Guyana
Haiti***
Honduras
Jamaica***
Maldives***
Mexico
Nicaragua
Panama
Paraguay
Peru
St. Kitts & Nevis***
St. Vincent &
  Grenadines***
St. Lucia***
Suriname
Trinidad & Tobago***
U.S.A.
Uruguay
Venezuela

EUROPE

Albania
Andorra
Austria
Belarus
Belgium
Bosnia & Herz.
Bulgaria
Croatia
Cyprus
Czech Rep.
Denmark
Estonia
Finland
France
Germany
Greece
Holy See
Hungary
Iceland
Ireland
Italy
Latvia
Liechtenstein
Lithuania
Luxembourg
Malta
Monaco
Netherlands
Norway
Poland
Portugal
Rep. of Moldova
Romania
Russian Fed.*
San Marino
Slovakia
Slovenia
Spain
Sweden
Switzerland
the former Yugoslav
  Rep. of Macedonia
Ukraine
United Kingdom
Yugoslavia

AFRICA

Algeria
Angola
Benin
Botswana
Burkina Faso
Burundi
Cameroon
Cape Verde
Cen. Afr. R.
Chad
Comoros**
Congo
Côte d'Ivoire
Djibouti
Egypt
Equat. Guinea
Eritrea
Ethiopia
Gabon
Gambia
Ghana
Guinea
Guinea-Bissau
Kenya
Lesotho
Liberia
Libyan A.J.
Madagascar
Mali
Malawi
Mauritania
Mauritius**
Morocco
Mozambique
Namibia
Niger
Nigeria
Rwanda
São Tomé & Príncipe
Senegal
Seychelles**
Sierra Leone
Samoa
South Africa
Sudan
Swaziland
Tanzania
Togo
Tunisia
Uganda
Zaire
Zambia

ASIA

Afghanistan
Armenia
Azerbaijan
Bahrain
Bangladesh
Bhutan
Brunei Dar.
Cambodia
China
D.P.R. Korea
Fiji +
Georgia
India
Indonesia
Iran
Iraq
Israel
Japan +
Jordan
Kazakhstan
Kiribati +
Kuwait
Kyrgystan
Lao P.D. Rep
Lebanon
Marshall Isl. +

Micronesia +
Myanmar
Mongolia
Nauru +
Nepal
Niue +
Pakistan
Palau
Philippines
Qatar
Rep. of Korea
Saudi Arabia
Singapore
Solomon
   Islands +
Syrian A. Rep.
Sri Lanka
Tajikistan
Thailand
Tonga +
Turkey*
Turkmenistan
Tuvalu +
Uzbekistan
Vanuatu +
Viet Nam
Yemen

AUSTRALIA

Australia
New Zealand
Papua N. Guinea ++

*	Eurasia
**	Indian Ocean
***	West Indies
+	Pacific Ocean
++	Oceania

226

International Covenant on Civil and Political Rights

Participant	Rsv.	Dates	NR
Afghanistan		24-01-1983 a	
Albania		04-10-1991 a	
Algeria		12-09-1989 r	
Angola		10-01-1992 a	
Argentina	15-1	08-08-1986 r	
Armenia		23-06-1993 a	
Australia	10-2a,b,3; 14-6; i	13-08-1980 r	
Austria	12-4; 10-3; 14; ii	10-09-1978 r	
Azerbaijan		13-08-1992 a	
Barbados	14-3d	05-01-1973 a	
Belarus		12-11-1973 r	
Belgium	iii, iv, 10-2a*, 3*; 14; 20; 20-1; 23-2	21-04-1983 r	
Benin		12-03-1992 a	
Bolivia		12-08-1982 a	
Bosnia & Herzeg.		01-09-1993 d	
Brazil		24-01-1992 a	
Bulgaria		21-09-1970 r	
Burundi		09-05-1990 a	
Cambodia		26-05-1992 a	
Cameroon		27-06-1984 a	
Canada		19-05-1976 a	
Cape Verde		06-08-1993 a	
Central African Rep.		08-05-1981 a	
Chad		09-06-1995 a	
Chile		10-02-1972 r	
Colombia		29-10-1969 r	
Congo	11	05-10-1983a	
Costa Rica		29-11-1968 r	
Côte d'Ivoire		26-03-1992 a	
Croatia		12-10-1992 d	
Cyprus		02-04-1969 r	
Czech Republic		22-02-1993 d	
Dem. P. Rep. Korea		14-09-1981 a	
Denmark	10-3; 14-1*; 5**;7; 20-1	06-01-1972 r	
Dominica		17-06-1993 a	
Dominican Republic		04-01-1978 a	
Ecuador		06-03-1969 r	
Egypt		14-01-1982 r	
El Salvador		30-11-1979 r	
Equatorial Guinea		25-09-1987 a	
Estonia		21-10-1991 a	
Ethiopia		11-01-1993 a	
Finland	10-2b,3; 14-7*; 20-1	19-08-1975 r	
France	v; vi; 4-1; 9; 13; 14-5**; 20-1*	04-11-1980 a	
Gabon		21-01-1983 a	
Gambia	14-3d	22-03-1979 a	
Georgia		03-05-1994 a	
Germany	ii; 14-3d*,5*; 15-1	17-12-1973 r	
Grenada		06-09-1991 a	
Guatemala		05-05-1992 a	
Guinea		24-01-1978 r	
Guyana	14-3d,6*	15-02-1977 r	
Haiti		06-02-1991 a	
Honduras		19-12-1996 s	
Hungary		17-01-1974 r	
Iceland	10-2b,3; 13*; 14-7*; 20-1	22-08-1979 r	
India		10-04-1979 a	
Iran (Isl. Rep.)		24-06-1975 r	
Iraq		25-01-1971 r	
Ireland	10-2; 14-6; 19-2; 20-1**; 23-4	08-12-1989 r	
Israel	vii	03-10-1991 r	
Italy	9-5; 12-4; 14-5**; 15-1**; 19-3	15-09-1978 r	
Jamaica		03-10-1975 r	
Japan		21-06-1979 r	
Jordan		28-05-1975 r	
Kenya		01-05-1972 a	
Kyrgyzstan		07-10-1994 a	
Latvia		14-04-1992 a	
Lebanon		03-11-1972 a	
Lesotho		09-09-1972 a	
Liberia		18-04-1967 s	
Libyan Arab Jamahiriya		15-05-1970 a	
Lithuania		20-11-1991 a	
Luxembourg	10-3; 14-3, 5+; 19-2; 20	18-08-1983 r	

Participant	Rsv.	Dates	NR
Madagascar		21-06-1971 r	
Malawi		22-12-1993 a	
Mali		16-07-1974 a	
Malta	13**; 14-2,6*; 19; 20*; 22	13-09-1990 a	
Mauritius		12-12-1973 a	
Mexico	13*; 25b	23-03-1981 a	
Mongolia		18-11-1974 r	
Morocco		03-05-1979 r	
Mozambique		21-07-1993 a	
Namibia		28-11-1994 a	
Nepal		14-05-1991 a	
Netherlands	10-2*, 3**; 12-1, 2, 4*; 14-3d**; 14-5++, 7*; 19-2; 20-1	11-12-1978 r	
New Zealand	10-2b, 3; 14-6*; 20*; 22	28-12-1978 r	
Nicaragua		12-03-1980 a	
Niger		07-03-1986 a	
Nigeria		29-07-1993 a	
Norway	10-2b*, 3**; 14-5***, 7; 20-1	13-09-1972 r	
Panama		08-03-1977 r	
Paraguay		10-06-1992 a	
Peru		28-04-1978 r	
Philippines		23-10-1986 r	

Participant	Rsv.	Dates	NR
Poland		18-03-1977 r	
Portugal		15-06-1978 r	
Rep. Korea	14-5+; 22*	10-04-1990 a	
Rep. Moldova		26-01-1990 a	
Romania		26-01-1993 a	
Russian Fed.		09-12-1974 r	
Rwanda		16-10-1973 r	
S. Vinc. & Grenadines		09-11-1981 a	
San Marino		18-10-1985 a	
São Tomé & Príncipe		31-10-1995 s	
Senegal		13-02-1978 r	
Seychelles		05-05-1992 a	
Slovakia		28-05-1993 d	
Slovenia		06-07-1992 d	
Somalia		24-01-1990 a	
South Africa		03-10-1994 s	
Spain		27-04-1977 r	
Sri Lanka		11-01-1980 a	
Sudan		18-03-1986 a	
Suriname	10-3**; 14-7; 20-1	28-12-1976 a	
Sweden	10-2b; 12-1*; 14-1**, 3d***, f, 5+; 20*; 25b; 26	06-12-1971 r	
Switzerland		18-06-1992 a	
Syrian A. Rep.		21-04-1969 a	
Togo	4-2; 10-2b, 3;	24-05-1984 a	
		21-12-1978 a	

Participant	Rsv.	Dates	NR
Trinidad & Tobago	12-2*; 14-5+, 6*; 15-1**; 21; 26	18-01-1994 d	
the former Yugoslav Rep. of Macedonia		18-03-1969 r	
Tunisia		21-06-1995 a	
Uganda		12-11-1973 r	
Ukraine		20-05-1976 r	
U. Kingdom	v; viii; 10-a**2b, 3; 11*; 12-1**; 4; 14-3d; 20*; 23-3; 24-3	11-06-1976 a	
U. Rep. of Tanzania	ix; x; 7;	08-06-1992 r	
U.S.A.	10-2b, 3; 14-4; 15-1***; 20-1	01-04-1970 r	
Uruguay		28-09-1995 a	
Uzbekistan		10-05-1978 r	
Venezuela	14-3d+	24-09-1982 a	
Vietnam		09-02-1987 a	
Yemen		02-06-1971 r	
Yugoslavia		01-11-1976 a	
Zaire		10-04-1984 a	
Zambia		13-05-1991 a	
Zimbabwe			

International Covenant on Civil and Political Rights

i
The State Party interprets the rights provided for by Article 19 [right to hold opinions without interference], 21 [right to peacefully assembly] and 22 [right to freedom of association with others including to form and join trade unions] as consistent with Article 20 [any propaganda for war, advocacy of national, racial or religious hatred that constitutes incitement to discrimination, hostility or violence shall be prohibited by law] and accordingly, having legislated with respect to the subject matter of the Article, reserve the right not to introduce any further legislative provision on these matters.

ii
The State Party interprets Articles 19 [right to hold opinions without interference], 21 [right to peaceful assembly] and 22 [right to freedom of association with others including to form and join trade unions] will be applied provided that they are not in conflict with legal restrictions as provided in Article 16 of the European Convention for the Protection of Human Rights and Fundamental Freedoms.

iii
The State Party interprets Articles 19 [right to hold opinions without interference], 21 [right to peaceful assembly] and 22 [right to freedom of association with others including to form and join trade unions] will be applied provided that they are not in conflict with legal restrictions as provided in Articles 10 and 11 of the European Convention for the Protection of Human Rights and Fundamental Freedoms.

iv
The State Party reserves the right to apply Articles 2 [to ensure the rights of the present Covenant to all individuals without discrimination], 3 [to ensure the equal right of men and women to the enjoyment of all civil and political rights] and 25 [the right to take part in the conduct of public affairs, to vote and be elected] in so far as they do not conflict with the State's Constitution under which the royal powers may be exercised only by males.

v
The State Party considers that, in accordance with Article 103 of the Charter of the United nations, in case of conflict between its obligations under the present Covenant and its obligations under the Charter the latter shall prevail.

vi
The State Party interprets Articles 19 [right to hold opinions without interference], 21 [right to peacefully assembly] and 22 [right to freedom of association with others including to form and join trade unions] will be applied provided that they are not in conflict with legal restrictions as provided in Articles 10, 11 and 16 of the European Convention for the Protection of Human Rights and Fundamental Freedoms.

vii
The State Party reserves the right not to be bound by any Article in the Covenant which refers to matters of personal status, in particular Article 23 [the right to marriage] as these are governed by the State's religious law.

viii
The State party reserves the right to apply to members of and persons lawfully detained in penal establishments of whatever character such laws and procedures as they may from time to time deem to be necessary for the preservation of service and custodial discipline and their acceptance of the provisions of the Covenant is subject to such restrictions.

ix
The State Party reserves the right, subject to its Constitutional constraints, to impose capital punishment on any person (other than a pregnant woman) duly convicted under existing or future laws.

x
The State Party entered some interpretative declarations regarding the following Articles: *Articles 26* [all persons are equal before the law] and *2–1* [all individuals are recognised the rights arisen from this Covenant without distinction of any kind] – distinctions based on race, colour, sex, language, etc. will be permitted when such distinctions are, at a minimum, rationally related to a legitimate governmental objective; *Article 4–1* [in case of public emergency State Parties may derogate from this Covenant to the extent strictly required by the situation provided that such measures do not involve discrimination] – cannot bar distinctions that may have a disproportionate effect upon persons of a particular status; *Articles 9–5* [right to compensation to victims of unlawful arrest] and *14–6* [right to compensation to victims of undue punishment] – victims of miscarriage of law can obtain compensation from either the responsible individual or the appropriate governmental entity; compensation may be subject to reasonable requirements of domestic law; *Article 10–2a* [accused persons shall, except in segregated circumstances, be segregated from convicted persons] – the reference to 'exceptional circumstances' is understood to permit the imprisonment of an accused person with convicted persons where appropriate in the light of the individual's overall dangerousness; *Article 10–3* [the essential aim of the penitentiary system shall be the reform and social rehabilitation of prisoners] – does not diminish the goals of punishment, deterrence and incapacitation as additional legitimate purposes for a penitentiary system; *Article 14–3b* [right to have adequate time for the preparation of a defence and to communicate with counsel of his own choosing] and *14–3d* [right to be tried in his presence and to defend himself in person or through legal assistance of his own choosing] – do not require the provision of a criminal defendant's counsel of choice when the defendant is provided with court-appointed counsel on grounds of indigence; *Article 14–e* [right to examine or have examined the witnesses against him and to obtain attendance and examination of witnesses] – does not prohibit a requirement that the defendant make a showing that any witness whose attendance he seeks to compel is necessary for his defence; *Article 47* [nothing in the Covenant shall be interpreted as impairing the inherent right of all peoples to enjoy and utilise fully and freely their natural wealth and resources] – may be exercised only in accordance with international law.

Article 4–1 [*in time of public emergency the State parties may take measures derogating from their obligations under the Covenant*]
The State Party reserves the right to have its domestic legislation understood as meeting the purpose of this Article.

Article 4–1 [*in time of public emergency the State parties may take measures derogating from their obligations under the Covenant*]
The State Party reserves the right to have its domestic legislation understood as meeting the purpose of this Article.

Article 4–2 [*no derogation from Articles 6, 7, 8, 11, 15, 16 and 18 may be made*]
The State Party reserves the right not to be bound by this Article.

Article 7 [*no one shall be subjected to torture or to cruel, inhuman or degrading treatment or punishment*]
The State Party reserves the right to interpret this provision as meaning 'the cruel and unusual treatment or punishment' prohibited by its Constitution.

Article 9 [*everyone has the right to liberty and security of person and no one shall be subject to arbitrary arrest or detention*]

The State Party reserves the right to apply this Article provided that legal regulations governing the proceedings and measures of deprivation of liberty as provided in the State's national law remain permissible.

Article 9–5 [anyone who has been victim of unlawful arrest or detention shall have a right to compensation]
The State Party reserves the right to interpret the above Article, in particular the expression 'unlawful' as exclusively referring to cases of arrest or detention contrary to the provisions of Article 9–1 [no one shall be subject to arbitrary arrest] of this Covenant.

Article 10–2 [accused juvenile persons shall be segregated from adults]
The State Party reserves the right to regard full implementation of the principles of this Article as objectives to be achieved progressively.

Article 10–2* [accused juvenile persons shall be segregated from adults]
The State Party reserves the right not to be bound by this Article.

Article 10–2a [accused persons shall, save in exceptional circumstances, be segregated from convicted persons and shall be subject to separate treatment]
The State Party reserves the right to apply this Article in so far as the principle of segregation is accepted as an objective to be achieved progressively.

Article 10–2a** [accused persons shall, save in exceptional circumstances, be segregated from convicted persons and shall be subject to separate treatment]
The State Party reserves the right not to apply this Article in Gibraltar, Montserrat and the Turks and Caicos Islands in so far as it requires segregation of accused and convicted persons.

Article 10–2b [accused juvenile persons shall be separated from adults]
The State Party accepts the obligation to segregate only to the extent that such segregation is considered by the responsible authorities to be beneficial to the juveniles or adults concerned.

Article 10–2b* [accused juvenile persons shall be separated from adults]
The State Party reserves the right not to be bound by this Article.

Article 10–3 [juvenile offenders shall be segregated from adults and be accorded treatment appropriate to their age and legal status]
The State Party accepts the obligation to segregate only to the extent that such segregation is considered by the responsible authorities to be beneficial to the juveniles or adults concerned.

Article 10–3* [juvenile offenders shall be segregated from adults and be accorded treatment appropriate to their age and legal status]
The State Party reserves the right to apply this Article only in so far as it is in accord with its own domestic legislation.

Article 10–3** [juvenile offenders shall be segregated from adults and be accorded treatment appropriate to their age and legal status]
The State Party reserves the right not to be bound by this Article.

Article 11 [no one shall be imprisoned merely on the ground of inability to fulfil contractual obligation]
The State Party reserves the right not to be bound by this Article.

Article 11* [no one shall be imprisoned merely on the ground of inability to fulfil contractual obligation]
The State party reserves the right not to apply this Article in Jersey.

Article 12–1 [the right to liberty of movement and freedom to choose residence]
The State Party declares that for the purposes of this Article it considers the Netherlands Antilles as a separate territory to that of its own.

Article 12–1* [the right to liberty of movement and freedom to choose residence]
The State Party reserves the right to apply this Article subject to its laws on aliens.

Article 12–1** [the right to liberty of movement and freedom to choose residence]
The State Party reserves the right to interpret this Article as applying separately to each of the territories comprising its State and dependencies.

Article 12–2 [the right to leave any country including its own]
The State Party declares that for the purposes of this Article it considers the Netherlands Antilles as a separate territory to that of its own.

Article 12–2* [the right to leave any country including his own]
The State Party reserves the right not to be bound by this Article.

Article 12–4 [no one shall be arbitrarily deprived of the right to enter his own country]
The State Party reserves the right to apply this Article in so far as it does not conflict with its domestic legislation.

Article 12–4* [no one shall be arbitrarily deprived of the right to enter his own country]
The State Party declares that for the purposes of this Article it considers the Netherlands Antilles as a separate territory to that of its own.

Article 13 [an alien lawfully in the territory of a State Party may be expelled therefrom only in pursuance with a lawful decision]
The State Party declares that this Article cannot derogate from national law concerning the entry into, sojourn of aliens and expulsion of aliens.

Article 13* [an alien lawfully in the territory of a State Party may be expelled therefrom only in pursuance with a lawful decision]
The State Party reserves the right not to be bound by this Article in so far as it inconsistent with its domestic legislation.

Article 13** [an alien lawfully in the territory of a State Party may be expelled therefrom only in pursuance with a lawful decision]
The State Party endorses this Article but declares that it cannot comply entirely with it.

Article 14 [the right of every person who is charged under criminal law to fair treatment]
The State Party reserves the right to have minor offences against military law dealt with summarily in accordance with current procedures which may not, in all respects, conform to the requirements of this Article.

Article 14–1 [all persons shall be equal before the courts and tribunals; everyone shall be entitled to a fair and public hearing]
The State Party reserves the right to apply this Article provided that legal regulations governing the proceedings and measures of deprivation of liberty as provided in the State's national law remain permissible.

Article 14–1* [all persons shall be equal before the courts and tribunals; everyone shall be entitled to a fair and public hearing]
The State Party reserves the right not to be bound by this Article.

Article 14–1** [all persons shall be equal before the courts and tribunals; everyone shall be entitled to a fair and public hearing]

The State Party reserves not to apply this Article to proceedings which involve a civil rights and obligations dispute or to the merits of the prosecution's case in a criminal matter.

Article 14–2 [everyone charged with a criminal offence shall have the right to be presumed innocent until proved guilt]
The State Party declares that the provisions of this Article cannot preclude any law from imposing upon any person charged the burden of proving particular facts.

Article 14–3 [in the determination of any criminal charge everyone shall be entitled: (a) to be informed promptly; (b) to have adequate time for the preparation of defence; (c) to be tried without undue delay; (d) to be tried in his presence and to defend himself or through legal assistance; (e) to examine or have examined the witnesses against him; (f) to have the free assistance of an interpreter, if needed; (g) not to be compelled to testify against himself nor to confess guilt]
The State Party reserves the right not to apply this Article to persons who, under its domestic law, are remanded directly to a higher court.

Article 14–3d [the right to be tried in his presence, and to defend himself in person or through legal assistance of his own choosing and to have legal assistance assigned to him without any payment by him]
The State Party reserves the right not to apply in full the guarantee of free legal assistance.

Article 14–3d [the right to be tried in his presence, and to defend himself in person or through legal assistance of his own choosing and to have legal assistance assigned to him without any payment by him]*
The State Party reserves the right to apply this Article in such a manner that it is for the court to decide whether an accused person held in custody has to appear in person at the hearing before the court of review.

*Article 14–3d** [the right to be tried in his presence, and to defend himself in person or through legal assistance of his own choosing and to have legal assistance assigned to him without any payment by him]*
The State Party reserves the statutory option of removing a person charged with a criminal offence from the courtroom in the interests of the proper conduct of the proceedings.

*Article 14–3d*** [the right to be tried in his presence, and to defend himself in person or through legal assistance of his own choosing and to have legal assistance assigned to him without any payment by him]*
The State Party reserves the right not to definitely exempt the beneficiary of legal assistance from defraying the resulting costs.

Article 14–3d+ [the right to be tried in his presence, and to defend himself in person or through legal assistance of his own choosing and to have legal assistance assigned to him without any payment by him]
The State Party reserves the right not to be bound by this Article.

Article 14–3 [the right to have assistance of an interpreter]
The State Party reserves the right not to definitely exempt the beneficiary of translating services from defraying the resulting costs.

Article 14–4 [the procedure for juveniles shall be such as to take account of their age and the desirability of promoting their rehabilitation]
The State Party reserves the right to, in exceptional circumstances, treat juveniles as adults.

Article 14–5 [everyone convicted of a crime shall have the right to his conviction and sentence being reviewed by a higher tribunal]
The State Party reserves the right not to apply this Article to persons, who, under its law, are convicted and sentenced to second instance following an appeal against their acquittal of first instance or who are brought directly before a higher tribunal.

Article 14–5* [everyone convicted of a crime shall have the right to his conviction and sentence being reviewed by a higher tribunal]
The State Party reserves the right to apply this Article in such a manner that (a) a further appeal does not have to be instituted solely on the grounds the accused person was convicted for the first time; (b) in the case of criminal offences of minor gravity the review by a higher court of a decision does not have to be admitted in all cases.

Article 14–5** [everyone convicted of a crime shall have the right to his conviction and sentence being reviewed by a higher tribunal]
The State Party interprets this Article as stating a general principle to which the law may make limited exceptions.

Article 14–5*** [everyone convicted of a crime shall have the right to his conviction and sentence being reviewed by a higher tribunal]
The State Party reserves the right not to be bound by this Article.

Article 14–5+ [everyone convicted of a crime shall have the right to his conviction and sentence being reviewed by a higher tribunal]
The State Party reserves the right to apply this Article only in so far as it does not conflict with its domestic legislation.

Article 14–5++ [everyone convicted of a crime shall have the right to his conviction and sentence being reviewed by a higher tribunal]
The State Party reserves the right to grant its Supreme Court to have sole jurisdiction to try certain categories of persons charged with serious offences.

Article 14–6 [when a person has by a final decision been convicted of a criminal offence and suffered punishment and when subsequently his conviction has been reversed the person shall be compensated according to law]
The State Party makes the reservation that the provision of compensation for miscarriage of justice may be by administrative procedures rather than pursuant to specific legal provision.

Article 14–6* [when a person has by a final decision been convicted of a criminal offence and suffered punishment and when subsequently his conviction has been reversed the person shall be compensated according to law]
The State Party reserves the right not to be bound by this Article.

Article 14–7 [no one shall be liable to be tried or punished again for an offence for which he has already been finally convicted or acquitted in accordance with the law of each country]
The State Party reserves the right not to be bound by this Article.

Article 14–7* [no one shall be liable to be tried or punished again for an offence for which he has already been finally convicted or acquitted in accordance with the law of each country]
The State Party reserves the right to pursue its present practice regarding this matter.

Article 15–1 [no one shall be guilty of any criminal offence on account of any act or omission which did not constitute a criminal offence at the time when it was committed]
The State Party declares that the application of this Article shall be subject to the principle laid down in Article 18 of its Constitution.

Article 15–1* [no one shall be guilty of any criminal offence on account of any act or omission which did not constitute a criminal offence at the time when it was committed]
The State Party reserves the right to apply this Article in such a manner that when provision is made by law for the imposition of a lighter penalty the hitherto applicable law may for certain exceptional cases remain applicable.

Article 15–1** [... if subsequent to the commission of the offence, provision is made by law for the imposition of a lighter penalty, the offender shall benefit thereby]
The State Party reserves the right to deem this provision to apply exclusively to cases in progress.

Article 15–1*** [... if subsequent to the commission of the offence, provision is made by law for the imposition of a lighter penalty, the offender shall benefit thereby]
The State Party reserves the right not to be bound by this Article.

Article 19 [the right to hold opinions without interference]
The State Party reserves the right to apply this Article subject to its domestic legislation.

Article 19–2 [the right to freedom of expression... in the form of art or through any other media]
The State Party reserves the right to confer monopoly on or require the licensing of broadcasting enterprises.

Article 19–3 [the right to freedom of expression subject to (a) the respect of the rights or reputations of others; (b) the protection of national security or public order]
The State Party declares that these provisions are compatible with the existing licensing system for national radio and television.

Article 20 [any propaganda for war, advocacy of national, racial or religious hatred that constitutes incitement to discrimination, hostility or violence shall be prohibited by law]
The State Party reserves the right to apply this Article taking into account the rights to freedom of thought and religion, freedom of opinion and freedom of assembly and association proclaimed in Articles 18, 19 and 20 of the Universal Declaration of Human Rights.

Article 20* [any propaganda for war, advocacy of national, racial or religious hatred that constitutes incitement to discrimination, hostility or violence shall be prohibited by law]
The State Party reserves the right not to introduce any legislation for the purposes of this Article.

Article 20–1 [advocacy of national, racial or religious hatred that constitutes incitement to discrimination, hostility or violence shall be prohibited by law]
The State Party reserves the right not to be bound by this Article.

Article 20–1* [advocacy of national, racial or religious hatred that constitutes incitement to discrimination, hostility or violence shall be prohibited by law]
The State Party declares that the term 'war' is to be understood to mean war in contravention of international law and considers that its domestic legislation in this matter is adequate.

Article 20–1** [advocacy of national, racial or religious hatred that constitutes incitement to discrimination, hostility or violence shall be prohibited by law]
The State Party reserves the right to postpone the application of this Article.

Article 21 [the right of peaceful assembly]
The State Party reserves the right not to be bound by this Article.

235

Article 22 [the right to freedom of association including the right to form and join trade unions]
The State Party reserves the right not to apply this Article to the extent that existing domestic law may not be fully compatible with it.

Article 22* [the right to freedom of association including the right to form and join trade unions]
The State Party reserves the right to apply this Article only in so far as it does not conflict with its domestic legislation.

Article 23–2 [the right of men and women of marriageable age to marry]
The State Party reserves the right to interpret this Article as presupposing not only that national law shall prescribe the marriageable age but also that it may regulate the exercise of that right.

Article 23–3 [no marriage shall be entered into without the free and full consent of the intending spouses]
The State Party reserves the right to postpone the application of this Article in regard to the Solomon Islands.

Article 23–4 [to ensure equality of rights and responsibilities of spouses as to marriage]
The State Party accepts this provision on the understanding that it does not imply any right to obtain a dissolution of marriage.

Article 24–3 [every child has the right to acquire a nationality]
The State Party reserves the right to apply this Article only in so far as it does not conflict with its domestic legislation.

Article 25b [the right to vote and to be elected by secret ballot]
The State Party reserves the right not to be bound by this Article in so far as it conflicts with its domestic legislation.

Article 25b [the right to vote and to be elected by secret ballot]
The State Party reserves the right to apply this Article only in so far as it does not conflict with its domestic legislation.

Article 26 [all persons are equal before the law and are entitled to equal treatment without discrimination]
The State Party reserves the right to apply this Article only in connection with other rights contained in this Covenant.

Article 26 [all persons are equal before the law and are entitled to equal treatment without discrimination]
The State Party reserves the right not to apply this Article in so far as it applies to the holding of property in its territory.

STATE PARTIES BY CONTINENTS

AMERICA

Argentina
Barbados***
Bolivia
Brazil
Canada
Chile
Colombia
Costa Rica
Dominica***
Dominican Rep.***
Ecuador
El Salvador
Grenada***
Guatemala
Guyana
Haiti***
Honduras
Jamaica***
Mexico
Nicaragua
Panama
Paraguay
Peru
St. Vincent &
   Grenadines***
Suriname
Trinidad & Tobago***
U.S.A.
Uruguay
Venezuela

EUROPE

Albania
Austria
Belarus
Belgium
Bosnia & Herz.
Bulgaria
Croatia
Cyprus
Czech Rep.
Denmark
Estonia
Finland
France
Germany
Hungary
Iceland

Ireland
Italy
Latvia
Lithuania
Luxembourg
Malta
Netherlands
Norway
Poland
Portugal
Rep. Moldova
Romania
Russian Fed.*
San Marino
Slovakia
Slovenia
Spain
Sweden
Switzerland
the former Yugoslav
Rep. of Macedonia
Ukraine
United Kingdom
Yugoslavia

AFRICA

Algeria
Angola
Benin
Burundi
Cameroon
Cape Verde
C. Afr. Rep.
Chad
Congo
Côte d'Ivoire
Egypt
Equatorial Guinea
Ethiopia
Gabon
Gambia
Guinea
Kenya
Lesotho
Madagascar
Malawi
Mali
Mauritius**
Morocco

Mozambique
Namibia
Niger
Nigeria
Rwanda
São Tomé & Príncipe
Senegal
Seychelles**
Somalia
South Africa
Togo
Tunisia
Uganda
U. Rep. Tanzania
Zaire
Zambia
Zimbabwe

ASIA

Afghanistan
Armenia
Azerbaijan
Cambodia
D.P.R. Korea
Georgia
India
Iran
Iraq
Israel
Japan
Jordan
Kyrgyzstan
Lebanon
Liberia
Libyan Arab J.
Mongolia
Nepal
Philippines
Rep. Korea
Sri Lanka
Sudan
Syrian A. Rep.
Uzbekistan
Vietnam
Yemen

AUSTRALIA

Australia
New Zealand

*   Eurasia
**   Indian Ocean
***   West Indies

237

International Covenant on Economic, Social and Cultural Rights

Participant	Rsv.	NR**	Dates
Afghanistan			24-01-1983 a
Albania			04-10-1991 a
Algeria	13-3, 4		12-09-1989 r
Angola			10-01-1992 a
Argentina			08-08-1986 r
Armenia			13-09-1993 a
Australia			10-12-1975 r
Austria			10-09-1978 r
Azerbaijan			13-08-1992 a
Barbados	i		05-01-1973 a
Belarus	2-2, 3		12-11-1973 r
Belgium			21-04-1983 r
Benin			12-03-1992 a
Bolivia			12-08-1982 a
Bosnia & Herz.			01-09-1993 d
Brazil			24-01-1992 a
Bulgaria			21-09-1970 r
Burundi			09-05-1990 a
Cambodia			26-05-1992 a
Cameroon			27-06-1984 a
Canada			19-05-1976 a
Cape Verde			06-08-1993 a
Central Af. Rep.			08-05-1981 a
Chad	13,3, 4		09-06-1995 a
Chile			10-02-1972 r
China		1	
Colombia			29-10-1969 r

Participant	Rsv.	NR**	Dates
Georgia			03-05-1994 a
Germany			17-12-1973 r
Greece			16-05-1985 a
Grenada			06-09-1991 a
Guatemala			19-05-1988 a
Guinea			24-01-1978 r
Guinea-Bissau			02-07-1992 a
Guyana			15-02-1977 r
Honduras			17-02-1981 r
Hungary			17-01-1974 r
Iceland			22-08-1979 r
India	ii		10-04-1979 a
Iran (Islamic Rep. of)			24-06-1975 r
Iraq	2-2*; 13-2a		25-01-1971 r
Ireland			08-12-1989 r
Israel			03-10-1991 r
Italy			15-09-1978 r
Jamaica	7d; 8-1d; 13-2b,c;		03-10-1975 r
Japan			21-06-1979 r
Jordan			28-05-1975 r
Kenya			01-05-1972 a
Kyrgyztan			07-10-1994 a
Latvia			14-04-1992 a
Lebanon			03-11-1972 a
Lesotho			09-09-1992 a
Liberia			18-04-1967 s
Libyan A.J.	13-2a*		15-05-1970 a

Participant	Rsv.	NR**	Dates
Paraguay			10-06-1992 a
Peru			28-04-1978 r
Philippines			07-06-1974 r
Poland			18-03-1977 r
Portugal			31-07-1978 r
Republic of Korea			10-04-1990 a
Rep. of Moldova			26-01-1993 a
Romania			09-12-1974 r
Russian Federation			16-10-1973 r
Rwanda			16-04-1975 a
St. Vincent & the Grenadines			09-11-1981 a
San Marino			18-10-1985 a
São Tomé Príncipe			31-10-1995 s
Senegal			13-02-1978 r
Seychelles			05-05-1992 a
Slovakia			28-05-1993 d
Slovenia			06-06-1992 d
Solomon Islands			17-03-1982 d
Somalia			24-01-1990 a
South Africa			03-10-1994 s
Spain			27-04-1977 r
Sri Lanka			11-06-1980 a
Sudan			18-03-1986 a
Suriname			28-12-1976 a

Country	Notes	Date
Congo		05-10-1983 a
Costa Rica		29-11-1968 r
Cote d'Ivoire		26-03-1992 a
Croatia		12-10-1992 d
Cyprus		02-04-1969 r
Czech Rep.	7d	22-02-1993 d
Dem. People's Rep. of Korea		14-09-1981 a
Denmark		06-01-1972 r
Dominica		17-06-1993 a
Dominican Rep.		04-01-1978 a
Ecuador		06-03-1969 r
Egypt		14-01-1982 r
El Salvador		30-10-1979 r
Equatorial Guinea		25-09-1987 a
Estonia		21-10-1991 a
Ethiopia		11-06-1993 a
Finland		19-08-1975 r
France		04-11-1980 a
Gabon		21-01-1983 a
Gambia		29-12-1978 a

cont....

Country	Notes	Date
Lithuania		20-11-1991 a
Luxembourg		18-08-1983 r
Madagascar		22-09-1971 r
Malawi	8-1d	22-12-1993 a
Mali		16-07-1974 a
Malta		13-09-1990 r
Mauritius		12-12-1973 a
Mexico		23-03-1981 a
Mongolia	8-1d*	18-11-1974 r
Morocco	iii	03-05-1979 r
Namibia		28-11-1994 a
Nepal		14-05-1991 a
Netherlands	8-1d**	11-12-1978 r
New Zealand		28-12-1978 r
Nicaragua		12-03-1980 a
Niger		07-03-1986 a
Nigeria		29-07-1993 a
Norway		13-09-1972 r
Panama		08-03-1977 r

Country	Notes	Date
Sweden	7d	06-12-1971 r
Switzerland		18-06-1992 a
Syrian A. Rep.		21-04-1969 a
the former Yugoslav Rep. of Macedonia		18-01-1994 d
Togo	iv	24-05-1984 a
Trinidad & Tobago		08-12-1978 a
Tunisia		18-03-1969 r
Uganda	i; 6; 9; v; 13-2a*	21-01-1987 a
Ukraine		12-11-1973 r
United Kingdom		20-05-1976 r
U. Rep. of Tanzania		11-06-1976 a
U.S. of America		05-10-1977 s
Uruguay		01-04-1970 r
Uzbekistan		28-09-1995 a
Venezuela		10-05-1978 r
Vietnam	13-2a*	24-09-1982 a
Yemen		09-02-1987 a
Yugoslavia		02-06-1971 r
Zaire		01-11-1976 a
Zambia		10-04-1984 a
Zimbabwe		13-05-1991 a

1

This Convention was signed on behalf of China. Some State Parties have written to the Secretary-General saying that their Government did not recognise the said signature as valid.

i

The State Party reserves the right to postpone the application of *Article 7-1a* in so far as it concerns the provision of equal pay to men and women for equal work; *Article 10-2* in so far as it relates to the special protection to be accorded mothers during a reasonable period during and after childbirth and *Article 13-2a* in so far as it relates to primary education.

ii

Articles 9 [the right to social security], 13 [the right to education], 4 [the rights granted under this convention can only be subject to such limitations as are determined by law], 8 [the right to form and join trade unions] and 7c [the right to equal opportunity to be promoted in employment] of this convention shall be applied as to be in consonance with the provision of the Constitution of India.

iii

The State Party reserves the right not to apply *Article 8* to the extent that existing legislative measures may not be fully compatible with this article. The State Party also reserves the right to postpone the application of *Article 10-2* as it relates to paid maternity leave or leave with adequate social security benefits.

iv

The State Party reserves the right to impose lawful and reasonable restrictions on the exercise of the rights granted under *Articles 8-1d and 8-2* [the right to strike] by personnel engaged in essential services.

v

The State Party reserves the right to postpone the application of *Article 7a(i)* in so far as it concerns the provision of equal pay to men and women for equal work in the private sector in Jersey, Guernsey, the Isle of Man, Bermuda, Hong Kong and the Solomon Islands; the right to postpone the application of *Article 9* [the right to social security] in the Cayman Islands and the Falkland Islands; the right to postpone the application of *Article 10-1* in regard to a small number of customary marriages in the Solomon Islands and *Article 10-2 in so far as it concerns paid maternity leave in Bermuda and the Falkland Islands.*

Article 2-2 [*The State Parties undertake to guarantee that the rights enunciated in this convention will be exercised without discrimination of any kind*]
The State Party interprets non-discrimination as to national origin as not necessarily implying an obligation on States automatically to guarantee to foreigners the same rights as to their nationals.

Article 2-2*
The State Party reserves the right to require, or give favourable consideration to, a knowledge of the Irish language for certain occupations.

Article 2-3 [*Developing countries may determine to what extent they would guarantee the economic rights recognised in this convention to non-nationals*]
The State Party declares that this provision cannot infringe the principle of fair compensation in the event of expropriation or nationalisation.

Article 6 [*The right to work*]
The State Party reserves the right to interpret this article as not precluding the imposition of restrictions based on place of birth or residence qualification on the taking of employment.

Article 7d (Remuneration for public holidays]
The State Party cannot for the time being undertake to comply with this article.

Article 8-1d [Trade unions are given the right to establish national federations or confederations and the right to join or form international trade union organisations]
The State Party reserves the right not to be bound to this article except in relation to sectors in which this right is accorded by the State Party's national laws.

Article 8-1d*
This Article shall not apply to the Netherlands Antilles with regard to its central and local government bodies.

Article 8-1d**
The State Party reserves the right not to be bound to this article to the effect that the current State's practice shall not be considered incompatible with the right to strike.

Article 13-2a [primary school shall be compulsory and available free for all]
The State Party reserves the right to allow parents to provide for the education of their children in their homes provided that certain standards are observed.

Article 13-2a*
The State Party reserves the right to postpone the application of this article. Under this article primary education shall be compulsory and available free to all.

Article 13-2b,c
The State Party shall not be bound by 'in particular by the progressive introduction of free education' referred to in these provisions.

Article 13-3, 4 [Parents have the right to choose any school so long as it conforms to the minimum educational standards laid down by the authorities and to ensure their child's religious and moral education]
The State Party declares that the provision under this article can in no case impair its right to freely organise its educational system.

STATE PARTIES BY CONTINENTS

AMERICA

Argentina
Barbados*
Bolivia
Brazil
Canada
Chile
Colombia
Costa Rica
Dominican Rep.*
Ecuador
El Salvador
Grenada*
Guatemala
Guyana
Honduras
Jamaica*
Mexico
Nicaragua
Panama
Paraguay
Peru
St. Vincent & Grenadines*
Suriname
Trinidad & Tobago*
U.S.A.
Uruguay
Venezuela

EUROPE

Albania
Austria
Belarus
Belgium
Bosnia & Herz.
Bulgaria
Croatia
Cyprus
Czech Rep.
Denmark
Estonia
Finland
France
Germany
Greece
Hungary
Iceland
Ireland
Italy
Latvia
Lithuania
Luxembourg
Malta
Netherlands
Norway
Poland
Portugal
Rep. of Moldova

Romania
Russian Fed.***
San Marino
Slovakia
Slovenia
Spain
Sweden
Switzerland
the former Yugoslav
   Rep. of Macedonia
Ukraine
U. Kingdom
Yugoslavia

AFRICA

Algeria
Angola
Benin
Burundi
Cameroon
Cape Verde
Central A. Rep.
Chad
Congo
Côte d'Ivoire
Egypt
Equat. Guinea
Ethiopia

Gabon
Gambia
Guinea
Guinea-Bissau
Kenya
Lesotho
Liberia
Libyan A.J.
Madagascar
Mali
Mauritius**
Mongolia
Morocco
Namibia
Niger
Nigeria
Rwanda
S. Tomé & Príncipe
Senegal
Seychelles***
Somalia
South Africa
Sudan
Togo
Tunisia
Uganda
U. Rep. Tanzania
Zaire
Zambia
Zimbabwe

ASIA

Afghanistan
Armenia
Azerbaijan
Cambodia
China
Dem. Rep.
   Korea
Georgia
India
Iran
Iraq
Israel
Japan
Jordan
Kyrgyztan
Lebanon
Malawi
Nepal
Philippines
Rep. of Korea
Syria A. Rep.
Uzbekistan
Vietnam
Yemen
Solomon Isl.****
Sri Lanka

AUSTRALIA

Australia
New Zealand

*   West Indies
**   Indian Ocean
***   Eurasia

Convention against Torture and Other Cruel, Inhuman or Degrading Treatment or Punishment

Participant	Rsv.	Dates	NR	Participant	Rsv.	Dates	NR	Participant	Rsv.	Dates	NR
Afghanistan	20; 30-1	01-04-1987 r	2000	Cambodia		15-10-1992 a	1997	Finland		30-08-1989 r	1998
Albania		11-05-1994 a	1999	Canada		24-06-1987 r	2000	France	30-1	18-02-1986 r	2000
Algeria		12-09-1989 r	1998	Cape Verde		04-06-1992 a	1997	Gabon		21-01-1986 s	—
Antigua & Barbuda		19-07-1993 a	1998	Chad		09-06-1995 a	2000	Gambia		23-10-1985 s	—
Argentina		24-09-1986 r	1999	Chile	20; 30-1	30-09-1988 r	1997	Georgia		26-10-1994 a	1999
Armenia		13-09-1993 a	1998	China	20; 30-1	04-10-1988 r	1997	Germany		01-10-1990 r	1999
Australia		08-08-1989 r	1998	Colombia		08-12-1987 r	1997	Greece		06-10-1988 r	1997
Austria	5-1c	29-07-1987 r	2000	Costa Rica		11-11-1993 r	1998	Guatemala		05-01-1990 a	1999
Belarus	20	13-03-1987 r	2000	Côte d'Ivoire		18-12-1995 a	2000	Guinea		10-10-1989 r	1998
Belgium		04-02-1985 s	—	Croatia		12-10-1992 d	1997	Guyana		19-05-1988 r	1997
Belize		17-03-1986 a	2000	Cuba	20; 30-1	17-05-1995 r	2000	Hungary		15-04-1987 r	2000
Benin		12-03-1992 a	1997	Cyprus		18-07-1991 r	2000	Iceland		04-02-1985 s	—
Bolivia		04-02-1985 s	—	Czech Rep.		22-02-1993 d	1998	Indonesia		23-10-1985 s	—
Bosnia & Herz.		01-09-1993 d	1997	Denmark		27-05-1987 r	2000	Ireland		28-09-1992 s	—
Brazil		28-09-1989 r	1998	Dominican Rep.		04-02-1985 s	—	Israel	20; 30-1	03-10-1991 r	2000
Bulgaria	20	16-12-1986 r	2000	Ecuador	i	30-03-1988 r	1997	Italy		12-01-1989 r	1998
Burundi		18-02-1993 a	1998	Egypt		25-06-1986 a	1999	Jordan		13-11-1991 a	2000
Cameroon		19-12-1986 a	2000	Estonia		21-10-1991 a	1996	Latvia		14-04-1992 a	1997
				Ethiopia		14-03-1994 a	1999	Libyan A.J.		16-05-1989 a	1998

243

Participant	Rsv.	Dates	NR
Liechtenstein		02-11-1990 r	1999
Luxembourg		29-09-1987 r	1999
Malta		13-09-1990 a	1996
Mauritius		09-12-1992 a	1999
Mexico		23-01-1986 r	1999
Monaco	30-1	06-12-1991 a	2000
Morocco	20	21-06-1993 r	1998
Namibia		28-11-1994 a	1999
Nepal		14-05-1991 a	1999
Netherlands		21-12-1988 r	1997
New Zealand	14	10-12-1989 r	1999
Nicaragua		15-04-1985 s	—
Nigeria		28-07-1988 s	—
Norway		09-07-1986 r	1999
Panama	30-1	24-08-1987 r	2000
Paraguay		12-03-1990 r	1999
Peru		07-07-1988 r	1999
Philippines		18-06-1986 a	1999

Participant	Rsv.	Dates	NR
Poland	20; 30-1	26-07-1989 r	1998
Portugal		09-02-1989 r	1998
Rep. of Korea		09-01-1995 a	2000
Rep. of Moldova		28-11-1995 a	2000
Romania		18-12-1990 a	1999
Russian Fed.		03-03-1987 r	2000
Senegal		21-08-1986 r	1999
Seychelles		05-05-1992 a	1999
Sierra Leone		18-03-1985 s	—
Slovakia		28-05-1993 d	1998
Slovenia		16-07-1993 a	1998
Somalia		24-01-1990 a	1999
South Africa		29-01-1993 s	—
Spain		21-10-1987 r	2000
Sri Lanka		03-01-1994 a	1999
Sudan		04-06-1986 s	—
Sweden		08-01-1986 r	1999
Switzerland		02-12-1986 r	1999

Participant	Rsv.	Dates	NR
Tajikistan		11-01-1995 a	2000
the former Yugoslav Rep. of Macedonia		12-12-1994 d	1996
Togo		18-11-1987 r	1997
Tunisia	30-1	23-09-1988 r	1997
Turkey		02-08-1988 r	2000
Uganda	20	03-11-1986 a	2000
Ukraine		24-02-1987 r	1997
United Kingdom	30-1; ii	08-12-1988 r	1999
U.S. of America		21-10-1994 r	2000
Uruguay		24-10-1986 r	2000
Uzbekistan		28-09-1995 a	2000
Venezuela		29-07-1991 r	1996
Yemen		05-11-1991 a	1996
Yugoslavia		10-09-1991 r	—

Article 20
The State Party does not consider itself bound by Article 20 under which if the Committee receives reliable information that torture is being systematically practised in the territory of a State Party, the Committee shall invite that State Party to cooperate in the examination of the information. The Committee may designate member(s) to make a confidential inquiry. After examination of the findings the Committee shall report back to the State Party with findings, comments and suggestions. A summary account of the results of the proceedings may be included in the Committee's annual report after consultation with the State Party concerned.

Article 30-1 [Any dispute concerning the interpretation or application of this Convention which cannot be settled through negotiation shall, at the request of one of the parties thereto, be submitted to arbitration]
The State Party does not consider itself bound to this Article to the extent that the settlement of disputes between the State Parties may be referred to arbitration or to the International Court of Justice with the consent of all the Parties concerned and not by one of the Parties only.

Article 5-1c
The State Party will only establish its jurisdiction under Article 5-1c if prosecution by a State having jurisdiction under para. 1a *[when the offences are committed in any territory under its jurisdiction or on board a ship or aircraft registered in that State]* or para. 1b *[when the alleged offender is a national of that State]* is not to be expected. Under Article 5-1c each State Party shall take such measures as may be necessary to establish its jurisdiction over the offences referred to in Article 4 *[all acts of torture, attempt to commit torture and complicity or participation in torture]* when the victim is a national of that State if that State considers it appropriate.

Article 14
The State Party reserves the right to award compensation to victims of torture, under Article 14, only at the discretion of its Attorney-General. Under Article 14, each State Party shall ensure in its legal system that the victim of an act of torture obtains redress and has an enforceable right to fair and adequate compensation.

i
The State Party reserves the right to award compensation to victims of torture, under Article 14, only at the discretion of its Attorney-General. Under Article 14, each State Party shall ensure in its legal system that the victim of an act of torture obtains redress and has an enforceable right to fair and adequate compensation.

i
The State Party will not permit extradition of its nationals.

ii
The State Party declares that the provisions of Article 1 to 16 are not self-executing.

STATE PARTIES BY CONTINENTS

AMERICA

Antigua & Barbuda
Argentina
Belize
Brazil
Canada
Chile
Colombia
Costa Rica
Cuba
Ecuador
Guatemala
Guyana
Mexico
Panama
Paraguay
Peru
U.S.A.
Uruguay
Venezuela

EUROPE

Albania
Austria
Belarus
Bosnia & Herz.
Bulgaria
Croatia
Cyprus
Czech Rep.
Denmark
Estonia
Finland
France
Germany
Greece
Hungary
Italy
Latvia
Liechtenstein
Luxembourg
Malta
Monaco
Netherlands
Norway
Poland
Portugal
Rep. of Moldova
Romania
Russian Fed.*
Slovakia
Slovenia
Spain
Sweden
Switzerland
the former Yugoslav
    Rep. of Macedonia
Ukraine
United Kingdom
Yugoslavia

AFRICA

Algeria
Benin
Burundi
Cameroon
Cape Verde
Chad
Côte d'Ivoire
Egypt
Ethiopia
Guinea
Libyan A.J.
Mauritius**
Morocco
Namibia
Senegal
Seychelles**
Somalia
Togo
Tunisia
Uganda

ASIA

Afghanistan
Armenia
Cambodia
China
Georgia
Israel
Jordan
Nepal
Philippines
Rep. of Korea
Sri Lanka
Tajikistan
Turkey*
Uzbekistan
Yemen

AUSTRALIA

Australia
New Zealand

*   Eurasia
**   Indian Ocean

Convention for the Suppression of the Traffic in Persons and of the Exploitation of the Prostitution of others

Participant	Rsv.	Dates	NR*	Participant	Rsv.	Dates	NR*	Participant	Rsv.	Dates	NR*
Afghanistan	22	21-05-1985 a		France	i	19-11-1960 a		Norway		23-01-1952 a	
Albania	22	06-11-1958 a		Guinea		26-04-1962 a		Pakistan		11-07-1952 r	
Algeria	22	31-10-1963 a		Haiti		26-08-1953 a		Philippines		19-09-1952 r	
Argentina		15-11-1957 a		Honduras		15-06-1993 r		Poland		02-06-1952 a	
Bangladesh		11-01-1985 a		Hungary		29-09-1955 r		Portugal		30-09-1992 a	
Belarus		24-08-1956 a		India		09-01-1953 r		Republic of Korea		13-02-1962 a	
Belgium		22-06-1965 a		Iran (Islamic Rep. of)		16-07-1953 s		Romania	22	15-02-1955 a	
Bolivia		06-10-1983 a		Iraq		22-09-1955 a		Russian Federation		11-08-1954 a	
Bosnia & Herzegovinia		01-09-1993 d		Israel		28-12-1950 a		Senegal		19-07-1979 a	
Brazil		12-09-1958 r		Italy		18-01-1980 a		Seychelles		05-05-1992 a	
Bulgaria		18-01-1955 a		Japan		01-05-1958 a		Singapore		26-10-1966 a	
Burkina Faso		27-08-1962 a		Jordan		13-04-1976 a		Slovakia		28-05-1993 d	
Cameroon		19-02-1982 a		Kuwait		20-11-1968 a		Slovenia		06-07-1992 d	
Central Afr. Rep.		29-09-1981 a		Lao People's D. Rep.	22	14-04-1978 a		South Africa		10-10-1951 r	
Congo		25-08-1977 a		Latvia		14-04-1992 a		Spain		18-06-1962 a	
Croatia		12-10-1992 d		Liberia		21-03-1950 s		Sri Lanka		15-04-1958 a	
Cuba		04-09-1952 a		Libyan Arab Jamahiriya		03-12-1956 a		Syrian Arab Rep.		12-06-1959 a	
Cyprus		15-10-1983 a		Luxembourg	22	05-10-1983 r		the former Yugoslav Rep. of Macedonia		18-01-1994 d	
Czech Republic		30-12-1993 d		Malawi		13-10-1965 a		Togo		14-03-1990 a	
Denmark		12-02-1951 s		Mali		23-12-1964 a		Ukraine		15-11-1954 a	
Djibouti		21-03-1979 a		Mauritania		06-06-1986 a		Venezuela		18-12-1968 a	
Ecuador		03-04-1979 r		Mexico		21-02-1956 a		Yemen		06-04-1989 a	
Egypt	22	12-06-1959 a		Morocco		17-08-1973 a		Yugoslavia		26-04-1951 r	
Ethiopia		10-09-1981 a		Myanmar		14-03-1956 s		Zimbabwe		15-11-1995 a	
Finland	09	08-06-1972 r		Niger		10-06-1977 a					

Article 22
The State Party does not consider itself bound to Article 22 (under which in the event of any dispute arising between the parties to the present Convention relating to its interpretation and application and if such dispute cannot be settled by other means, the dispute shall, at the request of *one* of the parties to the dispute, be referred to the International Court of Justice) to the extent that any disputes which may be referred to the International Court of Justice will require the agreement of *all* parties to the dispute.

Article 9
The State Party reserves the right to leave the decision whether its citizens will or will not be prosecuted for a crime committed abroad to the State Party's competent authority. Under Article 9, in States where the extradition of nationals is not permitted by law, nationals who have returned to their own State after the commission abroad of any of the offences referred to in Articles 1 and 2 [*procuring, enticing or leading away for purposes of prostitution another person; exploiting the prostitution of another; keeping or managing or knowingly financing or taking part in the financing of a brothel; knowingly renting or letting premises for the purpose of prostitution*] shall be prosecuted in and punished by the courts of their own State. This provision does not apply if, in a similar case between the parties the extradition of an alien cannot be granted.

i
The State Party declares that until further notice this Convention will only be applicable to its metropolitan territory.

STATE PARTIES BY CONTINENTS

AMERICA

Argentina
Bolivia
Brazil
Cuba
Ecuador
Haiti
Honduras
Mexico
Venezuela

EUROPE

Albania
Belarus
Belgium
Bosnia & Herz.
Bulgaria
Croatia
Cyprus
Czech Rep.
Denmark
Finland
France
Hungary
Italy
Latvia
Luxembourg

Norway
Poland
Portugal
Romania
Russian Federation*
Slovakia
Slovenia
Spain
the former Yugoslav
　　Rep. of Macedonia
Ukraine
Yugoslavia

AFRICA

Algeria
Burkina Faso
Cameroon
Central African Rep.
Congo
Djibouti
Egypt
Ethiopia
Guinea
Liberia
Libyan Arab
　　Jamahiriya
Mali
Mauritania

Morocco
Niger
Senegal
Seychelles**
South Africa
Togo
Zimbabwe

ASIA

Afghanistan
Bangladesh
India
Iran (Islamic Rep. of)
Iraq
Israel
Japan
Jordan
Kuwait
Lao People's Democ. Rep.
Malawi
Myanmar
Pakistan
Rep. of Korea
Singapore
Sri Lanka
Syrian Arab Rep.
Yemen

*　　Eurasia
**　　Indian Ocean

C4: TABLE OF MINIMUM AGE LEGISLATIVE STANDARDS FOR HAZARDOUS OCCUPATIONS

Minimum Age Legislative Standards for Hazardous Occupations and Industries

Occupation/Industry	Hazards	Min Age	Countries
Abattoirs & meat rendering	Injuries from cuts, burns, falls and dangerous equipment;	18	Central African Republic, Congo, Finland, Gabon, Luxembourg [1], Togo, USA, Zaire
	Exposure to infectious disease; Heat stress	16	Bahrain, Lebanon [2]
Acids	Risk of burns, inhalation of toxic fumes, eye injuries	18	Angola [1], Austria, Bolivia, Cameroon, Chad, Colombia [1], Congo, Cyprus, Denmark [1], France, Germany, Spain [7], Sudan, Togo
		16	Bahrain, Honduras, Mexico
Agriculture	Unsafe machinery, hazardous substances;	21	Uruguay
	Accidents;	18	Colombia [1, 4]
	Chemical poisoning; Arduous work;		Costa Rica [4], Spain [4, 7]
	Dangerous animals, insects and reptiles	17	Australia (Queensland) [3]
		16 or 18	France [4, 5]
		16	Denmark [4], United Kingdom [4], USA [3, 4]
Alcohol production and/or sale	Intoxication, addiction;	21	Chile
	Prejudicial to morals;	18	Argentina, Australia (Victoria)
	Risk of violence	18	Argentina, Australia (Victoria), Bolivia, Brazil, Burundi, Cameroon, Colombia, Costa Rica, Dominican Republic, Ecuador, Equatorial Guinea, Haiti, Italy, Luxembourg, Mexico, Panama, Peru, Portugal, Spain [7], Venezuela, Zaire
		16	Guatemala, Honduras, Mexico
		15	Jamaica, Thailand

Carpet weaving	Dust inhalation, poor lighting, poor posture, respiratory and musculo-skeletal disease;	14	India
	Eye strain and chemical poisoning		
Cement manufacture	Harmful chemicals, exposure to harmful dust;	18	Angola [1], Cameroon, Colombia [1]
	Arduous work;	14	India
	Respiratory and musculo-skeletal disease		
Circular saws and other dangerous machines	Accidents (loss of limb or life, danger from unprotected moving parts)	18	Argentina, Australia (Victoria), Austria, Bolivia, Cameroon [1], Colombia [1], Denmark [1], Djibouti, Ecuador, France, Gabon, India, Luxembourg, Madagascar, Mauritius, Nepal, Peru, Saudi Arabia, Spain, Trinidad, USA, Zaire
		17	Pakistan
		16	Burkina Faso, Chad, Central African Republic, Congo, Malaysia [1], Senegal, United Kingdom
Construction and/or demolition	Exposure to heat, cold, dust;	18	Austria, Bolivia, Burundi, Colombia [1, 11], El Salvador
	Falling objects;		France, Gabon
	Sharp objects;		Luxembourg, Madagascar [11], Netherlands, Peru [11], Spain [7], USA
	Accidents		
	Musculo-skeletal diseases	16	Bahrain, Barbados, Burkina Faso [11], Cameroon [11], Central African Republic, Chad, Congo, Côte d'Ivoire [11], Djibouti [11], France, Kenya, Morocco, Senegal [11], Somalia, UK
		15	Dominica, Jamaica
		14	Belize, Cyprus, India
Cranes, Hoists, Lifting Machinery	Accidents; falling objects; Musculo-skeletal diseases;	18	Argentina, Austria, Canada, Central African Republic, Chad, Colombia [1], Congo, Gabon, Japan, Luxembourg, Madagascar, Mauritius, Netherlands, USA, Zaire
	Risk of injury to others	16	Bahrain, Denmark, France, Israel

250

Crystal and/or Glass Manufacture	Molten glass; Extreme heat; poor ventilation;	18	Angola [1], Argentina, Austria, Bolivia, Cameroon
	Cuts from broken glass; Carrying hot glass; Burns		Côte d'Ivoire, Colombia [1], Cyprus [women], Denmark [1], Djibouti, Ecuador, Ireland, Madagascar, Senegal
	Respiratory disease;	17	Austria [4]
	Heat stress;	16 to 18	France [4, 5]
	Toxic dust	16	Bahrain
		15	Syrian Arab Republic
Domestic service	Long hours, physical, emotional and sexual abuse; Malnutrition; Insufficient rest; Isolation	16	Denmark
Electricity	Dangerous work with high voltage; risk of falling;	18	Angola [1], Cameroon, Colombia [1], France, Panama, Sweden, Uruguay, Zaire
	High level of responsibility for safety of others	16	Bahrain, Mexico
		15	Dominica, Jamaica
		14	Belize
Entertainment (clubs, bars, gambling, circuses)	Long, late hours;	21	Chile, Seychelles (casinos), Uruguay
	Sexual abuse; Exploitation; Prejudicial to morals	18	Angola, Austria, Bolivia, Brazil, Burundi, Cameroon, Colombia, Ecuador, El Salvador, Italy, Luxembourg, Panama, Peru, Philippines, Seychelles, Switzerland
		16	France, Honduras
		15	Thailand
Explosives (manufacture and handling)	Risk of explosion, fire, burns, mortal danger	18	Angola [1], Austria, Bolivia, Belgium, Burundi, Cameroon, Chad, Colombia [1], Congo, Costa Rica, Côte d'Ivoire, Cyprus, Denmark [1], Djibouti, Ecuador, El Salvador, Equatorial Guinea, Finland, France, Japan, Laos, Luxembourg, Madagascar, Netherlands, Panama, Peru, Philippines, Portugal, Senegal, Spain [7], Sweden, Switzerland, Thailand, Togo, USA, Zaire

251

		17	Canada (Federal)
		16	Bahrain, Dominican Republic, Honduras, Mexico
		14	India
Fumes, Dust, Gas and Other Noxious Substances	Chemical poisoning; Damage to eyes and respiratory system; Poisoning	18	Angola [1], Austria [1], Bolivia, Colombia [1], Congo, Czech Republic [1], Denmark [1], Ecuador, El Salvador, France, Germany [1], Japan, Laos, Luxembourg, Madagascar, Netherlands, Nicaragua, Peru, Portugal, Slovakia [1], Spain [7], Sudan, Sweden, Switzerland, Thailand, Togo
		17	Cuba
		16	Bahrain, Honduras, Mexico, Morocco, UK
		14	India
Hospitals and work with risk of infection	Infectious diseases; Responsibility for well-being of others	18	Austria, Bangladesh, Czech Republic [1], Luxembourg, Madagascar, Netherlands, Slovakia [1], Spain, Switzerland
		17	Israel [12]
Lead/zinc metallurgy; white lead; lead in paint	Cumulative poisoning; Neurological damage	21	Uruguay
		18	Australia (Queensland, Victoria), Austria, Barbados, Belgium, Bolivia, Cameroon, Colombia [1], Cyprus, Czech Republic [1], Denmark [1], Djibouti, Ecuador, France, Gabon, Germany, Ireland, Madagascar, Malta, Norway, Slovakia [1], Sudan, Sweden, Togo, Zaire
		16	Bahrain, Greece [lead accumulators], Honduras, Mexico, UK
		15	Syrian Arab Republic
Machinery in motion (operation, cleaning repairs)	Danger from moving engine parts;	21	Uruguay

252

	Accidents, cuts, burns, exposure to heat and noise; Noise stress; Eye and ear injuries	18	Argentina, Austria [1], Bolivia, Burundi, Cameroon, Central African Republic, Colombia, Chad, Congo, Côte d'Ivoire, Cyprus, Denmark [1], Djibouti, Dominica, Dominican Republic, El Salvador, Equatorial Guinea, France, Gabon, Greece, India, Ireland, Japan, Luxembourg, Madagascar, Malawi, Malta, Mauritius, Myanmar, Netherlands, Peru, Saudi Arabia, Spain, Sweden, Switzerland, Thailand, Zaire, Zambia
		17	Pakistan
		16	Bahrain, Bangladesh, Djibouti, Guyana, Jamaica, Malaysia [1], Morocco, Nigeria, Saint Lucia, Senegal, Singapore, UK
		15	Italy [14], Syrian Arab Republic
Maritime work	Accidents; Heat, burns; Falls from heights;	21	Brazil [10]
	Heavy lifting, arduous work, musculo-skeletal disease; Respiratory diseases	19	Denmark [1], Iceland
		18	Algeria, Argentina, Australia, Bahamas, Bangladesh, Belgium, Belize [6], Burundi, China, Congo, Côte d'Ivoire, Djibouti, Ecuador, El Salvador, Fiji, Gabon, Iraq, Ireland, Japan, Kenya, Liberia, Luxembourg, Malawi, Malta, Myanmar, Nigeria [6], Pakistan [6], Peru, Philippines, Romania, Sierra Leone [6], Singapore, Solomon Islands, Somalia, Sri Lanka, Sudan, Tanzania, Trinidad & Tobago, Tunisia, Zaire
		17	Canada (Federal), Cuba [10]

Mining, quarries, underground work	Exposure to dusts, gases, dirty conditions	21	Brazil
	Respiratory and musculo-skeletal diseases; Accidents; Falling objects; Arduous work, heavy loads	18	Afghanistan, Albania, Angola [1], Argentina, Australia (South and Western), Austria [1], Belgium, Bolivia, Botswana, Burundi, Belarus, Cameroon [1], Cape Verde, Central African Rep., Chad, Chile, Colombia [1], Congo, Cuba, Cyprus [13], Czech Republic [1], Denmark [1], Djibouti, Dominican Republic, Ecuador, El Salvador, Equatorial Guinea, Fiji, France, Gabon, Germany [1], Ghana, Greece, Guinea Bissau, India, Indonesia, Iraq, Ireland, Israel, Italy, Japan, Jordan, Laos, Luxembourg, Nicaragua, Panama, Peru, Philippines, Portugal, Russian Federation, Saudi Arabia, Slovakia [1], Somalia, Sudan, Swaziland, Switzerland, Tanzania, Thailand, Tunisia, Turkey, USA, Venezuela, Zaire, Zambia
		17	Australia (Victoria), Bangladesh, Canada (Federal), Jamaica, Myanmar [15], Pakistan
		16	Bahrain, Barbados, Burkina Faso, Côte d'Ivoire, Hungary, Kenya, Lesotho [2], Mexico, Nicaragua, Nigeria, Sierra Leone [2], Singapore, Solomon Islands [2], UK
		15	Dominica, Syrian Arab Republic
		14	Belize, Cyprus [13]

Radioactive substances or ionising radiation (work with)	Radiation	18	Argentina, Austria [1], Belgium, Colombia [1], Czech Republic [1], Denmark [1], Finland, France, Germany, India, Laos, Luxembourg, Malta, Netherlands, Panama, Philippines, Slovakia [1], Sudan, Thailand, USA
		17	Canada (Federal)
		16	Bahrain, Guyana, Honduras, UK
Rubber	Heat, burns, chemical poisoning	18	Angola [1], Cyprus
		16	Mexico
Street trades	Exposure to drugs, violence, criminal activity, heavy loads;	18	Austria, Bolivia, Brazil, Peru [7]
	Musculo-skeletal diseases; Sexual diseases;	16	Burkina Faso, Cyprus, Djibouti [women], Dominican Republic, Italy, UK
	Accidents	15	Costa Rica [14]
		14	Sri Lanka
Tanneries	Chemical poisoning;	18	Chad, France, Gabon, Zaire
	Sharp instruments;	17	Austria
	Respiratory diseases	16	Dominican Republic, Mexico
	Tar, asphalt, bitumen; Exposure to heat, burns;	15	Syrian Arab Republic
	Chemical poisoning,	14	India
	Respiratory diseases	18	Angola [1], Czech Republic, Luxembourg, Slovakia [1]
		15	Syrian Arab Republic
Transportation, operating vehicles	Accidents; Danger to self and passengers	18	Austria, Burundi, Central African Republic, Chad, Congo, Denmark [1], Equatorial Guinea, Gabon, Pakistan [9], Panama, Peru, Philippines, Spain [7], USA, Zaire
		16	Barbados, Dominican Republic, Israel, Kenya, UK
		15	Dominica, Jamaica
		14	Belize, Cyprus

255

Underwater	Decompression illness; Dangerous fish;	18	Austria, Colombia [1], El Salvador, Laos, Sudan, Sweden, Thailand, Turkey
	Death or injury	16	Dominican Republic, Mexico
Weights and loads	Physical stress and strain; Musculo-skeletal diseases	14 to 18	Australia (Victoria), Belgium, Belize, Bolivia, Botswana, Burkina Faso, Burundi, Cameroon, Central African Republic, Chad, Congo, Côte d'Ivoire, Cuba, Cyprus, Czech Republic, Djibouti, Ecuador, Gabon, India, Israel, Italy, Niger, Russian Federation, Slovakia, Spain, Switzerland, Ukraine, Uruguay, Zaire
Welding and smelting	Exposure to extreme heat of metals; Flying sparks and hot metal objects;	18	Argentina, Austria [1], Bolivia, Cameroon, Colombia [1], Ecuador, Luxembourg, Spain [7], Sudan, Sweden, USA
	Metalworking accidents; Eye injuries; Heat stress	16	Bahrain

NOTES

[1] Except for apprenticeships
[2] Medical certificate required
[3] Application of agricultural chemicals (min. age 17 in Queensland; 16 in USA)
[4] For specified tasks only
[5] Different minimum age depending on the type of work
[6] Where a person over 18 is unavailable for a trimmer and stoker position this may be filled by two 16-year-olds
[7] Minimum age of 18 for men and 21 for women
[8] Provision is made in legislation for maximum loads per age grouping
[9] Minimum age of 21 in road transport services requiring the driving of a vehicle
[10] Applies only to stevedoring
[11] Applies only to work on scaffolding
[12] Applies only to work involving contact with TB, leprosy or mental patients
[13] Minimum age of 18 for underground work; 14 in other mines and quarries
[14] Minimum age of 15 for men, 18 for women (applies to street trades in Costa Rica for unmarried women only)
[15] Minimum age of 17 for underground work; 15 for other work in mines, quarries

Original Source: Conditions of Work Digest Vol. 10, 1/1991, Part II, Annexe 3

Reproduced from 'First Things First in Child Labour'

National Legislation on the Minimum Age for Admission to Employment or Work

Annexe 1: Africa

Country	Compulsory education required to age	Minimum age — Basic minimum age	Minimum age — Light work	Minimum age — Dangerous work	Exceptions to coverage — Categories of work excluded	Exceptions to coverage — Sectors of activity excluded
Algeria	15	16	None; authorisation necessary <2>	16 to 18 <1>	Domestic service, homeworkers	None
Angola	15	14	—	18	Family undertakings	None
Benin	11	14	12	18	None	None
Botswana	—	15	14	15 to 18 <3>	Domestic service, family undertakings, other exclusions possible <2>	Commerce, non-commercial agriculture, etc.
Burkina Faso	14	14	12	16 to 18 <4>	Exclusions possible <2>	None
Burundi	13	16	12	18	Family undertakings, domestic work in family, other exclusions possible <2>	None
Cameroon	12	14	—	18	Exclusions possible <2>	None
Cape Verde	13	14 to 15 <5>	12	16 to 18	Family undertakings, self-employment, etc. <5>	None
Central African Republic	14	14	12	16 to 18	Family undertakings, other exclusions possible <2>	None
Chad	14	12 to 14 <6>	12	16 to 18	Family undertakings, other exclusions possible	None
Comoros	16	15	—	— <7>	— <8>	None
Congo	16	16	12	16 to 18	Family undertakings, other exclusions possible <2>	None
Côte d'Ivoire	13	14	12	16 to 18	Domestic service	None

(continued)

257

Country	Compulsory education required to age	Minimum age Basic minimum age	Minimum age Light work	Minimum age Dangerous work	Exceptions to coverage Categories of work excluded	Exceptions to coverage Sectors of activity excluded
Djibouti	15	14	–	16 to 18	None	None
Egypt	15	12	–	15 to 17	Domestic service, family undertakings	Agriculture
Equatorial Guinea	14	–	12 to 13	16	None	None
Ethiopia	13	14	–	18	Self-employment	None
Gabon	16	16	–	18	Family undertakings, other exclusions possible	None
Ghana	16	15	No limit	18	Family undertakings	None
Guinea	13	16 <19>	–	–	Self-employment, etc. <9>	None
Guinea Bissau	13	14 <10>	–	18	None	None
Kenya	–	16 <11>	–	16	Family undertakings (industry), various <11>	Agriculture, commerce, etc. <11>
Lesotho	13	15 <12>	–	16	Family undertakings, self-employment, domestic service, etc. <12>	Agriculture <12>
Liberia	16	14 to 16 (by sector) <13>	–	18	None	None
Libyan Arab Jamahiriya	15	15	–	18	Family undertakings, domestic service	Agriculture, maritime
Madagascar	13	14 to 15 (by sector) <14>	–	16 to 18	Exclusions possible <2>	None
Malawi	14	14 to 15 (by sector) <15>	12	18	Family undertakings, domestic service, self-employed <15>	Agriculture, commerce, etc. <15>

					domestic service, other exclusions possible <2>	
Mauritania	—	14 to 15 (by sector) <14>	—	18	Exclusions possible <2>	None
Mauritius	—	15	—	18	None	None
Morocco	14	12	—	16	None	None
Mozambique	14	15	—	18	None	None
Namibia	16	14 <16>	—	16	Domestic service, self-employment, etc. <16>	Agriculture, commerce, etc. <16>
Niger	15	14	12	16 to 18	Exclusions possible <2>	None
Nigeria	12	12 to 15 (by sector) <17>	12	16 to 18	None	None
Rwanda	15	14	—	—	None	None
São Tomé and Príncipe	14	14 to 15	12	16 to 18	Family undertakings	None
Senegal	13	14 to 15 (by sector) <14>	12	16 to 18	Exclusions possible <2>	None
Seychelles	15	15	12	18	None	None
Sierra Leone	—	12 to 16 (by sector) <18>	No limit <19>	16 to 18	Family undertakings	None
Somalia	14	15	12	16 to 18	Family undertakings, other exclusions possible	None
Sudan	—	12	—	18	Family undertakings	None
Swaziland	—	13 to 15 (by sector) <20>	—	18	Family undertakings, self-employment	Agriculture <20>
Tanzania	14	12 to 15 (by sector) <21>	10	18	Family undertakings (maritime), other exclusions possible <2>	None

Country	Compulsory education required to age	Minimum age			Exceptions to coverage	
		Basic minimum age	Light work	Dangerous work	Categories of work excluded	Sectors of activity excluded
Togo	12	14	–	18	Exclusions possible <2>	None
Tunisia	–	13 to 15 (by sector) <22>	13	18	Family undertakings, domestic service, self-employment	Commerce, etc. <22>
Uganda	–	– <23>	12	16 to 18	–	–
Zaire	12	16	14	18	None	None
Zambia	14	14 <11>	–	19	Family undertakings, domestic service, self-employment	Agriculture, commerce, etc. <11>

<1> 16 for work that is dangerous, unhealthy or detrimental to morals; 18 for work in the maritime industry.
<2> Determined by the competent authority.
<3> 15 for work involving lifting, carrying or moving anything heavy; 18 for underground work and dangerous or harmful work.
<4> General minimum age for hazardous work is 16 years; 18 for work exceeding strength and harmful to morality.
<5> Minimum age of 14 for contract as a permanent worker; 15 for work in industry.
<6> General minimum age is 14 years; 12 years for specified agricultural work.
<7> Age limits and nature of work prohibited to adolescents to be determined by ministerial decision.
<8> Applies only to enterprises.
<9> Applies only to industry and contractual employment.
<10> Or upon completion of compulsory schooling.
<11> Basic minimum age applies only to industry.
<12> Basic minimum age applies only to commerce and industry.
<13> General minimum age is 14 years; 15 for work on fishing vessels and on school ships; 16 for work in industry, agriculture and on ships.
<14> General minimum age is 14 years; 15 for work at sea.
<15> Minimum age of 14 for work in industry; 15 for work at sea.
<16> Minimum age applies only to work in factories and mines.
<17> General minimum age is 12 years; 15 for work in industry and shipping (except family undertakings).
<18> General minimum age is 12 years; 15 for work in industry and at sea; 16 for work in mines.
<19> Authorised only where the work is not harmful to the child. Authorisation for light work is subject to approval by the competent authority.
<20> Minimum age of 13 in commercial undertakings; 15 in industrial undertakings.
<21> General minimum age is 12 years; 15 for work in industry.
<22> 13 years for work in agriculture; 15 for work in industry, fishing and work at sea.
<23> A person under the apparent age of 18 shall not be employed other than as provided for by decree.

Country	Compulsory education required to age	Minimum age			Exceptions to coverage	
		Basic minimum age	Light work	Dangerous work	Categories of work excluded	Sectors of activity excluded
Antigua and Barbuda	16	16 <1>	14	–	Family undertakings, domestic service	Commerce <1>
Argentina	14	14	–	18	Family undertakings <2>, domestic service, other exclusions possible <3>	None
Bahamas	14	14 <4>	–	16 to 18	Family undertakings, domestic service, self-employment	Agriculture, commerce, etc. <4>
Barbados	16	15 to 16 <5>	–	18	Family undertakings, domestic service, self-employment	Agriculture, commerce, etc. <5>
Belize	14	12 to 15 (by sector) <6>	–	18	None	None
Bolivia	13	14	–	18	None	None
Brazil	14	14 <7>	–	18 to 21 <8>	None	None
Canada: Federal	16	– <9>	–	17 <10>	–	– <9>
Provinces	–	Various <11>	–	16 to 18	Various (e.g. family undertakings in some provinces)	Agriculture (most provinces)
Chile	13	15	14	18 to 21 <21>	None	None
Colombia	14	14	12	18	None	Commerce, fishing
Costa Rica	15	12 to 15 <13>	12	18	Domestic service	None

261

Country						
Cuba	11	15	—	17 to 18	None	None
Dominica	15	15 <14>	—	18	Family undertakings, domestic service, self-employment	Agriculture, commerce, etc. <14>
Dominican Republic	14	14	—	18	—	Agriculture (except dangerous work)
Ecuador	14	12 to 15 <15>	—	18	Domestic service	None
El Salvador	15	14	—	18	Exclusions possible <3>	None
Guatemala	14	14	—	16	Exclusions possible <3>	None
Guyana	14	14	—	16 to 18	Family undertakings	None
Haiti	12	12 to 15	—	18	None	None
Honduras	13	14	—	16	Exclusions possible <3>	Small agricultural undertakings <17>
Jamaica	12	12 to 15 (by sector) <18>	No limit	16 to 17 <18>	Family undertakings (maritime)	None
Mexico	14	14	—	16	None	None
Nicaragua	12	14 <4>	—	18	Various <4>	Agriculture, commerce, etc. <4>
Panama	15	14 to 16 <20>	12	18	None	None
Paraguay	13	15	12	18	Family undertakings	None
Peru	12	14 to 16 (by sector) <21>	—	18	Family undertakings, domestic service	Small agricultural undertakings <22>
Saint Lucia	15	12 to 14 (by sector) <23>	No limit	14 to 16	Family undertakings	None

Suriname	12	14	—	18	Family undertakings (agriculture), other exclusions possible <24>	None
Trinidad and Tobago	11	12 to 16 (by sector) <25>	—	14 to 18	Family undertakings	None
United States (Federal)	16	16	—	16 to 18	Family undertakings, domestic service, other exclusions possible <24>	Agriculture
Uruguay	14	15	12	18 to 21	None	None
Venezuela	14	14	—	18	Domestic service	Agriculture

<1> Minimum age applies only to agriculture and industrial undertakings and for work on ships.

<2> On condition that the work is not harmful or dangerous and that the hours do not interfere with primary schooling.

<3> The competent authority may authorize exceptions if it is essential for the maintenance of the person concerned or that person's family and on condition that minimum education is completed, or work does not interfere with minimal education requirements.

<4> Minimum age applies only to industrial undertakings.

<5> Minimum age applies only to industrial undertakings or ships, including work in mines and quarries, construction, transportation. Minimum age of 15 only if compulsory schooling is finished.

<6> General minimum age is 12 years; 14 for work in industry, mines and quarries, construction, transportation, etc.; 15 for work at sea.

<7> Except apprentices above the age of 12.

<8> Minimum age of 21 for stevedoring and underground work.

<9> The Canada Labour Code does not set an absolute minimum age for employment. It provides that an employer may employ a person under 17 years in (a) occupations as may be specified by regulation, and (b) subject to the conditions and at a wage of not less than the minimum wage prescribed, and (c) provided that persons under 17 years are not required by provincial law to be in attendance at school (the youngest age for leaving school as provided by the provinces is 15). (Branches and undertakings governed by federal jurisdiction include communications, international and national transport, broadcasting, banking, uranium extraction and nuclear energy, and also certain branches by Parliament to be of interest to the nation. Federal legislation covers 10 per cent of the active population.)

<10> Persons under 17 years cannot be employed in specified jobs or at night.

263

<11> According to province, or territory, and sector. In certain provinces and territories, the employment of young persons is prohibited for various sectors only during school hours.

<12> Minimum age of 21 for work in cabarets, etc., presenting live performances and offering alcoholic beverages.

<13> Minimum age of 12 only if compulsory schooling has been completed or work does not prevent its completion, and not for more than five hours a day. Minimum age of 15 to 18 for work no exceeding seven hours a day.

<14> Minimum age applies only to industrial undertakings, including mining, manufacturing, shipbuilding, electrical utilities, construction and transportation.

<15> General minimum age is 14; 12 for minors who are obliged to work for their or their family's living; 15 for work on fishing vessels.

<16> General minimum age is 15 years; 12 for domestic service.

<17> Undertakings employing less than ten workers.

<18> General minimum age is 12 years; 15 for work in industry, mines and quarries, construction, transportation, and work at sea.

<19> 16 years for work in sugar factories and work with machinery in motion; 17 for mining.

<20> General minimum age is 14 years; 15 years where the child has not yet finished school; 16 for work on ships.

<21> 14 years for agriculture and non-industrial work; 15 for work in industry; 16 for industrial fishing. Regulations apply to all work.

<22> Which do not possess agricultural machinery.

<23> General minimum age is 12 years; 14 for work in industry and on ships. No work may be performed during school hours, if the child is still completing schooling.

<24> Determined by the competent authority.

<25> General minimum age is 12 years; 14 for work in industry; 16 for work on ships.

264

Annexe 1: Asia

Country	Compulsory education required to age	Minimum age			Exceptions to coverage	
		Basic minimum age	Light work	Dangerous work	Categories of work excluded	Sectors of activity excluded
Afghanistan	15	15	–	18	Domestic service, etc. <1>	Agriculture, commerce, etc. <1>
Australia	16	Varies according to province and sector <2>	–	16 to 18	–	–
Bahrain	–	14	–	16	Family undertakings, domestic service	Agriculture, maritime
Bangladesh	10	12 to 15 (by sector) <3>	–	16 to 18 <4>	Family undertakings (maritime), domestic service, various <5>	Small factories <5>, agricultural undertakings other than tea plantations <3>
China	16	16	–	18	Family undertakings	–
Fiji	–	12 to 15 (by sector) <6>	No limit	16 to 18	Family undertakings, other exclusions possible <7>	Exclusion of ships allowed
India	14	14 <8>	–	18	Family undertakings, various <8>	Agriculture, commerce, etc. <8>
Indonesia	13	14 <9>	–	18	Various <9>	Various <9>
Iran	10	15	–	18	None	None
Iraq	12	15	–	18	Family undertakings	None

(continued)

Country	Compulsory education required to age	Minimum age			Exceptions to coverage	
		Basic minimum age	Light work	Dangerous work	Categories of work excluded	Sectors of activity excluded
Israel	16	15	–	16 to 18	None	Agriculture, commerce
Japan	15	15	12	18	Family undertakings, domestic service	None
Jordan	15	13	–	15	Family undertakings, domestic service	Agriculture
Kuwait	14	14	–	18	Casual or temporary work, domestic service	None
Lao People's Democratic Republic	15	15	–	18	None	None
Lebanon	–	13	8	16	Family undertakings, domestic service	Non-commercial agriculture
Malaysia	14	14	No limit	16	None	None
Mongolia	16	16	–	18	None	Agriculture
Myanmar	10	13 <10>	–	15 to 18	Domestic service, self-employment	Agriculture, small factories <10>
Nepal	11	14 <11>	–	18	Various <11>	Agriculture, commerce, etc. <11>
New Zealand	15	15 <12>	–	15 to 21	None	Agriculture, commerce, etc. <13>

Pakistan	—	14 to 15 (by sector) <14>	—	16 to 21	Various <15>	Small factories, agriculture; other exceptions possible <15>
Papua New Guinea	—	14 to 16	—	16	Family undertakings <16>	None
Philipines	13	15	No limit	18	Family undertakings	None
Qatar	—	12	—	—	Family undertakings, domestic service	None
Saudi Arabia	—	13	—	18	Family undertakings, domestic service	Agriculture
Singapore	—	12 to 14 (by sector)	12	16 to 18	—	—
Solomon Islands	—	12 to 15 (by sector) <17>	No limit	16 to 18	Family undertakings	None
Sri Lanka	15	14 to 15 (by sector) <18>	No limit	16 to 18	Family undertakings	None
Syrian Arab Republic	11	12 to 13 (by sector) <19>	—	15	Family undertakings, domestic service	Small undertakings <19>
Thailand	15	12 <20>	12	15 to 18	Various <20>	Agriculture
United Arab Emirates	12	15 <21>	—	18	Family undertakings, domestic service	Agriculture, small undertakings <21>
Yemen	—	12	—	—	Domestic service, temporary work	Agriculture

<1> Applies only to industry, administrations and co-operatives.
<2> Regulations cover only work at sea (16 years). Certain states and territories impose a minimum age in certain sectors; others merely prohibit the employment of young persons during school hours.
<3> Minimum age of 12 for work in shops and on tea plantations; 14 for work in factories; and 15 for work at sea.
<4> 16 for work in factories with machinery in motion; 17 for mining; 18 for work at sea as trimmers and stokers.
<5> According to the size of the undertaking. The Factories Act governs all undertakings which employ or have employed at least ten workers during the previous 12 months. Regulations apply in particular to tea plantations with a surface area of more than 25 acres (ten hectares) which employ at least 30 workers.
<6> General minimum age is 12 years; 15 for work in industry.
<7> Determined by the competent authority.
<8> Minimum age applies only to designated occupations.
<9> Children below 14 may work with the permission of parents or guardians up to four hours a day.
<10> Applies only to certain factories (those where motive power is installed which employ less than ten workers, and those without motive power employing less than 20 workers are excluded), commerce, the merchant navy and mineworks.
<11> Minimum age applies only to factories. Exemptions of factories possible.
<12> Minimum age applies only to factories, work at sea, fishing and railways.
<13> No child may be employed during school hours or where this hinders or prevents the child from attending school.
<14> Minimum age of 14 for work in factories, shops and commerce, and work at sea; 15 for work in mines and on railways.
<15> Legislation in factories applies only to those employing at least ten workers. The competent authority may authorize the exclusion of any region or establishment from the scope of legislation concerning commerce.
<16> Minimum age of 11 for family undertakings.
<17> General minimum age is 12 years; 15 for work in industry and at sea.
<18> General minimum age is 14 years; 15 for work at sea.
<19> General minimum age is 12 years; 13 for work in industry. Applies only to undertakings with more than ten employees.
<20> Minimum age applies only to employment relationships.
<21> Minimum age applies only to undertakings with more than five employees.

268

Annexe 1: Europe

Country	Compulsory education required to age	Minimum age			Exceptions to coverage	
		Basic minimum age	Light work	Dangerous work	Categories of work excluded	Sectors of activity excluded
Albania	13	15	—	18	Domestic service, etc. <1>	Agriculture, commerce, etc. <1>
Austria	15	15	12 <2>	16 to 18	Domestic service	None
Belgium	18	14 <3>	—	16 to 21	Domestic service	None
Bulgaria	16	16	15	18	None	None
Cyprus	15	13 to 16 (by sector) <4>	No limit	16 to 18	Family undertakings, domestic service	Agriculture
Czechoslovakia	16	16	—	18	None	None
Denmark	15	15	10 to 13 (according to the work)	16 to 18	Self-employment	None
Finland	16	15 <3>	14	16 to 18	Home work	None
France	16	16 <3>	12 to 14	16 to 18	Family undertakings	None
Germany	18	15 <5>	13	18	None	None
Greece	15	15	—	16 to 18	Family undertakings (agriculture only)	None
Hungary	16	15 <3>	14	16 to 18	None	None
Iceland	15	15 <6>	14	18 to 19	Domestic work, home work, self-employment, etc. <6>	Agriculture, commerce, etc. <6>
Iceland	15	15 <3>	14	18	Exclusions possible <7>	Agriculture

(continued)

Country	Compulsory education required to age	Minimum age			Exceptions to coverage	
		Basic minimum age	Light work	Dangerous work	Categories of work excluded	Sectors of activity excluded
Italy	13	14 or 15 (by sector) <8>	14	15 to 18	None	None
Luxembourg	15	15 <3>	–	18	None	None
Malta	16	15 to 16 (by sector) <9>	–	18	Family undertakings	None
Netherlands	16	15	13 to 15	18	None	None
Norway	15	15 to 16 (by sector) <10>	13	18	None	None
Poland	14	15	15	18	None	None
Portugal	14	14	–	18	None	None
Romania	16	16	–	16 to 18	None	None
Spain	15	16	–	18	None	None
Sweden	16	16	13	18	None	None
Switzerland	15	15	13	16 to 18	Family undertakings, domestic service	Agriculture
Turkey	14	15	13	18	Family undertakings, domestic service, home work and janitorial services	Agriculture
United Kingdom	16	13 to 16 (by sector) <11>	–	16 to 18	None	None
USSR	17	16	–	18	None	None
Yugoslavia	15	15	–	18	None	None

<1> Minimum age applies only to enterprises, institutions and handicraft co-operative societies.
<2> No minimum age in agriculture.
<3> Provided compulsory schooling has been completed.
<4> General minimum age is 13 years; 14 for work in industry; 16 for work at sea (except vessels where only members of a single family are employed).
<5> Child must have compulsory schooling. Minimum age applied not only to employment relationships, but to all work, including the self-employed.
<6> Minimum age applies only to factories and transport. The child must have also completed compulsory schooling.
<7> Determined by the competent authorities on condition that well-being, safety and health are not endangered.
<8> General minimum age is 15 years; 14 for work in agriculture or to assist the family.
<9> General minimum age is 16 years; 15 for work on ships.
<10> General minimum age is 15 years and the completion of compulsory schooling; 16 to work in merchant shipping.
<11> General minimum age is 13 years; 16 for work in industry. Children below the age of 16 may not work during school hours or for more than two hours a day.

271

National Legislation on the Minimum Age for Admission to Employment or Work

Annexe 2: Legislative provisions for light work by minors

Definition of light work	Minimum age	Country
General, i.e. not restricted to any particular sectors	15	Bulgaria <1, 9, 13, 14>
	14	Antigua and Barbuda, Botswana <1, 2, 10, 11, 12, 19>, Chile <1, 2, 9 or 15, 17>, Finland <8, 13, 14, 20>, France <20>, Hungary <20>, Iceland, Tunisia <1, 2, 5, 7>, Zaire <1, 2, 23>
	13	Cyprus <11, 15>, Equatorial Guinea <1, 2>, Germany <1, 8, 17, 21>, Norway <1, 2, 15>, Sweden <1, 2>, Thailand <15>, Turkey <1, 2>
	12	Brazil <1, 2>, Burundi <1, 2, 12, 15, 16>, Colombia <9, 15, 23>, Cyprus <6, 11, 15>, France <1, 2, 11>, Malawi <15>, Singapore <13>, Somalia <1, 22>, Uganda <15>
	None	Malaysia <7, 11, 12>, Philippines <1, 2>
Light work of a non-industrial nature	15	Netherlands <2>
	14	Ireland <2>, Italy <1, 2>
	13	Switzerland <1, 2, 6, 8>, Tunisia <1, 2>, United Kingdom <1, 2, 6, 8>
	12	Chad <9, 15>, Central African Republic <9, 13, 15>, Congo <9, 15>, Japan <2, 7, 9>, Mali <15, 23>, Niger <2, 6, 7, 15>, Thailand <16>, Uruguay <15, 17, 18>
	8	Lebanon
	None	Jamaica <11>, Solomon Islands <11, 15>
Non-agricultural work, occasional, light assistance, of short duration and not equivalent to that of an employee	12	Austria <1, 2, 5, 6, 7, 8, 9>, Seychelles
Light agricultural, horticultural or plantation work	13	Germany <2, 8, 9, 24, 25>, Netherlands <6>
	12	Benin, Burkina Faso, Burundi <1, 2, 9, 12, 16>, Cape Verde, Central African Republic <9, 13, 15>, Congo <1, 9, 15>, Côte d'Ivoire <9, 23>, Equatorial Guinea <15>, Fiji <4>, Guinea Bissau, Mali <15, 23>, Niger <2, 6, 7>, Nigeria <11, 15>, Panama <2, 15>, Paraguay <1, 2, 7, 9, 13, 15, 23>, São Tomé and Príncipe
	10	Denmark, Tanzania <8, 11, 15, 23>

	None	Austria <1, 4>, Belize <4>, Ghana <11>,Jamaica <11>, Saint Lucia <4>, Sierra Leone <6, 8, 11, 15>, Sri Lanka <4, 11>, United Kingdom <1, 2, 6, 8>
Domestic service	14	Botswana <1, 12>, Italy <1, 2, 4>
	12	Benin, Belize, Burkina Faso, Burundi <1, 2, 9, 12>, Central African Republic <9, 13, 15>, Chad <9, 15>, Congo <9, 15>, Côte d'Ivoire, Haiti <15>, Jamaica <11>, Mali <15, 23>, Niger <2, 6, 7>, Nigeria <11, 15>, Panama <2, 15>
	None	Sierra Leone <6, 8, 11, 15>
	Not covered by legislation	Afghanistan, Albania, Algeria, Antigua and Barbuda, Austria, Bahamas, Bahrain, Bangladesh, Cape Verde, Comoros, Costa Rica, Dominica, Ecuador, Egypt, India, Japan, Jordan, Kenya, Kuwait, Lebanon, Lesotho, Libyan Arab Jamahiriya, Malawi, Myanmar, Namibia, Nepal, Nicaragua, Pakistan, Peru, Qatar, São Tomé and Príncipe, Saudi Arabia, Swaziland, Turkey, United Arab Emirates, Venezuela, Zambia
Shop assistants, work in launderies, ticketing goods, kiosks, bakeries, green-grocers, packing and sorting light articles, newspaper sale and delivery	15	Netherlands <2, 5>
	13	Denmark <6, 14>
Seasonal and intermittent work	15	Poland <15>
	12	Senegal <9>

<1> Work must not expose the minor to risk of accident, endanger physical or mental health or development, or jeopardize morals.
<2> Work must not interfere with school instruction/not during school hours.
<3> Not in industry, commerce or commercial agriculture.
<4> Only on parents' or guardians' lands, gardens or plantation.
<5> No work on weekly rest day or religious or statutory holidays.
<6> Work must not exceed two hours a day.
<7> Combined school and work hours must not exceed seven in any day.
<8> No work between 20:00 and 08:00/19:00 and 06:00, or similar time periods.
<9> Consent of a parent or guardian is required.
<10> Domestic service only where suitable accommodation is provided.
<11> Work allowed if performed for a member of the family, in a family undertaking or under parental supervision.
<12> No more than six hours a day or 30 hours a week.
<13> Medical examination required, either before acceptance for employment or on a regular basis during employment.
<14> Must have an interruption of at least 12 or 14 hours between days of work.
<15> Work must be authorized by the labour inspector or appropriate authority.
<16> Weight limits imposed for loads which may be lifted by minors.
<17> Provided compulsory schooling has been completed.

<18> Work is essential to the existence of the family.

<19> Child must return each night to parents' or guardians' residence.

<20> Work to be done only during school holidays and for a restricted time during the holidays.

<21> Light work up to seven hours a day and 35 hours a week.

<22> Work must be essential to the learning of the trade/apprenticeship.

<23> Work must not exceed four or four-and-a-half hours a day.

<24> No work before school on school days.

<25> Work must not exceed three hours a day.

C5: CONTACT NAMES AND ADDRESSES

Amnesty International
1 Easton Street, London WC1X 8DJ, UK
Tel: (44) 171 413 5500
Fax: (44) 171 956 1157
Email: amnestyis@amnesty.org

15, route des Morillons, 1218 Grand-
Saconnex, Geneva, SWITZERLAND
Tel: (44) 22 798 2500
Fax: (41) 22 791 0390

Defence for Children International
P.O. Box 88, CH 1211 Geneva 20,
Switzerland
Tel. (41) 22 734 0558
Fax. (41) 22 740 1145
Email: dci-hq.pingnet.ch

**International Federation of Human Rights
(Federation des droits de L'Homme-
FIDH)**
14 Passage Dubail, 75010 Paris, FRANCE
Tel: (33) 1 40 37 54 26
Fax: (33) 1 44 72 05 86

Human Rights Internet
8 York St, Suite 202, Ottawa, Ontario
KIN 6N5, CANADA
Tel: (1-613) 789 7407
Fax: (1-613) 789 7414
Email: hri@hri.ca

International Human Rights Law Group
1601 Connecticut Avenue, NW Suite 700,
Washington DC 20009, USA
Tel: (1-202) 232 8500
Fax: (1-202) 232 6731 or 9518

Lawyers Committee for Human Rights
330 Seventh Avenue – 10th Floor,
New York, NY 10001, USA
Tel: (1-212) 629 6170
Fax: (1-212) 967 0916

Human Rights Watch
485 Fifth Avenue – 3rd Floor, New York,
NY 10017, USA
Tel: (1-212) 972 8400
Fax: (1-212) 972 0905
Email: whitman@hrw.org

Minnesota Advocates for Human Rights
Suite 1050, 400 Second Avenue South,
Minneapolis, Minnesota 55402
Tel: (1-612) 341 3302
Fax: (1-612) 341 2971

Radda Barnen
Torsgaten 4, S-107 88, Stockholm, SWEDEN
Tel: (46-8) 698 9000
Fax: (46-8) 698 9010
Email: carl.vonessen@rb.se

Save the Children (SCF)
Mary Datchelor House, 17 Grove Lane,
Camberwell, London, SE5 8RD, UK
Tel: (44) 171 703 5400
Fax: (44) 171 703 2278
Email: scfuk.org.uk

International Labour Organisation (ILO)
Application of Standards Branch,
CH-1211, Geneva 22, SWITZERLAND
Tel: (41) 22 799 7154
Fax: (41) 22 798 8685

**International Confederation of Free Trade
Unions**
37-41 rue Montagne-aux-Herbes-
Potagares, B-1000 Bruxelles, BELGUIM
Tel: (32) 217 80 85
Fax: (32) 218 84 15

**International Committee of the Red Cross
(ICRC)**
17 Avenue de la Paix, 1211 Geneva,
SWITZERLAND
Tel: (41) 22 374 6001
Fax: (41) 22 734 8280

Casa Alianza UK
The Coach House, Grafton Underwood,
Kettering, Northants NN1 3AA, UK
Tel: (44) 1536 330 550
Fax: (44) 1536 330 718
Email: casalnza@gn.apc.org

Casa Alianza Latin America Regional Office
SJO 1039/PO Box 025216, Miami, Florida
33102 - 5216 USA
Tel: (506) 2535439
Fax: (506) 244 5689
Email: bruce@casa-alianza.org

The Child Rights Information Network (CRIN)
c/o Save the Children UK, 17 Grove Lane,
London SE5 8RD, UK
Tel: (44) 171 703 5400
Fax: (44) 171 793 7630
Email: crin@mail.pro-net.co.uk

Consortium for Street Children
Thomas Clarkson House, The Stableyard,
Broomgrove Road, London SW9 9TL
Tel/Fax: (44) 171 274 0087
Email: cscuk@gn.apc.org

Jubilee Campaign
St Johns, Cranleigh Road, Wonersh,
Surrey GU5 0QX, UK
Tel: (44) 1483 894 787
Fax: (44) 1483 894 797
Email: info@jubileecampaign.demon.co.uk

MEDICAL

Physicians for Human Rights (PHR)
100 Boylston St, Suite 702, Boston MA
02116, USA
Tel: (1-617) 695 0041
Fax: (1-617) 695 0307

RULE OF LAW

International Commission of Jurists ICJ
PO Box 160, 26 Chemin de Joinville,
1216 Cointrin, Geneva, SWITZERLAND
Tel: (41) 22 788 4747
Fax: (41) 22 788 4880

International Bar Association
2 Harewood Place, Hanover Square,
London W1R 9HB, UK
Tel: (44) 171 629 1206
Fax: (44) 171 409 0456
Email: donna.field@int-bar.org

International Association of Judges
Palazzo di Giustizia, Piazza Cavour,
00193 Rome, ITALY

Interights
Lancaster House, 33 Islington High Street,
London N1 9LH, UK
Tel: (44) 171 278 3230
Fax: (44) 171 278 4334
Email: interights@compuserve.com

MINORITIES

Minority Rights Group
379 Brixton Road, London SW9 7DE, UK
Tel: (44) 171 978 9498
Fax: (44) 171 738 6265
Email: minority.rights@mrgmail.org

SLAVERY

Anti-Slavery International for the Protection of Human Rights
Thomas Clarkson House, The Stableyard,
Broomgrove Road, London SW9 9TL
Tel: (44) 171 924 9555
Fax: (44) 171 738 4110
Email: antislavery@gn.apc.org

TORTURE

Organisation Mondiale Contre la Torture – SOS Torture (OMCT)
PO Box 119, CH-1211 Geneva 20,
SWITZERLAND
Tel: (41) 22 733 3140
Fax: (41) 22 733 1051
Email: OMTC@iprolink.ch

UNITED NATIONS

UN NGO Liaison Office Room 176-2,
Palais des Nations, CH-1211 Geneva 10,
SWITZERLAND
Tel: (41) 22 917 2127
Fax: (41) 22 917 0001
Email: Rmartineau@unog.ch

NGO Liaison Office in the Centre for Human Rights
Room A-505, Palais des Nations (as
above)
Tel: (41) 22 917 1143

International Service for Human Rights
1 rue de Varembe, PO Box 16, 1211
Geneva, SWITZERLAND
Tel: (41) 22 733 5123
Fax: (41) 22 733 0826

UN Center for Human Rights
United Nations Office at Geneva, 8-14
Avenue de la Paix, 1211 Geneva 10,
SWITZERLAND
Tel: (41) 22 917 4211
Fax: (41) 22 917 0123
Human Rights Fax Hotline: (41) 22 917 0092

REGIONAL

Inter-American Court of Human Rights
Apto 6906–100
San Jose, Costa Rica
Tel: (506) 234 0581 225 3333
Fax: (506) 234 0589
Email: corteidh@sol.racsa.co.cr

European Commission of Human Rights
Conseil de l'Europe, BP 431 R6,
67006 Strasbourg Cedex, FRANCE
Tel: (33) 88 61 49 61
Fax: (33) 88 36 70 57 or 35 19 61

For Asia and Middle East:
Contact Human Rights Watch in New
York (address above)

**African Network for the Prevention and
Protection of Child Abuse and Neglect
(ANPPCAN)**
PO Box 71420, Nairobi, Kenya
Tel: (254) 2 72 24 96
Fax: (254) 2 72 19 99
Email: anppcan@arcc.or.ke

**African Commission on Human and
People's Rights**
Kairaba Ave, PO Box 673, Banjul,
THE GAMBIA
Tel: (220) 392 962
Fax: (220) 390 764

RELATED WEBSITES

It is advisable to contact the Child Rights Information Network, on **http://www.crin.ch** and Human Rights Internet on **http://www.hri.ca** for email links and updated information on new websites. Both organisations also produce useful directories of human rights and child-focused organisations.

Amnesty International: http://www/amnesty.org
Anti-Slavery International http://www.charitynet.org~asi
Casa Alianza: http://www.casa-alianza.org
Consortium for Street Children UK: http://www.cscuk.org
Defence for Children International: http://www.childhub.ch/webpub/dcihome
European Network for Street Children Worldwide: http://knooppunt.be/~enscw/intro.html
Human Rights Information and Documentation System International:
   http://www.homepage.iprolink.ch/~huridocs
International Bar Association: http://www.iba.net.org
International Committee of the Red Cross: http://www.icrc.ch
International Labour Organisation: http://www.ilo.org
Save the Children UK: http://www.savethechildren.org.uk
Minority Rights Group: http://www.minorityrights.org
Radda Barnen: http://www.rb.se
UN Centre for Human Rights: http://www.unhchr.ch
UNICEF: http://www.unicef.org
University of Minnesota Human Rights Library: http://umn.edu/humanrts

NGO in Special Consultative Status with the Economic and Social Council of the United Nations

The Consortium for Street Children UK is a network of British development agencies and individuals which provide operational partnership and campaigning support to projects with street children throughout the world.

The objectives of the CSC are to:

1. Build a network of information and expertise through which agencies can share the most efficient and cost effective strategies for working with street children.

2. To increase public awareness of the issues that affect street and working children.

3. To lobby and advise national and international policy makers and legislators.

4. To monitor and promote children's rights in line with the Convention on the Rights of the Child.

President
Lord Dubs of Battersea

Chair
Ana Capaldi

Vice-Chair
Clare Hanbury

Member Agencies
Action UK
AHRTAG
CARF
Casa Alianza UK
Childhope UK
Children of the Andes
The Child to Child Trust
Estrela Nova North East
Hope for Children
International Child Development
  Programme
International Childcare Trust
International Children's Trust
Jubilee Action
Let the Children Live!
Link Romania
Merdeka
New Ways
The Railway Children
SKCV Children's Trust
The Society of Friends of the Lotus
  Children
Street Child Africa
Street Kids International
Child Studies Unit, University of Cork
Womankind Worldwide
World Association of Girl Guides and
  Girl Scouts

World Vision UK
YCare International

Observer Members
Amnesty International (British Section)
Anti-Slavery International
ECPAT UK
Save the Children Fund UK
UK Committee for UNICEF

Individual Members
Lion Len Aldridge
Iain Byrne
Trudy Davies
James Gardner
Clare Hanbury
David Shilling
Dr Richard Slater

Honorary Members
Baroness Flather of Maidenhead
Lord McNally of Blackpool
Dario Mitidieri

Director
Anita Schrader

Campaigns Officer
Richard Wakelam

Address:
Consortium for Street Children UK
Thomas Clarkson House
The Stableyard
Broomgrove Road
London SW9 9TL

Tel. & Fax: +44 0171 274 0087
Email: cscuk.advocacy@gn.apc.org
Website: www.csc.uk